The Anthropocene: Politik—Economics—Society—Science

Volume 3

Series editor

Hans Günter Brauch, Mosbach, Germany

More information about this series at http://www.springer.com/series/15232
http://www.afes-press-books.de/html/APESS.htm
http://www.afes-press-books.de/html/APESS_03.htm

Audley Genus
Editor

Sustainable Consumption

Design, Innovation and Practice

Springer

Editor
Audley Genus
Small Business Research Centre
Kingston University
Kingston upon Thames, Surrey
UK

Cover photo: © Mr. Narongrit Vannarat, Bangkok, Thailand who painted and photographed the cover photo and granted the permission to use it for this book cover. The paintings of this Thai painter are at: https://www.facebook.com/narongrit.n.vannarat and his Email address is at: nop2.17@gmail.com.

More on this book is at: http://www.afes-press-books.de/html/APESS_03.htm

ISSN 2367-4024 ISSN 2367-4032 (electronic)
The Anthropocene: Politik—Economics—Society—Science
ISBN 978-3-319-29663-0 ISBN 978-3-319-29665-4 (eBook)
DOI 10.1007/978-3-319-29665-4

Library of Congress Control Number: 2016930050

Copyediting: PD Dr. Hans Günter Brauch, AFES-PRESS e.V., Mosbach, Germany

Printed on acid-free paper

This Springer imprint is published by SpringerNature
The registered company is Springer International Publishing AG Switzerland

Acknowledgments

The publication of this edited volume could not have been achieved without the help and support of numerous people and organizations. I would like to acknowledge the YTL Corporation. The YTL funding has allowed me to participate in a range of networks and activities involving researchers and practitioners, of which the *Sustainable Consumption Research and Action Initiative* (SCORAI) is just one. I would not have undertaken and could not have realized this book project without the support of SCORAI colleagues.

I hope those I do not name in the following list will forgive me but among those who have helped to develop my thinking about sustainable consumption and innovation are: Maurie Cohen; Frances Fahy; Sylvia Lorek; Henrike Rau; Marlyne Sahakian; Edina Vadovics; and Philip Vergragt. I also wish to acknowledge the work of the chapter authors who worked so well under the pressure of time I put on them.

I also wish to say a heartfelt 'thank you' to my colleagues at Kingston University, London, for their general support but also for seminars and discussions which have informed my thinking about innovation and sustainable behaviour and practices. Just some of these colleagues include: Ruth Rettie, Tim Harries, John Kitching, Rob Blackburn, Eva Kasperova and Mara Iskandarova; I should also mention past colleagues Kevin Burchell, Alessandro Giudici and Arif Attar. Other researchers who have suggested ideas, references to follow up and in some cases contributed a chapter to the book include Anne-Marie Coles, Athena Piterou (of University of Greenwich) and Adrian Smith (SPRU, University of Sussex).

I am most certainly indebted to those practitioners, some of whom I have worked with in the Transition Town movement, who have helped to shape my thinking about environmental activism and the roles of academic researchers therein. Of the many I could name perhaps the following deserve a special mention: Tom Henfrey; Frances Hinton; Mandy Meikle; and Ann Thorpe. Of course, none of this work could ever have been possible without the support and love of my family. Accordingly, a very large vote of thanks goes to Claire and Alex.

My sincere thanks go to Dr. Hans Günter Brauch, who commissioned and copyedited the book, Dr. Johanna Schwarz and Janet Sterritt-Brunner of Springer in Heidelberg (Germany) and the production team in Chennai (India), without whom the realization and production of the book would not have been possible.

Surrey, UK
August 2015

Audley Genus

Contents

Abbreviations

ABC	Attitude, Behaviour and Choice model (E. Shove)
ABC	Attitude, Behaviour, Context model (P. Stern)
CAD	Computer-aided Design
CAP	Community Action Plan
CNG	Compressed Natural Gas
CSA	Community Supported Agriculture
CSR	Corporate Social Responsibility
DESIS	Design for Social Innovation and Sustainability
DIY	Do-it-Yourself
FAO	Food and Agriculture Organization
FAQ	Frequently Asked Questions
FEASTA	Foundation for the Economics of Sustainability
GDP	Gross Domestic Product
IEA	International Energy Agency
IPCC	Intergovernmental Panel on Climate Change
IPPR	Institute for Public Policy Research
JAC	Japanese Agricultural Cooperative
JOAA	Japanese Organic Agriculture Association
MAFF	Ministry of Agriculture, Forestry and Fisheries (Japan)
MW	Megawatt
OECD	Organisation for Economic Co-operation and Development
OSCR	Office of the Scottish Charity Regulator
OSE	Open Source Ecology
RACE	Reach, Act, Convert, Engage
SCIO	Scottish Charitable Incorporated Organisation
SCORAI	Sustainable Consumption and Research Action Initiative
SLOC	Small, Local, Open and Connected
SSSI	Site of Special Scientific Interest

TRACES	Track, Reach, Act, Convert, Engage, Synergy
UCG	Unconventional Gas
WATIF	Woolfords, Auchengray and Tarbrax Improvement Foundation
WCED	World Commission on Environment and Development
WRAP	Waste and Resources Action Programme

Chapter 1
Introduction

Audley Genus and Ann Thorpe

Abstract This opening chapter of the book presents an overview of the main themes and issues to be covered in the volume. It identifies the principal challenges connected with sustainable consumption and situates these in relation to developments in academic thinking in innovation, design, economics and environmental sociology, and in connection with public policy-making, market development and consumerism and 'bottom up' initiatives. The chapter lays the foundations of the book in terms of its concern with the contribution of design and environmental activism, innovation and changing social practices towards reducing unsustainable consumption, and with the nature and extent of emerging phenomena related to the sharing economy, DIY design and 'prosumption'.

Keywords Consumption · Consumerism · Design activism · Innovation · Social practice

1.1 Introduction

The manuscript for this book went into production several months prior to the start of negotiations due to take place at the Conference of Parties meeting (COP21) in Paris in December 2015, concerning possible international agreement on actions to tackle climate change. Much of the book was drafted before the announcement by the IEA (2015) that preliminary data showed an unexpected stabilization in energy-related CO_2 emissions in 2014 compared with 2013. This possibly temporary pause is thought to be due to lower coal consumption in China as well as one-off factors to do with weather conditions during the year, for instance. Further,

Audley Genus, Ph.D., YTL Professor of Innovation and Technology Management, Small Business Research Centre, Kingston University, London, UK; E-mail: a.genus@ kingston.ac.uk.

Ann Thorpe, Ph.D., Programme Officer (Master's Programme in Public Administration, University College London) and design activist/author, University College London; E-mail: ann@designers-atlas.net.

A. Genus (ed.), *Sustainable Consumption*, The Anthropocene: Politik—Economics—Society—Science 3, DOI 10.1007/978-3-319-29665-4_1

the stabilization of energy-related CO_2 emissions is notable and unusual for occurring at a time when world economies are growing (though the increases in economic growth experienced by China in the 1990s and 2000s have not been as dramatic recently). However, this apparent energy-related emissions success should be treated with great care, bearing in mind the more typical and generally alarming increases in global greenhouse gas emissions experienced over a number of decades, including the last decade.

Since the publication of the fourth assessment report of the Intergovernmental Panel and Climate Change, in 2007, annual global greenhouse gas emissions have continued to grow to a level not seen previously—'49.5 billion tonnes (giga tonnes or Gt) of *CO_2 equivalents* (CO_{2eq}) in the year 2010' (Victor et al. 2014: 113). According to the IPCC there is 'robust evidence' that over 70 % of global emissions are produced by ten large industrialized and developing countries (with the EU counted as one 'country'). The IPPC (Victor et al. 2014: 114) states that to achieve deep cuts in emissions requires actions involving technology, policy, institutions and 'changes in human behaviour and consumption'. Indeed consumption is one of the key drivers of anthropogenic climate change and, like other interventions to tackle the challenge, will require the efforts of a diverse array of actors operating locally, nationally and internationally. It is widely thought that the sectors which contribute most to greenhouse gas emissions are: food; passenger transport; and those connected with housing (including heating and leisure activities). These are responsible for about 75 % of total life cycle impacts of consumption. Of the other sectors clothing is responsible for the highest share of impact (see European Commission 2006; Reisch/Thøgersen in press). Concerned about the challenges presented above and the response of researchers and others to them, a two-day workshop on Sustainable Consumption was held in London in the Autumn of 2014, at the Royal Society for the Encouragement of the Arts, Manufactures and Commerce. This book reports and reflects upon the event. The workshop was the latest in a series of events organized by the SCORAI research network, which consists of the regional affiliates SCORAI Europe, SCORAI North America and SCORAI China (SCORAI standing for *Sustainable Consumption Research and Action Initiative*). The SCORAI network comprises around 500 researchers worldwide. It has grown substantially since its beginnings in 2008/9, in Europe as a development of the EU SCORE! project, and in the USA, as a result of activities originating in the Tellus Institute, Boston (see: Cohen et al. 2013 for further details of the historical development of SCORAI). The aims of the SCORAI networks are to: 1. share and support innovative research; 2. develop and promote collaboration between SCORAI regional affiliates, and with related organizations and networks such as the degrowth movement, One Earth, the European Roundtable for Sustainable Consumption and Production, the Global Research Forum for Sustainable Production and Consumption (and through this to the United Nations Environment Programme), and DESIS (*Design for Social Innovation and Sustainability*); and 3. to provide a bridge connecting academic research, social movements, and policy-making relevant to sustainable consumption.

Table 1.1 List of delegates attending SCORAI London workshop on Sustainable Consumption, 2014

Name of delegate	Affiliation (as of September 30, 2014)
Maurie Cohen	New Jersey Institute of Technology
Anne-Marie Coles	University of Greenwich
Karin Dobernig	WU—Vienna University of Economics and Business
Frances Fahy	National University of Ireland, Galway
Audley Genus	Kingston University, London
Mike Goodman	University of Reading
Mary Greene	National University of Ireland, Galway
Tom Henfrey	Schumacher Institute
Claudia Henninger	University of Sheffield
Frances Hinton	Transition Town Gosforth, Newcastle upon Tyne
Marfuga Iskandarova	Kingston University, London
Charlotte Jensen	Aalborg University
Steven R. McGreevy	Research Institute for Humanity and Nature, Kyoto
Mandy Meikle	WATIF (Woolfords, Auchengray and Tarbrax Improvement Foundation) South Lanarkshire, Scotland
Mariale Moreno	Nottingham Trent University
Sarah Netter	Copenhagen Business School
Athena Piterou	University of Greenwich
Giuseppe Salvia	Nottingham Trent University
Adrian Smith	Science Policy Research Unit, University of Sussex
Ann Thorpe	Design activist, ex-LUUM Architecture

Source The authors

The London workshop was attended by a diverse mix of practitioners and academics and included researchers from the fields of design, marketing, innovation, science and technology studies, geography and sociology. A number of practitioners participated, including a design activist, and environmental and community activists connected with the Transition Town movement and other groups. The 20 delegates came from the UK, other EU countries, USA and Japan (see Table 1.1 for a list of delegates). The broad aims of the London workshop were to: (1) Develop our understanding of innovative approaches to sustainable consumption; (2) Share and reflect upon contemporary research and practice; and (3) Build upon previous SCORAI events. Thus delegates at the London event shared and reflected upon research and practice relevant to themes suggested by participants in recent SCORAI Europe workshops in connection with the challenges posed by current patterns of unsustainable consumption and the crisis of global climate change. This book presents selected contributions from the workshop, pulling together various strands of the workshop discussions and highlighting their significance to current thinking about the challenges of sustainable consumption. The following sub-section further discusses the nature of these challenges.

1.2 Challenges of Sustainable Consumption

The workshop on which this book is based was informed by research, policies and practical initiatives that have aimed to expose and address challenges of sustainable consumption and economic growth. There has for a long time been widespread concern that conventional thinking misses the fundamental point that the pursuit and achievement of increasing economic growth is necessarily and directly linked to ever-increasing resource exploitation (Georgescu-Roegen 1971, 1975). Moreover concerns about such matters have tended to be painted as predominantly economic in character and dominated by the pursuit of increases in GDP, while neglecting socio-cultural, social justice, gender, environmental and ecological aspects (Martínez-Alier 2012; Schneider et al. 2010). A number of novel ways to measure well-being have been developed, intended to reduce reliance on *gross domestic product* (GDP) indicators. For example indexes which seek to measure well-being or social progress include the Index for Human Development, the Genuine Progress Indicator and the Index of Social Health. However, trends show a divergence between generally increasing economic growth, as measured by GDP, an indicator of well-having, and indications of well-being (the recent financial crisis not withstanding) (Latouche 2010). The question has been posed as to whether non-material growth is possible, and demands for investments which foreground ‘social impact’ juxtaposed with the difficulties that have been experienced with the development of suitable alternate measures of well-being (Thorpe 2012; New Economics Foundation 2009).

There has been increasing attention to ideas pertaining to the steady state economy (Daly 1973, 1992) the ‘Blue Economy’ (Pauli 2009), the ‘Circular Economy’ (Ellen MacArthur Foundation 2012) and the limits of economic growth (Jackson 2009; Meadows et al. 1972; Victor 2008). Moreover there has been marked debate between advocates of steady state growth and those who argue for policies and initiatives for economic ‘degrowth’. Working in French, Georgescu-Roegen (1994) used the word ‘décroissance’, which in English means something like ‘a-growth’, as in anti-GDP reliant economic growth or ‘grow less, well’ (c.f. Kerschner 2010; Latouche 2010). It has become identified with notions of ‘downshifting’ and ‘voluntary simplicity’, though implications of what it means or takes to ‘degrow’ have not been fully appreciated or spelled out, whilst there remains scepticism about the ‘less is more’ approach entailed (e.g. Schor 2010 emphasizes getting ‘more from less’ by increasing the productivity of self-provisioning). For example, the degrowth movement has been criticized for over-attention to localized initiatives, at the expense of a more thoroughgoing appreciation of global capitalism, and for presenting economic growth as 'homogenized'. With respect to the latter it is argued that degrowth theorists have failed to grapple with the intricacies and contradictions of contemporary capitalism, which would lead them to spell out in which activities 'good' growth is necessary, in order for certain ecological and social objectives to be realized (Schwartzman 2012). Further such a blanket view may lead to a failure to properly appreciate which opportunities carry the best potential for the pursuit of social change and economic/ecological development (Schwartzman 2012 refers to 'green urbanism' in this regard and to social media as a conduit for diffusing supportive policies and practices, and enabling a transnational green movement). Fundamentally, it is not clear whether advocates of degrowth wish to 'exit' the capitalist economy or radically transform it (Schwartzman 2012), or moderate its worse effects to present a greener face. Moreover the question arises as to whether some of the local or 'solidarity economy' initiatives which tend to feature in discussions about degrowth (or the steady state) will remain the province of the few who have the time, money and other resources to indulge in them and about how related practices may be scaled up, replicated and developed inclusively and judiciously.

1.2.1 Unsustainable Consumption

What are commonly viewed as 'better' forms of consumption including that of green, ethical or organic products, or sharing are yet to be established as the 'new normal', and in the aftermath of the recent financial and economic crisis have even been the subject of reductions in demand. The following tables and figures tell a disappointing tale, related in terms of data on purchases made rather than consumption 'practices', of which further discussion follows later. The story begins by noting the tiny share assumed by consumption of alternative fuels of total vehicle fuel consumption in the USA (see Table 1.2; Table 1.3 presents the data using percentage terms).

In relation to energy consumption the structure of the energy market in some countries is highly concentrated, dominated by large energy utilities and characterized by low levels of penetration of 'green' energy. In the UK, for example, the

Table 1.2 Estimated consumption of vehicle fuels in thousand gasoline equivalent gallons, by fuel type, 2007–2011

Fuel type	Year				
	2007	2008	2009	2010	2011
Alternative	414,715	430,329	431,107	457,755	515,920
Replacement	5,062,068	6,767,110	7,677,942	8,797,538	9,474,809
Traditional	185,179,000	176,078,904	172,087,071	174,006,229	170,526,914
Total	185,593,715	176,509,233	172,518,178	174,463,984	171,042,834

Source U.S. Energy Information Administration (2011)

Table 1.3 Estimated consumption of vehicle fuels, percentage of total consumed by fuel type, 2007–2011

Fuel type	Year				
	2007	2008	2009	2010	2011
Alternative	0.22	0.24	0.25	0.26	0.3
Replacement	2.73	3.83	4.45	5.04	5.54
Traditional	97.05	95.93	95.3	94.7	94.16

Source U.S. Energy Information Administration (2011)

'big 6' energy suppliers occupy over 90 % of the domestic retail market for electricity and in 2012 largely opted out of offering green tariffs to new domestic customers. In the USA, as of 2011 less than 8 % of energy consumers subscribed to green energy programmes, while green energy suppliers have continued to have difficulties in gaining purchase in the energy markets of most US states. According to the OECD (2014: 62) renewables' share of total energy supply 'remained relatively stable' in the first decade of the twenty-first century at around 8 %, while in 2011 renewable sources accounted for about 20 % of electricity generated worldwide.

Turning to consumption of food and drink the story is similar. Thus global sales of organic food and drink remain small. The USA is the country with the largest proportion of global organic food and drink sales (44 %), yet recent estimates (in 2012) put the organic market at only 4.3 % of the USA's total sales of food and drink. Further, Denmark has the highest share of organic food and drink as a proportion of national total sales in the world, though even here organic product sales account for less than 8.0 % of the national total (Soil Association Organic Market Report 2014: 20). In agriculture it is sobering to note that, according to a report by Textile Exchange (2014; see also The Guardian 27 January 2015), organic cotton represents only 0.4 % of global cotton production, compared with 0.1 % in 2004. In terms of land area farmed, organic agriculture made up 0.73 % of the world total agriculture in 2009, according to the latest available data from the Food and Agriculture Organisation http://faostat3.fao.org/search/organic%20farming/E

1.3 Research on Sustainable Consumption

The book's concern for (un)sustainable consumption should be understood as one about the nature and roots of consumerism in contemporary societies. Research on this is diverse. From an economic point of view consumption is vital to growth and behavioural approaches in economics and psychology have put the (one-off and rationally calculated) purchasing decisions of the sovereign consumer centre-stage. From a sociological perspective consumption is often wrapped up with considerations of identity, distinction, what it means to be normal and what people do and say by way of consumption practices (Schatzki 2011). Whilst not working on sustainable consumption *per se* research on the sociology of taste and distinction put centre stage matters of social class and identity which loom large in our concepts of ourselves and others and what we wear and eat, how we travel and so on (Bourdieu 1984; c.f. Schor 1998 on the role of status in purchasing decisions). In explaining the notions of fields, habitus and capital he employs, Bourdieu (Bourdieu/Wacquant 1992; Wacquant 1989) remarks on the emergence of the 'economic field' in societies, substantiated by economic relations rather than ones of 'friendship or love' (Wacquant 1989: 39). The social, human and economic capital which give power over the economic field are intimately bound up in and perpetuate these relations. The dominant dispositions (the 'habitus' or 'sense of the game') emphasising the accumulation of material goods and conspicuously consumptive lifestyles mediate between field-level relations and practices, and are themselves relational. Schor (2004) argues that, primarily in connection with the commercialization of childhood in the USA, we are 'born to buy', this apparent condition is better thought of in terms the working out of myriad relationships in the economic field which make patterns of contemporary consumerism seem 'natural'. From a design perspective consumerism has been identified as increasingly about stimulation in the short-term in a world where the pace of life is forever hastening and consumer product life cycles are short, obsolescence being built in order to create gaps for firms to exploit with new product introductions or upgrades. Thorpe (2012) identified four design-related challenges of consumerism:

1. Many important social and environmental values don't have prices.
2. The number, allure, and frequency of immediate rewards from consuming have all increased—what is more such goods and services have become ever cheaper, widely available and easier to use or access.
3. Traditional strategies for building commitment and social solidarity have become outmoded but replacement strategies aren't yet available or haven't become firmly and widely institutionalized.
4. Private purchases form an element of our social language, turning some important aspects of societal meaning and purpose over to profit-seeking entities.

There is a 'field of struggles' (Wacquant 1989), in which some actors have developed and are continuing to develop alternative positions on consumerism and consumption, and are acquiring and mobilising kinds of capital which potentially may combat these challenges. For example, it is recognized that there is much more to consumption than merely individualized purchase and ownership of goods, since there is a need to understand what has been labelled positional consumption (or 'shownership') and the implications of social and economic organization for design and how this relates to consumption and production. Further 'active' design practice can help to make visible the (un)sustainability of consumption, as well as providing collective rather than individual approaches to design. Such practice, it is argued, may also help to slow the pace of consumption that many people have come to live with, while contributing positively to their well-being and identity (Thorpe 2012). The book is concerned to highlight the nature of active or DIY design in practice as well as to reflect on the above claims for it.

In recent literature on the sociology of consumption aspects of collective behaviour come into view; for example Reisch/Thøgersen (in press) point to the relationship between collective agency and everyday routines, and the relationship between the everyday performance of practice and the macro-institutional context as forming the terrain on which sustainable consumption research will build, informed by theories of practice. The analysis of consumption is the source of much contention particularly between, on one hand, proponents of practice theory (as represented in the work of Schatzki 2011; Schatzki et al. 2001; Warde 2005; Warde/Southerton 2012; Shove 2003, 2011; Shove/Walker 2014) and, on the other hand, those who argue for cultural theory (such as espoused by Spaargaren 2003, 2011). One of the key points of the argument concerns the proper unit, or focal point, of analysis. In practice theory, this is the 'practice' connected with what is being consumed i.e. rather than the 'thing', the artefact, itself. Theories of practice have asserted the commingling of the material and the symbolic with what users know, do and say in relation to consumption, and whether and how these are transformed. In cultural theories the unit of analysis is, for example, national culture and the problem to be addressed framed in terms of the significance of national culture to shaping phenomena such as trust, which in turn may affect consumption practices understood as the habits connected with buying food, for example (McGreevy and Akitsu, Chap. 7, this volume). From the standpoint of practice theory, however, such habits are not best understood as the internalization of culture. Broadly speaking, habits are created through learned, repeated practice, necessitating personal embodied skill and knowledge and things in the external environment (Warde/Southerton 2012). Further, both doings and sayings are constituents of practice, whereas there is a focus on the act of purchase in approaches rooted in the analysis of values and attitudes and the requirements for eliciting individual behaviour change.

There are divergent views within both cultural theory and practice theory perspectives, which is of interest here since the differences of approach and emphasis are somewhat the product of disciplinary differences, and with respect to the researchers involved the SCORAI London workshop brought together a collection of contributors from a variety of academic fields. In the chapters below readers will see different approaches to addressing culture and agency, with certain contributions emphasising the importance of (national) culture in shaping consumer and other consumption-related behaviour. Others bring agency to the fore, focusing on the work of entrepreneurs or activists, for example in relation to DIY design and the sharing economy. Thus most chapters of the book are informed by either practice theory or cultural theory, typically employed in contrast with or complementary to other approaches. A relational dimension is apparent, involving relations among producers, designers and citizens/consumers. An institutional dimension applies to some contributions, sometimes implicitly. Apart from academic interest in identifying and evaluating factors implicated in consumption and how and why they change, there are possible policy implications to consider, a discussion of which appears in the concluding chapter. It may also be insightful to consider what institutional theory, complemented by discourse analysis can offer (Genus in press,

2014a; Hajer 1993; Hajer/Versteeg 2005). This is because certain discourse-institutional approaches, which have emerged in recent years in parallel with practice theory, are variously concerned with the implications of routine, habit and language (rule-*like* phenomena) for environmentally sustainable social transformation. The potential of such approaches is another thread to be picked up in the book's conclusion.

A large body of research has examined environmental sustainability and social change informed by the cognate fields of systems innovation, science and technology studies, and transition management. Much of this has been occupied with questions concerning novelty (and novelties), including the identification of interlocking systemic factors which enable or inhibit the development and diffusion of renewable energy or microgeneration technologies, and the relationship between innovative socio-technical niches, including grassroots movements, and the mainstream. Arguably the systems focus of much of this work has tended to hide from view more local or mundane phenomena to do with routine or institutionalized use of technology, especially where this is unsustainable. Moreover, to the extent that such research privileges the promises or benefits of innovation(s) and how artefacts are embedded in society there is a risk that it neglects failure of innovation to meet social challenges (Coles Chap. 8, this volume, Ellul 1964). Indeed it has been argued that failure to realize the transition to sustainability through socio-technical innovation may entail a shift towards adaptation rather mitigation-orientated climate change policies (Hess 2013).

The book sits at the junction of a number of themes, practitioner activities and academic disciplines. The following is a list of the themes specified in the call for papers for the workshop, which reflect the primary considerations of the SCORAI Europe network during 2014:

1. Actions for developing and diffusing sustainable consumption practice;
2. Relations among and roles for researchers and practitioners in enabling sustainable consumption;
3. New perspectives and research methods, mindful of the increasing calls for inter- or multi-disciplinary research to tackle societal 'grand challenges', and the potential and limitations associated with working across academic disciplines; and
4. Integrating sustainable consumption and production.

The themes concerning actions in practice and relations between non-researchers and academic researchers are central to SCORAI and pertinent to the formulation of research agenda, the openness or insularity of related networks and research questions considered to be important or 'not asked' (Shove 2010). The book reflects SCORAI's aspiration (and reflects on the demand) that researchers work with activists, entrepreneurs and policy actors (something which was emphasized in open space sessions of the London workshop). The problems as well as opportunities raised by this in undertaking action research and engagement with non-academic stakeholders are not always acknowledged or effectively addressed, something to which the book will return. Prevailing priorities of universities and funders may lead to shallow or short-term engagement, more to do with pursuing the 'impact' agenda or changing organization culture than fostering more fulsome relations between university researchers and others (Genus 2014b). A similar point applies to another key characteristic of SCORAI work, concerning multi-, inter- or transdisciplinarity. Some researchers in the SCORAI network have emphasized the need for and the potential of working across disciplines (Brown et al. 2013), and this is borne out in a number of the chapters below. However, the difficulties and limitations of doing so are not to be ignored (Shove 2011). In terms of the scope and focus of research the origins of the SCORAI network may be traced in part to the observation (correct at the time) that sustainability-related—and especially innovation—research over-emphasized technology (i.e. as artefact) and production. Here there is a determination to reconnect consumption with production. Fundamentally, this corrective is necessary to reassert SCORAI's association with the critique and transformation of unsustainable modes of production in which consumption is elemental but, moreover, to encourage those for whom production and technology tend to be primary foci to recognize the symbiosis of consumption and production (and consumers and producers) in a more sustainable society.

The book draws on and interweaves concerns that inhabit the domains of design, innovation studies, science and technology studies, marketing, sociology, history and geography. These explicitly or implicitly variously address issues such as: the nature of consumerism, and the importance of consumption in conferring a sense of belonging, pride and meaning to consumers in 'affluent societies'; the work of professional and DIY designers and design activism (Offer 2006); the phenomenon of the sharing economy; the work of environmental activists and entrepreneurs; the significance of culture and agency to the promotion and diffusion of sustainability-related consumption practices; the promise and limitations of sustainable consumption-related technology development and innovation; and the role of social networks and 'availability cascades' (Kuran/Sunstein 1999) in innovating sustainable consumption practices or in inhibiting their diffusion and institutionalization. The contributions below address various aspects of these aforementioned challenges and themes. Section 1.4 now outlines the content of the specific chapters comprising this volume.

1.4 The Structure of the Book

The remaining chapters of the book continue to lay out the conceptual terrain underpinning its work, while presenting new empirical data, typically based on rich analyses of particular practices, sectors and/or geographical and temporal spaces. In Chap. 2 Giuseppe Salvia and Tim Cooper examine the role of design and designers in the growth of sustainable DIY design, conceptualising DIY design as practices which should not be assumed to be more environmental sustainable. They do consider however in what ways and how the practice of design(ers) can contribute to reducing non-sustainable consumption. In Chap. 3, in a chapter based on the workshop presentation made by Mariale Moreno, Piscicelli et al. set out social psychological and social practice approaches to understanding consumption. They then develop a framework, which they argue may be employed as a design tool in 'participatory design workshops' to promote and understand sustainable consumer behaviour. Chapter 4 is by Athena Piterou and Fred Steward, who are concerned with the sociotechnical practice of reading. Piterou and Steward employ the concept of the 'communication circuit' (Darnton 1982) to examine the interaction of actors involved in book production and consumption. They consider the implications for consumption and dematerialization of the socio-technical system of book publishing of the move from print-on-paper to digitization. Chapter 5, by Sarah Netter, provides background on the notion of the sharing economy, as she develops her application of availability cascades to understanding the increasing popularity of concepts invoking the language of the sharing economy. Chapter 6 is by Henninger et al., who provide insights into sustainable consumption and production rooted in an examination of the slow-fashion industry and the marketing activities of micro-organizations therein. Chapter 7, by Steven R. McGreevy and Motoki Akitsu, discusses sustainable food consumption in Japan and the centrality of trust in relationships that 'bind' food consumers and producers. In Chap. 8 Anne-Marie Coles discusses the potential for sustainable production and consumption in the context of the 'technological society', her analysis being informed by the work of Ellul (1964, 1980). In Chap. 9 Mandy Meikle focuses on factors inhibiting and promoting sustainable consumption in rural Scotland, and represents a 'view from the ground' from an activist struggling to engage fellow residents in environmental or community activism. Chapter 10 summarizes the main findings from the foregoing chapters of the book, which are discussed in relation to wider literature and practice and in reflecting further on the workshop presentations and discussions. This concluding chapter considers the developments and requirements of sustainable or lower consumption in terms of future research, the activities of researchers and activists and implications for policy, recognising that local context may undercut the application of generalized prescriptions across national and regional boundaries. It sets the content of the book's chapters in the context of a discussion of perspectives which variously put centre stage user practices, behaviour, socio-technical systems, discourses and institutional rules in accounts of social transformation connected with the ecological challenges we face.

References

Bourdieu, P., 1984: *Distinction: A Social Critique of the Judgement of Taste* (R. Nice, Trans.) (Cambridge, MA: Harvard University Press).

Bourdieu, P.; Wacquant, L.J.D., 1992: *An Invitation to Reflexive Sociology* (Cambridge: Polity Press).

Brown, H.; Vergragt, P.; Cohen M., 2013: "Societal Innovation in a Constrained World: Theoretical and Empirical Perspectives", in: Cohen, M.; Brown, H.; Vergragt, P. (Eds.):

Innovations in Sustainable Consumption: New Economics, Socio-technical Transitions and Social Practices (Cheltenham: Edward Elgar): 1–27.
Cohen, M.; Brown, H.; Vergragt, P., 2013: *Innovations in Sustainable Consumption: New Economics, Socio-technical Transitions and Social Practices* (Cheltenham: Edward Elgar).
Daly, H.E., 1973: *Towards a Steady-State Economy* (San Francisco: Freeman).
Daly, H.E., 1992: *Steady-State Economics* (London: Earthscan Publications).
Darnton, R., 1982: "What is the History of Books?", in: *Daedalus*, 111,3: 65–83.
Ellen MacArthur Foundation, 2012: Towards the Circular Economy. Ellen MacArthur Foundation; at: http://www.mvonederland.nl/system/files/media/towards-the-circular-economy.pdf (20 June 2015).
Ellul, J., 1964: *The Technological Society* (New York: Vintage Books).
Ellul, J., 1980: *The Technological System* (New York: Continuum).
European Commission, 2006: *Environmental Impact of Products (EIPRO)—Analysis of the Life Cycle Environmental Impacts Related to the Final Consumption of the EU-25*. Main Report EUR 22284 (Brussels: Institute of Prospective Technology Studies/European Science and Technology Observatory).
Genus, A., in press: "Sustainability Transitions: A Discourse-Institutional Perspective", in: Brauch, H.G. (Ed.): *Handbook on Sustainability Transition* (Berlin: Springer).
Genus, A., 2014a: "Governing Sustainability: A Discourse-Institutional Approach", in: *Sustainability*, 6,1: 283–305.
Genus, A., 2014b: "'Co-inquiry' for Environmental Sustainability: A Review of the UK Beacons for Public Engagement", in: *Environment and Planning C: Government and Policy*, 32,3: 491–508.
Georgescu-Roegen, N., 1971: *The Entropy Law and the Economic Process* (Cambridge, Mass.: Harvard University Press).
Georgescu-Roegen, N., 1975: "Energy and Economic Myths", in: *Southern Economic Journal*, 41,3: 347–381.
Georgescu-Roegen, N. 1994: *La décroissance* (Introduction and translation by J. Grinevald, and I. Rens) (Paris: Sang de la terre).
Hajer, M., 1993: "Discourse Coalitions and the Institutionalization of Practice: The Case of Acid Rain in Britain", in: Fischer, F.; Forrester, J. (Eds.): *The Argumentative Turn in Policy Analysis and Planning* (Durham, NC: Duke University Press): 43–76.
Hajer, M.; Versteeg, W., 2005: "A Decade of Discourse Analysis of Environmental Politics: Achievements, Challenges, Perspectives", in: *Journal of Environmental Policy and Planning*, 7,3: 175–184.
Hess, D.J., 2013: "Sustainable Consumption, Energy and Failed Transitions: The Problem of Adaptation", in: Cohen, M.; Brown, H.; Vergragt, P. (Eds.): *Innovations in Sustainable Consumption: New Economics, Socio-technical Transitions and Social Practices* (Cheltenham: Edward Elgar): 159–178.
IEA, 2015: Global Energy Related Emissions of Carbon Dioxide Stalled in 2014. Press release; at: http://www.iea.org/newsroomandevents/news/2015/march/global-energy-related-emissions-of-carbon-dioxide-stalled-in-2014.html (16 March 2015).
Jackson, T., 2009: *Prosperity Without Growth* (London: Earthscan).
Kerschner, C., 2010: "Economic De-growth vs. Steady-State Economy", in: *Journal of Cleaner Production*, 18: 554–551.
Kuran, T.; Sunstein, C.R., 1999: "Availability Cascades and Risk Regulation", in: *Stanford Law Review*, 51,4: 683–768.
Latouche, S., 2010: "Editorial", in: *Journal of Cleaner Production*, 18: 519–522.
Martínez Alier, J., 2012: "Environmental Justice and Economic Degrowth: An Alliance Between Two Movements", in: *Capitalism Nature Socialism*, 23,1: 51–73.
Meadows, D.H.; Meadows, D.L.; Randers, J.; Behrens, W., 1972: *The Limits to Growth. A Report for The Club of Rome's Project on the Predicament of Mankind* (New York: Universe Books).
New Economics Foundation, 2009: *National Accounts of Well-Being: Bringing Real Wealth onto the Balance Sheet* (London: New Economics Foundation).

OECD (Organisation for Economic Co-operation and Development), 2014: *Green Growth Indicators* (Paris: OECD).
Offer, A., 2006: *The Challenge of Affluence: Self-Control and Well-Being in the United States and Britain Since 1950* (Oxford: Oxford University).
Pauli, G., 2009: *The Blue Economy: 10 Years, 100 Innovations, 100 Million Jobs*. Report to the Club of Rome (Taos, NM: Paradigm).
Reisch L.A.; Thøgersen, J., in press: "Research on Sustainable Consumption: Introduction and Overview", in: Reisch, L.A.; Thøgersen, J. (Eds.): *Handbook of Research on Sustainable Consumption* (London: Edward Elgar Publishing).
Schatzki, T.R., 2011: *Where the Action Is (on Large Social Phenomena such as Sociotechnical Regimes)*. Working paper no. 1, Sustainable Practices Working Group. Sustainable Practices Working Group; at: http://www.sprg.ac.uk/uploads/schatzki-wp1.pdf (20 June 2015).
Schatzki, T.R.; Knorr-Cetina, K.; Savigny. E. (Eds.), 2001: *The Practice Turn in Contemporary Theory* (London: Routledge).
Schneider, F.; Kallis, G.; Martínez-Alier, J., 2010: "Crisis or Opportunity? Economic Degrowth for Social Equity and Ecological Sustainability. Introduction to this Special Issue", in: *Journal of Cleaner Production*, 18: 511–518.
Schor J., 1998: "The Overspent American: An Interview with Juliet Schor", in: *The Multinational Monitor* (September): 21–24.
Schor J., 2004: *Born to Buy: The Commercialized Child and the New Consumer Culture* (New York: Simon and Schuster).
Schor, J., 2010: *Plenitude: The New Economics of True Wealth* (New York: Penguin Press).
Schwartzman, D., 2012: "A Critique of Degrowth and Its Politics", in: *Capitalism Nature Socialism*, 23,1: 119–125.
Shove, E., 2003: *Comfort, Cleanliness and Convenience: The Social Organization of Normality* (Oxford: Berg).
Shove, E., 2010: "Social Theory and Climate Change Questions Often, Sometimes and not yet Asked", in: *Theory, Culture and Society*, 27,2–3: 277–288.
Shove, E., 2011: "Commentary. On the Difference Between Chalk and Cheese: A Response to Whitmarsh et al.'s Comments on "Beyond the ABC: Climate Change Policy and Theories of Social Change"", in: *Environment and Planning A*, 43: 262–264.
Shove, E.; Walker, G., 2014: "What Is Energy For? Social Practice and Energy Demand", in: *Theory, Culture and Society,* 31,5: 41–58.
Soil Association, 2014: *Organic Market Report* (Bristol: Soil Association).
Spaargaren, G., 2003: "Sustainable Consumption: A Theoretical and Environmental Policy Perspective", in: *Society and Natural Resources*, 16: 1–15.
Spaargaren, G., 2011: "Theories of Practices: Agency, Technology, and Culture. Exploring the Relevance of Practice Theories for the Governance of Sustainable Consumption Practices in the New World-Order", in: *Global Environmental Change*, 1: 813–822.
Textile Exchange, 2014: 2013 Organic Cotton Report—From Farm to Market; at: https://29244d.campgn4.com/2014-OCMR-Executive-Summary (15 March 2015).
The Guardian, 2015: Organic Cotton Demand Still on the Rise (27 January).
Thorpe, A., 2012: *Architecture and Design Versus Consumerism: How Design Activism Confronts Growth* (Abingdon: Earthscan/Taylor and Francis).
US Energy Information Administration, 2011: Renewable and Alternative Fuels Alternative Fuel Vehicle Data, 2011; at: http://www.eia.gov/renewable/afv/index.cfm (15 March 2015).
Victor, P.A., 2008: *Managing Without Growth: Slower by Design, not Disaster* (Cheltenham: Edward Elgar).
Victor, D.G.; Zhou, D.; Ahmed, E.H.M.; Dadhich, P.K.; Olivier, J.G.J.; Rogner, H.-H.; Sheikho, K.; Yamaguchi, M., 2014: "Introductory Chapter", in: Edenhofer, O.; Pichs-Madruga, R.; Sokona, Y.; Farahani, E.; Kadner, S.; Seyboth, K.; Adler, A.; Baum, I.; Brunner, S.; Eickemeier, P.; Kriemann, B.; Savolainen, J.; Schlömer, S.; von Stechow, C.; Zwickel, T.; Minx, J.C. (Eds.): *Climate Change 2014: Mitigation of Climate Change. Contribution of*

Working Group III to the Fifth Assessment Report of the Intergovernmental Panel on Climate Change (Cambridge, UK—New York, NY: Cambridge University Press).

Wacquant, L.J.D., 1989: "Towards a Reflexive Sociology: A Workshop with Pierre Bourdieu", in: *Sociological Theory*, 7,1: 26–63.

Warde, A., 2005: "Consumption and Theories of Practice", in: *Journal of Consumer Culture*, 5,2: 131–153.

Warde, A.; Southerton, D., 2012: "Introduction", in: Warde, A.; Southerton, D. (Eds.): *The Habits of Consumption* (Helsinki: Open Access Book Series of the Helsinki Collegium for Advanced Studies): 1–25.

Chapter 2
The Role of Design as a Catalyst for Sustainable DIY

Giuseppe Salvia and Tim Cooper

Abstract Amateurs committed to self-production (i.e. DIY) are reshaping the relationship between production and consumption, leading to a 'new DIY age' (Hoftijzer 2009). The spreading of this trend suggests scenarios in which non-professional people are, or will be, able to create artefacts supported by innovative technologies, networks and, perhaps, companies with new business models. Easy access for consumers to the production system could lead to inefficient resource use and increased waste, however, and so the sustainability of this trend has been debated. Nonetheless, recent research by Salvia (2013) envisages this contemporary self-production phenomena as a 'window of opportunity' to foster positive environmental and social impact, through activities intended to prolong product lifetimes, e.g. *re-using, re-pairing, re-purposing and re-appropriating*—collectively named RE-DIY. This chapter addresses the role of design as catalyst for sustainable RE-DIY. Four scenarios portray the possible role of professional designers as educators or facilitators in the relationship with RE-DIY practitioners, at both a global and local scale. On the basis of a review of the current 'state of the art', cases of design-led sustainable initiatives promoting RE-DIY are explored to highlight the potential and feasibility of novel relationships between producers and consumers. Finally, barriers to the evolution of RE-DIY towards sustainable patterns are identified and discussed, and triggers for scaling up this practice on a broader societal level are proposed.

Keywords Co-design · DIY design · Fablabs · Hackerspaces · RE-DIY

Giuseppe Salvia, Ph.D., Research Fellow, Politecnico di Milano, Italy; E-mail: Giuseppe.Salvia@polimi.it.

Tim Cooper, Ph.D., Professor of Sustainable Design and Consumption and co-Director, INDEMAND Research Centre, Nottingham Trent University, Nottingham, UK; E-mail: t.h.cooper@ntu.ac.uk.

A. Genus (ed.), *Sustainable Consumption*, The Anthropocene: Politik—Economics—Society—Science 3, DOI 10.1007/978-3-319-29665-4_2

2.1 Introduction

At the Rio+20 conference, many Heads of State and Government renewed their commitment to sustainable development (United Nations 2012). Decades of declared intentions for environmental sustainability (WCED 1987) and the pursuit of Sustainable Consumption and Production (SCP) (United Nations 2002) generated limited or even negative practical responses (Frascara, in Cipolla/Peruccio 2008; Krantz 2010). Governmental institutions adopted weak actions (Fuchs/Lorek 2005), producers pursued eco-efficiency with consequential rebound effects (Hertwich 2005), and individuals were encouraged to change their behaviour with little notable success (Lilley 2009).

Furthermore, a higher level of consumption is, paradoxically, decoupled from perceived happiness by people in industrialized hyper-consumerist countries (Easterlin 1974; Lipovetsky 2006; Porritt 2003). A revised and hopefully more sustainable interpretation of well-being (Manzini, in Bœuf et al. 2006) is required in order to encourage people towards alternative forms of satisfaction in which well-being is disconnected from a perceived need (and, even, perceived right) to increase consumption indefinitely (Cooper 2005; Thorpe 2010).

For this purpose, a multidisciplinary approach is fundamental to influencing the complex system of production and consumption towards an alternative, low resource-demanding form. Such a goal may sound extremely ambitious; however, strategies integrating technological efficiency with sufficiency-driven lifestyles have been explored (Cooper 2005; Stahel 1997; Tukker et al. 2010) and a resulting increase in perceived happiness verified (e.g. Mont/Plepys 2008).

Reduced consumption has been pursued as a means to achieve greater happiness by several communities, namely for down-shifting and 'voluntary simplicity'. These niches or 'local discontinuities' have been described as laboratories of successful solutions for SCP that should be observed and potentially catalysed by design action (Manzini 2010).

2.1.1 DIY as a Promising Area of Intervention

Low resource-demanding practices in the above niches have been explored in order to identify components leading to individual happiness or satisfaction. Past research findings suggest that communities of voluntary simplicity commonly practice self-production and repairing, motivated by the rewarding sensation they receive and the longer-lasting relationships they can establish with artefacts (Marchand/Walker 2008; Marchand et al. 2010). Recently concluded research by Salvia (2013) addressed contemporary practice of self-production and repairing (i.e. Do It Yourself or DIY) through the sociological perspective of practice theory (Shove 2006; Warde 2005). This theory proved supportive in the systematic and detailed description of DIY and people's main motivations for engaging in practicing DIY ('meanings' in practice theory), such as monetary savings or individual attitudes and lifestyles (Salvia 2013). Perceived satisfaction gained in the DIY practice appears to be the crucial component motivating pursuance and accomplishment of the task, regardless of the level of the individual's commitment and ability. In other words, less committed and skilled 'DIYers' are very likely to gain levels of enjoyment and satisfaction comparable to highly committed practitioners when a task is accomplished.

Based on four major observations, DIY appears to merit further design-led research:

1. DIY has been identified as a major trend in contemporary society (Anderson 2012) deserving further research (Watson/Shove 2008);
2. DIY may contribute to the provision of individual and social empowerment (Manzini 2003) while reducing the consumption of resources (Lorek/Spangenberg 2014);
3. DIY's inventive nature and the implied 'design thinking' (Cross 2011) facilitate interventions by designers and their dialogue with DIYers;
4. Design for DIY can represent a business opportunity (Fox 2013).

Everyone can—and does—design (Cross 2011: 3). Concepts have emerged to describe this contemporary phenomenon, such as the 'new' DIY age (Hoftijzer 2009), the 'post-professional era' (Atkinson 2010) and a paradigm shift to DIY-led invention (Fox 2013). Engaged individuals have been described as 'craft consumers' (Campbell 2005), 'lead users' (von Hippel 2005), 'professional amateurs' (Leadbeater/Miller 2004) and 'prosumers' (Anderson, in Toffler 1980). Such individuals are united by the will and ability to create artefacts that they desire and may be supported by innovative technologies (e.g. Atkinson et al. 2008), networks (e.g. Leadbeater 2008) and, perhaps, companies with new business models (e.g. Franke et al. 2006).

The spreading of physical and virtual places where people can undertake creative activities is enabling the coalescing of committed individuals who support each other in 'communities of practice' (Lave/Wenger 1991) or even 'creative communities', i.e. groups of people who cooperatively invent, enhance and manage innovative solutions for new ways of living (Manzini, in Bœuf et al. 2006).

Nevertheless, the spreading of DIY risks generating unwanted rebound effects on the environment. Facilitated access to the production system by consumers could, in theory, lead to inefficient resource use and increased waste, and thus the sustainability implications of this trend are still being debated (Troxler, in Abel et al. 2011; Watson/Shove 2006).

Self-designing and crafting of artefacts may still depend on systems of mass production (Watson/Shove 2008). The disruptive innovation brought about by these trends then risks being reduced to a different form of production and consumption of more goods: essentially a new form of capitalism (Ritzer/Jurgenson 2010).

The question is then how to align the current DIY trend with sustainability targets. Research by Salvia (2013) envisaged this contemporary phenomenon as a '*window of opportunity*' to foster positive sustainability impacts through, for example, personal growth, community empowerment and waste reduction. The research addressed self-production as a means to prolong product lifetimes by re-using, re-pairing, re-purposing, and re-appropriating, hereafter named 'RE-DIY', i.e. RE-activities in DIY practice. In addition, grassroots innovations—as also happening in contemporary DIY—are recognized as incubators of the social change that is needed to minimize future environmental harm (O'Brien, cited in Feola/Nunes 2014). In fact, there is a growing and diverse population applying the DIY approach to the replication, repair, regeneration, redesign, or refunctionalization of products (e.g. fixers, remakers, refurbishers, customizers and hackers) (Bianchini/Maffei 2013).

2.1.2 *Aim*

The spreading of this 'social and participatory innovation' may have significant implications for design (Abel et al. 2011). The objective of this chapter is thus to identify and evaluate the possible contribution of the design profession to contemporary self-production practices that foster a positive impact on the environment and society. The focus is on RE-DIY practice applied to the most voluminous bulky waste, i.e. furniture and other domestic products (apart from electrical and electronic equipment).[1] These account for around 60 % of landfilled waste in the United Kingdom (*Waste and Resources Action Programme* [WRAP] 2012) and other European countries, e.g. Italy (Centro di Ricerca Economica e Sociale Occhio del Riciclone 2010), the majority of which are in such good condition when discarded that reuse has become a key policy area for the European Union (Beasley/Georgeson 2014).

The chapter explores the potential transition of RE-DIY from niche to broader levels of engagement in society. In the following sections the role of design for SCP is briefly depicted and its application in the realm of self-production is then addressed.

2.2 The Role of Design in SCP and RE-DIY

Design is widely considered to have a major influence on whether SCP is realized: it has been estimated that 80 % of the impact of products, services and infrastructure is defined at the design stage (Design Council 2002). On this basis, the EU 7th Action Programme gave priority to promoting resource efficient products, namely by intervening on durability, reparability, re-usability and recyclability (European Parliament 2013).

[1]Electric and electronic equipment was excluded because of different implications, e.g. technological obsolescence and safety issues.

The environmental crisis is thus, in many ways, a design crisis (van der Ryn and Cowan, in Marchand/Walker 2006) and, indeed, there has long been interest from the design profession in the development of strategies to prompt change and transition under the umbrella of Design for Sustainability (Spangenberg et al. 2010; Walker/Giard 2013). Such approaches, also known as Green- or Eco-design, have challenged paradigms of design and industrial production and consumption previously taken for granted (Madge 1997). However, it has been argued that design is mostly absent from discourse on sustainable consumption (Thorpe 2010). An exception is Manzini (1994), who describes how design gives form to a changing world and offers opportunities for new types of behaviour, calling on designers to move from being part of the problem to become part of the solution (Manzini 2006).

Although it is technically possible to design more durable products, economic, institutional and psychological factors seem to prevent their success (Mont 2008; Cooper 2010), and a more structured and systematic approach is required. Recent guidelines on sustainable design have highlighted the need to frame the design contribution at several concurrent levels, ranging from product improvement to the creation of new lifestyle scenarios (Barbiroli 2008; Lewis/Gertsakis 2011; Giudice et al. 2006).

Vezzoli/Manzini (2008) propose four levels of design action for the creation of a (positive) 'sustainable impact', ranging from intervention on the production side to new scenarios for a sustainable and satisfactory quality of life. Such design actions could support the spreading of a perceived quality of life and wellbeing that is not reliant on material consumption (Evans/Jackson 2008).

The involvement of final users gradually increases at each of the four levels, ultimately becoming co-creators of the results that they want to achieve. At each level, the design profession can contribute in redirecting contemporary self-production trends towards low resource-demanding RE-DIY practice, without a loss of perceived wellbeing (Cooper 2005; Manno 2002).

RE-DIY practice has already received interest from the design community (Redström 2006; Brandes/Erlhoff 2006; Rosner/Bean 2009; Akah/Bardzell 2010; Coskun/Dogan 2010; Aguirre 2010; Jencks/Silver 1972). In the following section, opportunities of design interventions in RE-DIY are considered from a broader perspective and mapped.

2.2.1 The Four Scenarios

A review of current RE-DIY practice identified several elements that appeared to offer scope for positive impacts on the environment: the channels used for collection of artefacts, suitability of the place where the practice is performed, and the means by which information is gathered (Salvia 2013). It is evident that designers can contribute towards each by designing 'enabling solutions', i.e. "systems of tangible and intangible elements (such as technologies, infrastructures, legal frameworks and modes of governance and policy making) that enable individuals or communities to use their skills and abilities to best advantage and, at the same time, make a proposed solution more effective, more accessible and therefore more likely to spread" (Manzini, in Boeuf et al. 2006: 13).

Cases of design-led sustainability initiatives promoting RE-DIY have thus been identified as examples of good practice in the reduction of resource consumption with active and formative involvement of the user.

In these cases designers can support RE-DIYers either as collaborators with experts or as facilitators (or even educators) with less experienced practitioners, according to the creativity level of the RE-DIYer (Sanders/Stappers 2008). As collaborators, designers bring an equal contribution into a project shared with practitioners. As facilitators, designers support the development of the project drafted (or defined) by the practitioners.

The interaction between the design and the practitioner is necessarily influenced by the means of contact, e.g. in person, or web-based platform dialogue. The four cases presented below are grouped according to the scale of action (i.e. geographical level of intervention) and proximity. In this research, the value of locality is fostered within a globally connected framework, as proposed in the SLOC (Small, Local, Open and Connected) model of Manzini (2010), to address novel and visionary, yet viable, scenarios for sustainable design.

Designers can support RE-DIYers locally by:

- assisting RE-DIY designers over the creative process
- co-designing with municipalities for citizen engagement

and on a global level by:

- designing 'enabling products'
- networking between activists, researchers, professionals and DIY designers.

Each of these four scenarios is described in more detail below.

2.3 Local Level: Assisting RE-DIY Designers in the Creative Process

In the last decade many DIY workshops equipped with user-friendly devices have spread globally (e.g. 373 FabLabs, 1,801 Hackerspaces, over 1,000 Men's Sheds, plus Community Garages, TechShops, etc.[2] Generally aiming at providing facilities for self-production, these workshops offer members the opportunity to share skills, knowledge and projects with others passionate about DIY. Although the efficacy of

[2]FabLabs https://www.fablabs.io/labs, Hackerspaces http://hackerspaces.org/wiki/List_of_Hacker_Spaces Men's Sheds http://mensshed.org, 100 k Garages http://www.100kgarages.com, TechShops (http://www.techshop.ws/locations.html (7 September 2014).

this model towards sustainability is still debated (Troxler, in Abel et al. 2011), significant efforts have been addressed to this end by organizations such as The Restart Project[3] and ReFab Space[4]; both are social enterprises that promote the extension of electric and electronic equipment lifespans by teaching and sharing repair and maintenance skills, either in their premises or during workplace events, as an empowering practice.

The focus on repairing is currently also pursued by grassroots initiatives such as Fixit Clinic or Repair Café,[5] local, community-led initiatives of amateurs supporting citizens wishing to repair their items. In these cases, designers can facilitate the process, bringing knowledge (e.g. about materials and technology) and competences (e.g. design thinking) to address the problem of minimizing resource consumption and, especially, empowering and educating individuals. An example is offered by Fixperts, a project which promotes creative and social values through design; designers will support people with small fixing tasks that a non-professional person may find difficult to accomplish, thus giving confidence to the individual facing a challenge.[6]

2.4 Local Level: Co-designing with Municipalities for Citizen Engagement

Self-production initiatives take place on a wider scale, while still at the local level, through groups of citizens contributing to community projects (e.g. Transition Towns). There is a tradition of designers engaged in collaboration with local communities (Meroni 2007).

The Italian design studio Controprogetto,[7] for example, has been actively involved in initiatives for the engagement of non-professional people in social enterprises and community projects. Its particular studio expertise is design and manufacturing using scrap materials as an opportunity to promote a culture of doing, individual creativity, engagement with diversity (of people and disciplines), and a sense of ownership of public spaces.

The vision is reflected in their project Parteciparco, a playground designed and created with a co-operative that is intended to engage its members (mostly 16 to 30 years old) in the creative process of participatory construction with reclaimed materials. The Controprogetto designers operate as catalyst for people's ideas and energies, raising them to visionary levels. This experience nurtured the creativity of

[3]http://therestartproject.org/.

[4]http://www.refab-space.org/w/doku.php.

[5]http://repaircafe.org/en/.

[6]http://fixperts.org.

[7]http://www.controprogetto.it/.

subsequent users of the space, eventually stimulating a sense of respect towards this shared infrastructure (Salvia 2013).

Similar results have been encountered in a bigger project, ParkUrka[8] with enthusiastic members of a neighbourhood in Taranto, Italy, to transform part of the town. The project aimed at strengthening inhabitants' sense of belonging towards the public space through collaborative, formative, but still enjoyable, experiences.

Designers operating at a local level can support RE-DIY practitioners in the development of their ideas through direct contact. They can contribute their skills in managing meta-design and problem-solving issues to extend product lifetimes, at the same time catalysing the process of increasing people's awareness of material, processing and, perhaps, environmental issues relating to artefacts. Operating at a local level provides the designer with an opportunity to receive instant feedback from the 'RE-DIYer' and allows for an iterative process of refinement according to the practitioner's response.

A different approach is required in the case of design interventions involving RE-DIYers at a global level, without direct contact.

2.5 Global Level: Designing 'Enabling Products'

RE-DIY practice is being nurtured by accessibility to information through the web, typically through online tutorials and instructions guiding users wishing to repair technological devices. Beyond the more widely known platforms for generic purposes (e.g. YouTube), iFixIt[9] is an on-line platform and community that supports the repair of all sorts of electrical and electronic devices by providing guides and selling parts. iFixIt thus aims at contributing to the extension of product lifespan and empowers people willing to repair faulty products.

Support provided in the form of communicating manual skills through virtual means does, however, face inherent limitations as direct feedback is generally lacking. Moreover, practitioners may be inhibited from undertaking a repair by a perception of lack of skills and competence, the latter "conventionally defined as a characteristic of the human subject [but] perhaps better understood as something that is in effect distributed between practitioners and the tools and materials they use" (Watson/Shove 2008: 77) .

Some studies are addressing this challenge (Fox et al. 2011). Meanwhile, designers have been creating practical means by which practitioners are able to undertake RE-DIY tasks, in the form of 'enabling products', indicating products—within the realm of 'enabling solutions' defined above—that limit the chance of error and enhance the confidence of users. RE-DIY practice has thus been facilitated by design professionals at different levels of competence through the

[8]https://labuat.wordpress.com/2009/09/08/immagini-dal-cantiere-di-park-urka/.

[9]https://www.ifixit.com/.

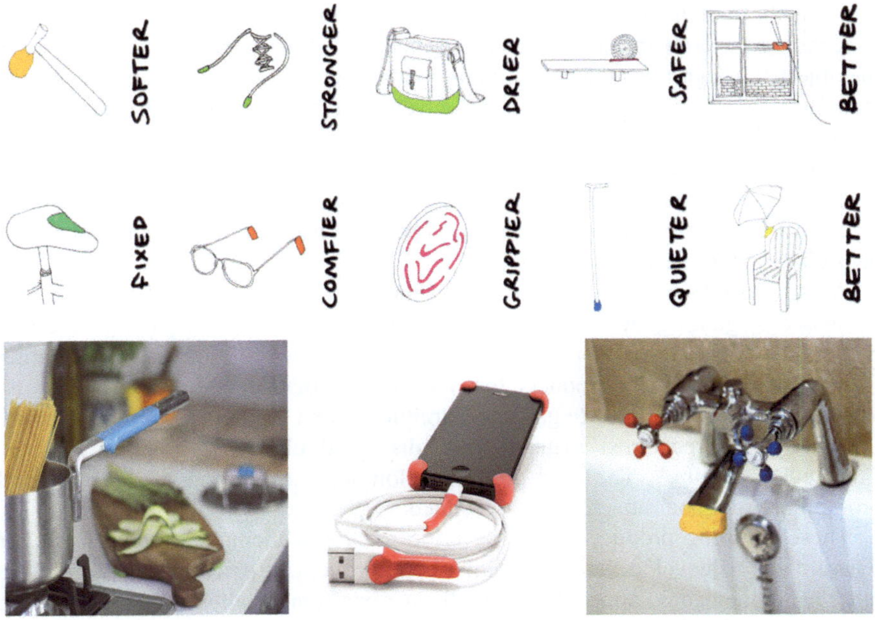

Fig. 2.1 Illustrations of some early Sugru repair products. *Source* Sugru.com (used with permission)

invention of new materials (e.g. Sugru, Woolfiller and Kintsugi),[10] technologies (e.g. customization kits for consumers) and products (e.g. Project_RE).[11]

For example, Sugru,[12] is a silicon-based material invented by a designer to support people willing to repair—or improve the status and use of—a wide range of products. These include improving the grip and heat resistance of pan handles, making cables for mobile phones more durable and making bath taps safer (see Fig. 2.1). Similar to plasticine, Sugru can be shaped according to the practitioner's taste and need. Once applied to any surface, it dries in the air and the object can be used as normal. Its attributes of self-adhesion, waterproofness and flexibility, together with aesthetic versatility (in shape and colour), make Sugru an accessible means for practitioners to restore or extend an empathic relation with objects.

A French design studio, 5.5 designstudio, addressed the challenge of designing components that facilitate reusing and repurposing practices in the project 'Réanim—the medicine of objects'[13]: prosthetic seats and legs allow for the recovery of

[10]More information about Sugru at http://sugru.com/, Woolfiller at http://www.woolfiller.com/, Kintsugi at http://humade.nl/products/new-kintsugi-1.

[11]http://project-re.blogspot.it.

[12]http://sugru.com/.

[13]http://www.5-5designstudio.com/en/project/2004-55designers-reanim.

products through the use of adjustable devices that fit (almost) every chair. The task of repairing the artefact (i.e. connecting components of the chair) is shared between the object (through the adjustable joining system) and the user (with simple manual skills to connect the components). A conventional method of repairing a broken chair would normally require practitioners to have the ability to choose, saw, plane or lathe, sand, nail and finish a piece of wood. The solution developed by 5.5 design studio enables people with different levels of manual capability to accomplish the repair task by distributing the competences between user and object, with an almost negligible chance of error.

As suggested above, limiting the likelihood of mistakes in RE-DIY is also addressed by guiding the practitioner through some or all of the steps in the creative process. Designers have been considering the involvement of final users in creating (or finalizing) RE-DIY products through on-line platforms for consumer customization (Schreier 2006) (e.g. Indie Furniture[14]) and guidelines on how to make furniture using reclaimed materials and discarded objects (e.g. Open Chair,[15] Cuisine D'Objects).[16] The final goal is prolonging the lifespan of materials and promoting emotional attachment to products.

These enabling products might be criticized for reducing the opportunity for practitioners to develop their acquisition or improvement of competences. On the other hand, they could appeal to and motivate practitioners who might otherwise be deterred from RE-DIY because they do not consider a task to be feasible with their level of competence. Watson/Shove (2008: 77) suggest that such devices should not be seen as instruments of de-skilling but as "agents that rearrange the distribution of competence within the entire network of entities that must be integrated to accomplish the job in hand."

2.6 Global Level: Networking Between Activists, Researchers, Professionals and DIY Designers

The establishment of the Internet, web 2.0 and social media has contributed to the spreading of groups who collaborate on a wide scale, often at a global level, for shared purposes. This is an example of commons-based peer production, whereby "large groups of individuals…co-operate effectively to provide information, knowledge or cultural goods without relying on either market pricing or managerial hierarchies to co-ordinate their common enterprise" (Benkler/Nissenbaum 2006: 394). It has led to several phenomena, initiatives and communities (e.g. open source, peer-to-peer, etc.) emerging with the aim of contributing to a more community-oriented society. Peer production has been envisaged as "an

[14]http://www.indie-furniture.org/configurator/.

[15]http://www.jamestooze.com/open-design/open-source-chair/.

[16]http://www.5-5designstudio.com/en/project/2009-cuisine-dobjets.

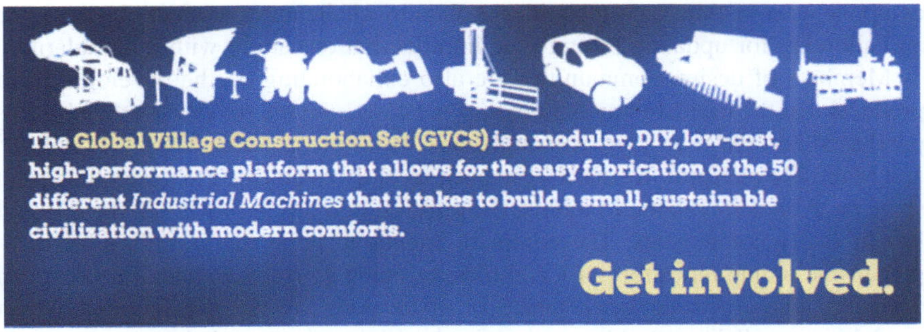

Fig. 2.2 Process for the generation of Open Structures components. *Source* Picture from http://blog.makezine.com/2010/02/23/open-structures-help-create-an-open/

opportunity for more people to engage in practices that permit them to exhibit and experience virtuous behavior" (Benkler/Nissenbaum 2006: 394).

Abilities in communication and compromise are likely to prove crucial for a successful output. Participants from different backgrounds need to establish a common terminology and understanding of each other's experiences. *Open Source Ecology* (OSE),[17] for instance, is a wiki platform connecting farmers, engineers and volunteers in order to develop the main parts for high-performance machinery collaboratively.

In another example aimed at facilitating collaboration between people involved in designing products, design studio Infrastructures[18] developed Open Structures,[19] an experimental construction system based on modules that can be designed collaboratively. The size and dimensional features of parts, components and products are based on a grid that allows for the creation, modification and integration of modular and compatible elements of a shared 'library'. The Open Structures approach is based on a few defined principles[20] aimed at supporting personal growth, product longevity and resource conservation (see Fig. 2.2). The project seeks to initiate "a new standard for sustainable and democratic design that, based on the principles of open-source software, facilitates the re-use of objects, parts and components and allows us to build things together".[21] An open, modular system of this kind has the potential to stimulate re-use cycles of various parts and

[17]http://opensourceecology.org.

[18]http://www.intrastructures.net.

[19]http://www.openstructures.net.

[20]'Standardize dimensions', 'Allow disassembly', 'Exchange skills', 'Allow hacking', 'Stimulate growth', 'Transform waste'.

[21]http://www.intrastructures.net/Intrastructures/Analysis_files/flyer_final-ENG.pdf. Further information in Lommee, Thomas (edited by). 2010. Yes! we're open. Open design for sustainable innovation. Exhibition catalogue. Kortrijk, Belgium.

components over time on a global level, thereby challenging product obsolescence and allowing for updating through the introduction of variety within modularity.

Members of design communities are also collaborating on the development of products that the user can buy online; in some cases, the file rather than the object is purchased and the user sources manufacture locally (e.g. Shapeways,[22] Ponoko.[23] and Make Me platform. Kazzata[24] has been recently established to design and print spare parts on demand, thus avoiding the disposal of a whole product in the event of lost or faulty components. The company intends to build the world's most comprehensive online repository of CAD files, bringing consumers, manufacturers and designers into a virtual marketplace of spare parts. If the file required is not available, it will be possible to send in the broken item and the company will produce a virtual replica.

Collaboration between practitioners and design professionals on a wider scale has resulted in groups forming to share experiences and disseminate knowledge in order to support a culture of product longevity or, more specifically, repair. From the late 1990s, the Dutch Eternally Yours Foundation operated for several years as a design-led multidisciplinary group investigating the topics of product longevity and emotional attachment to products, resulting in two books (Van Hinte 2004, 1997); a similar role was played in Britain by the Network on Product Life Spans.[25] Subsequent design-led efforts have introduced communities of researchers and activists to promote product longevity (e.g. Platform 21, Mend*RS). However, a lack of long term resilience in such initiatives raises questions about possible barriers to bringing the topic from an area of niche interest to higher levels of action.

2.7 Barriers and Triggers for Spreading RE-DIY

The cases presented above provide strong evidence of the role of design, at both local and global levels, to redirect contemporary DIY trends towards patterns of SCP, especially by promoting product longevity through interventions of repair, re-use, re-purpose and re-appropriation. The resulting design-led RE-DIY practice fosters not only a reduction in resource consumption but has a positive impact on individuals and the social fabric, e.g. a preference for local resources and craftsmanship, skilling processes and environmentally conscious behaviour, encouraging collaboration. However, these potential benefits may be undermined by certain factors discussed below.

[22]http://www.shapeways.com.

[23]http://www.ponoko.com/.

[24]http://kazzata.com/.

[25]http://gow.epsrc.ac.uk/NGBOViewGrant.aspx?GrantRef=GR/S87645/01.

2.7.1 Availability and Suitability of Local Resources

The four scenarios demonstrate interventions that may involve making use of locally available resources and products to, for instance, repair products. Countries or localities with limited means could, however, be strongly challenged in this respect. Nevertheless, optimization of available resources contributed to success in some cases, namely as a driver for variety and even innovation. In fact, historical evidence suggests that cultures constrained by limited resources may in such circumstances demonstrate inventiveness, performance, efficiency or beauty, as in ancient Japan with the Urawaza (Juniper 2003), England during the Great Depression and World Wars with 'Make-Do-and-Mend' (Ministry of Information 2007), Russia with contemporary folk artefacts (Arkhipov 2006), and the current Cuba with the Rikimbili (Oroza 2009).

In recent times, designers have been exploring the condition of limited resource availability as a business (and environmental) opportunity. One of the most notable cases is Swiss manufacturer Freitag,[26] which reuses discarded truck coverings and car safety belts for unique high-performance bags. In short, designers can support the interpretation and utilization of locally available resources to meet people's needs.

2.7.2 The Aesthetics of Imperfection

Artefacts resulting from RE-DIY practice generally show signs of age that may accelerate a desire to replace them with shiny new objects. However, they can gain value through design-led contributions, as seen in particular in the case of enabling products. The positive implication envisaged is a new aesthetic paradigm: the provision of dignity to 'imperfect' appearance and the acceptance—or even appreciation—of mutable, physically degrading products (Salvia et al. 2010). Signs of imperfection due to wear and use bear witness to the shared existence of an artefact and its user, potentially strengthening their relationship.

Design has increasingly addressed strategies for emotional attachment (Mugge et al. 2010; Lilley 2009; Scott et al. 2009; Van Hinte 2004; Chapman 2005; Woolley 2003) with products that evolve with the user, e.g. by adaptation to new needs, visual traces of use, or ageing gracefully. The object then becomes the representation of its user's identity and story, embedding significant and valuable components and memories, and making the user more willing to keep and take care of it for longer.

---

[26]http://www.freitag.ch/.

2.7.3 *Possible Side-Effects of 'Green Consumption'*

Products that are intended to support a shift to sustainable consumption may nonetheless be treated as commodities and risk offering no more than a greener form of consumerism, even triggering the acquisition of new goods, the 'Diderot effect' (McCracken 1990). This risk can be limited by strengthening the pro-environmental information and experience that the item embeds or favours. The provision of a clear and engaging message, stimulating enquiry about skills acquisition and environmental questions, can trigger or amplify the trend towards SCP. For instance, Sugru (described above) has a web-gallery showcasing possible uses of this material at different levels of complexity, thus encouraging people to use it according to their personal level of skill. Likewise the online stores for collaboratively designed products presented above could inform buyers about the environmental and social benefits of their products if the client opts for purchasing the file and manufacturing the product locally rather than purchasing the product and requesting delivery.

According to Shove/Warde (2001: 237), "the Diderot effect could be appropriated in support of less wasteful consumer practices, by restoring value to durability, by encouraging the matching of those items whose production and distribution is not a threat to sustainability, and so forth." In other words, promoting the consumption of one type of less environmentally harmful product could encourage the purchase of other types of less environmentally harmful product, thereby accelerating progress towards SCP.

The provision of enabling solutions allowing for successful results may increase self-confidence in practitioners, thus "setting and moving the boundary between what amateurs are and are not willing to do for themselves, and in permitting and sustaining innovations in practice" (Shove et al. 2007: 66). As a consequence, practitioners may become keen to extend the range of RE-DIY activities in which they engage, with further potentially positive effects on the environment.

2.8 Discussion and Conclusion

The four scenarios presented above demonstrate that design can redirect contemporary DIY practice towards SCP through a focus on RE-activities. Some barriers that might prevent its evolution or spreading have been identified and possible ways to overcome them proposed.

Current RE-DIY trends with design involvement can be elements of innovation in (potentially) sustainable practices. The positive results collected in what are relatively small scale projects should encourage adoption more widely. Even so, RE-DIY practices need to be nurtured. The design-led cases presented above represent opportunities for innovation, either at a local or global level, but effort and resources are required to support these and similar cases, namely by introducing them into the daily life of current (and possibly future) practitioners. This could enable the transition of RE-DIY from niches—where it currently it resides—to a broader level. Salvia (2013) proposes the introduction of RE-DIY culture and practice in education programs (e.g. modules in schools of Design), social enterprises and repair workshops.

Policy-makers can play a crucial role in encouraging design-led initiatives involving local and global communities in SCP projects. However, grassroots innovations such as the DIY trend discussed in this chapter are sometimes either not visible to them or do not attract their support, and consequently their potential remains largely underdeveloped (Feola/Nunes 2014). This is unfortunate, as governments could act to catalyse the innovation brought by the RE-DIY niches in wider societal levels arising from the interest of manufacturers (e.g. of rapid prototyping machineries), development of technologies (e.g. Web 2.0) and emergent networks (e.g. repair communities). Governments could, for example, offer support for establishing or developing infrastructure to facilitate RE-DIY (e.g. local workshops) and for deepening relationships between local communities and industry (e.g. through public funding for collaboration). These are topics that merit further investigation.

References

Abel, B. van; Klaassen, R.; Evers, L.; Troxler, P. (Eds.) 2011: *Open Design Now: Why Design Cannot Remain Exclusive* (Amsterdam: BIS Publishers).

Aguirre, D., 2010: "Design for Repurposing: A Sustainable Design Strategy for Product Life and Beyond", in: *Industrial Designers Society of America 2010 Conference,* 1–25.

Akah, B.; Bardzell, S., 2010: "Empowering Products: Personal Identity through the Act of Appropriation", in: *CHI'10 Conference* (Atlanta, GA, USA: ACM): 4021–4026. doi:10.1145/1753846.1754096. http://dl.acm.org/citation.cfm?id=1754096.

Anderson, C., 2012: *Makers: The New Industrial Revolution* (Toronto: McClelland and Stewart). http://books.google.co.uk/books/about/Makers.html?id=L5zxn5JFIeQC&pgis=1.

Arkhipov, V., 2006: *Home-Made: Contemporary Russian Folk Artifacts* (London: Fuel Publishing). http://books.google.com/books?id=HLi0AAAAIAAJ&pgis=1.

Atkinson, P., 2010: "Boundaries? What Boundaries? The Crisis of Design in a Post-Professional Era", in: *The Design Journal,* 13,2: 137–155.

Atkinson, P.; Unver, E.; Marshall, J.; Dean, L.T., 2008: "Post Industrial Manufacturing Systems: The Undisciplined Nature of Generative Design", in: *Proceedings of the Design Research Society Conference,* Sheffield Hallam University, 194/1-194/17. Sheffield. http://eprints.hud.ac.uk/5628/1/Atkinson_et_al_DRS2008_194.pdf.

Barbiroli, G., 2008: "Profile of Products' Enduring Quality Over Long Periods as Strategic Factor to Increase their Utilisation Rate", in: *International Journal of Product Development,* 6,3/4: 450–467. http://inderscience.metapress.com/index/J877K19201143093.pdf.

Beasley, J.; Georgeson, R., 2014: *Advancing Resource Efficiency in Europe: Indicators and Waste Policy Scenarios to Deliver a Resource Efficient and Sustainable Europe* (Brussels: European Environmental Bureau).

Benkler, Y.; Nissenbaum, H., 2006: Commons-Based Peer Production and Virtue. in: *Journal of Political Philosophy,* 14,4 (December): 394–419. doi:10.1111/j.1467-9760.2006.00235.x; http://onlinelibrary.wiley.com/doi/10.1111/j.1467-9760.2006.00235.x/full.

Bianchini, M.; Maffei, S., 2013: "Microproduction Everywhere: Defining the Boundaries of the Emerging New Distributed Microproduction Socio-Technical Paradigm", in: *Social Frontiers: The Next Edge of Social Innovation Research*: 1–21; Available at: http://www.researchgate.net/profile/Stefano_Maffei3/publication/269996138_Microproduction_everywhere._Social_local_open_and_connected_manufacturing/links/549dd6d90cf2fedbc3119a04.pdf (11 June 2015).

Bœuf, J.Le.; Amatullo, M.; Breitenberg, M.; Maffei, S.; Villari, B.; Menzi, R.; Loetscher, M.; Fleming, D.; Lynch, G., 2006: *Cumulus Working Papers*. 16/06. Publication Series G. Nantes.

Brandes, U.; Erlhoff, M., 2006: *Non Intentional Design* (Cologne: DAAB).

Campbell, C., 2005: "The Craft Consumer: Culture, Craft and Consumption in a Postmodern Society", in: *Journal of Consumer Culture,* 5,1 (March 1): 23–42. http://joc.sagepub.com/content/5/1/23.

Centro di Ricerca Economica e Sociale Occhio del Riciclone, 2010: "Rapporto Nazionale Sul Riutilizzo 2010" (in Italian). Centro di Ricerca Economica e Sociale Occhio del Riciclone; Available at: http://www.occhiodelriciclone.com/attachments/article/1211/RAPPORTO%20NAZIONALE%20SUL%20RIUTILIZZO%202014.pdf (20 June 2015).

Chapman, J., 2005: *Emotionally Durable Design: Objects, Experiences and Empathy* (London: Routledge).

Cipolla, C.; Peruccio, P.P. (Eds). 2008: "Changing the Change", in: *Changing the Change: Design, Visions, Proposals and Tools* (Torino: Allemandi).

Cooper, T., 2005: Slower Consumption: Reflections on Product Life Spans and the 'Throwaway Society'", in: *Journal of Industrial Ecology*, 9,1–2: 51–67. doi:10.1162/1088198054084671.

Cooper, T. (Ed.) 2010: *Longer Lasting Products: Alternatives to the Throwaway Society* (Farnham: Gower).

Coskun, A.; Dogan, C., 2010: "Post-Use Design Thinking Presenting Insights into a Design Research for Sustainability", in: *Proceedings of LeNS Conference*, Bangalore, India. (Sheffield, UK: Greenleaf Publishing): 368–381.

Cross, N., 2011: *Design Thinking: Understanding How Designers Think and Work* (Oxford: Bloomsbury Academic). http://books.google.co.uk/books/about/Design_Thinking.html?id=Ndu48n8Ik9UC&pgis=1.

Design Council, 2002: *Design Council Annual Review 2002. Review Literature and Arts of The Americas* (London: Design Council).

Easterlin, R., 1974: "Does Economic Growth Improve the Human Lot? Some Empirical Evidence", in: Paul, A.D.; Reder, W.M. (Eds.): *Nations and Households in Economic Growth: Essays in Honour of Moses Abramovitz* (New York: Academic Press): 89–125.

European Parliament (2013). Decision no. 1386/2013/EU of the European Parliament and of the Council of 20 November 2013 on a General Union Environment Action Programme to 2020 "Living Well, within the Limits of Our Planet." *Official Journal of the European Union*. http://eur-lex.europa.eu/legal-content/EN/TXT/PDF/?uri=CELEX:32013D1386&from=EN.

Evans, D.; Jackson, T., 2008: *Sustainable Consumption: Perspectives from Social and Cultural Theory*. RESOLVE Working Paper 05–08.

Feola, G.; Nunes, R., 2014: "Success and Failure of Grassroots Innovations for Addressing Climate Change: The Case of the Transition Movement", in: *Global Environmental Change*, 24: 232–250. doi:10.1016/j.gloenvcha.2013.11.011. http://www.sciencedirect.com/science/article/pii/S0959378013002197.

Fox, S., 2012: "The New Do-It-Yourself Paradigm: Financial and Ethical Rewards for Businesses", in: *Journal of Business Strategy,* 33,1: 21–26. doi:10.1108/02756661211193785. http://www.emeraldinsight.com/10.1108/02756661211193785.

Fox, S., 2013: "Paradigm Shift: Do-It-Yourself (DIY) Invention and Production of Physical Goods for Use or Sale", in: *Journal of Manufacturing Technology Management*, 24,2: 218–234. doi:10.1108/17410381311292313. http://www.emeraldinsight.com/10.1108/17410381311292313.

Fox, S.; Ehlen, P.; Purver, M., 2011: "Enabling Distributed Communication of Manual Skills", in: *International Journal of Managing Projects in Business,* 4,1: 49–63. doi:10.1108/17538371111096881; http://www.emeraldinsight.com/10.1108/17538371111096881.

Franke, N.; von Hippel, E.; Schreier, M., 2006: "Finding Commercially Attractive User Innovations: A Test of Lead-User Theory", in: *Journal of Product Innovation Management*, 23,4: 301–315. doi:10.1111/j.1540-5885.2006.00203.x; http://doi.wiley.com/10.1111/j.1540-5885.2006.00203.x.

Fuchs, D.A., Lorek, S., 2005: "Sustainable Consumption Governance: A History of Promises and Failures", in: *Journal of Consumer Policy*, 28,3: 261–288. doi:10.1007/s10603-005-8490-z; http://www.springerlink.com/index/10.1007/s10603-005-8490-z.

Giudice, F.; La Rosa, G.; Risitano, A., 2006: *Product Design for the Environment: A Life Cycle Approach* (Boca Raton, FL: CRC Press).

Hertwich, E.G., 2005: "Consumption and the Rebound Effect: An Industrial Ecology Perspective", in: *Journal of Industrial Ecology,* 9,1: 85–98. http://onlinelibrary.wiley.com/doi/10.1162/1088198054084635/abstract.

Hoftijzer, J., 2009: "DIY and Co-creation: Representatives of a Democratizing Tendency", in: *Design Principles and Practices, An International Journal,* 3,6: 69–81.

Jencks, C.; Silver, N., 1972: *Adhocism: The Case for Improvisation* (New York: Doubleday).

Juniper, A., 2003: *Wabi Sabi: The Japanese Art of Impermanence* (Boston: Tuttle Publishing).

Krantz, R. (2010). "A New Vision of Sustainable Consumption", in: *Journal of Industrial Ecology,* 14,1 (January): 7–9. doi:10.1111/j.1530-9290.2009.00220.x; http://blackwell-synergy.com/doi/abs/10.1111/j.1530-9290.2009.00220.x.

Lave, J.; Wenger, E., 1991: *Situated Learning: Legitimate Peripheral Participation* (Cambridge: Cambridge University Press). http://books.google.co.uk/books/about/Situated_Learning.html?id=CAVIOrW3vYAC&pgis=1.

Leadbeater, C., 2008: *We-Think: Mass Innovation, Not Mass Production* (London: Profile Books).

Leadbeater, C.; Miller, P., 2004: *The Pro-Am Revolution: How Enthusiasts Are Changing Our Economy and Society* (London: Demos).

Lewis, H.; Gertsakis, J. (Eds.) 2011: "Electronic and Electronical Products", in: Lewis, H.; Gertsakis, J. (Eds.): *Design and Environment: A Global Guide to Designing Greener Goods* (Sheffield, UK: Greenleaf): 164–184.

Lilley, D., 2009: "Design for Sustainable Behaviour: Strategies and Perceptions", in: *Design Studies*, 30,6: 704–720. doi:10.1016/j.destud.2009.05.001; http://linkinghub.elsevier.com/retrieve/pii/S0142694X09000301.

Lipovetsky, G., 2006: *Le Bonheur Paradoxal: Essai Sur La Société D'hyperconsommation* (Paris: Gallimard).

Lorek, S.; Spangenberg, J., 2014: "Sustainable Consumption Within a Sustainable Economy—Beyond Green Growth and Green Economies", in: *Journal of Cleaner Production*, 63: 33–44. doi:10.1016/j.jclepro.2013.08.045; http://www.sciencedirect.com/science/article/pii/S0959652613006008.

Madge, P., 1997: "Ecological Design: A New Critique", in: *Design Issues*, 13,2: 44–54. http://www.jstor.org/stable/1511730.

Manno, J., 2002: "Commoditization: Consumption Efficiency and an Economy of Care and Connection", in: Princen, T.; Maniates, M.; Conca, K. (Eds.): *Confronting Consumption* (Cambridge: MIT Press): 67–87.

Manzini, E., 1994: "Design, Environment and Social Quality: From 'Existenzminimum' to 'Quality Maximum'", in: *Design Issues*, 10,1: 37–43. http://www.jstor.org/stable/1511653.

Manzini, E., 2003: "Scenarios of Sustainable Wellbeing", in: *Design Philosophy Papers*, 1,1: 5–21. doi:10.2752/144871303X13965299301434; http://www.ingentaconnect.com/content/bloomsbury/dphp/2003/00000001/00000001/art00002.

Manzini, E. (2006). "Design Research for Sustainable Social Innovation", in: Michel, R. (Ed.): *Design Research Now: Essays and Selected Projects* (Board of International Research in Design) (Basel: Birkhäuser): 233–245.

Manzini, E., 2010: "Small, Local, Open and Connected. Design Research Topics in the Age of Networks and Sustainability", in: *Proceedings of LeNS Conference*, Bangalore, India, 14–18.

Marchand, A.; Walker, S., 2006: "Designing Alternatives: Sustainable Consumption, Lifestyles and 'Responsible Consumers'", in: *Proceedings of Changes to Sustainable Consumption. Workshop of the Sustainable Consumption Research Exchange (SCORE!) Network*, Copenhagen, 253–264.

Marchand, A.; Walker, S., 2008: "Product Development and Responsible Consumption: Designing Alternatives for Sustainable Lifestyles", in: *Journal of Cleaner Production*, 16,11: 1163–1169. doi:10.1016/j.jclepro.2007.08.012; http://linkinghub.elsevier.com/retrieve/pii/S0959652607001837.

Marchand, A.; Walker, S.; Cooper, T., 2010: "Beyond Abundance: Self-Interest Motives for Sustainable Consumption in Relation to Product Perception and Preferences", in: *Sustainability*, 2,5: 1431–1447. doi:10.3390/su2051431; http://www.mdpi.com/2071-1050/2/5/1431/.

McCracken, G.D., 1990: *Culture and Consumption: New Approaches to the Symbolic Character of Consumer Goods and Activities* (Bloomington: Indiana University Press). http://books.google.com/books?id=szALv30Usi0C&pgis=1.

Meroni, A., 2007: *Creative Communities. People Inventing Sustainable Ways of Living* (Milano: POLI.design). http://books.google.com/books?id=ClSXPAAACAAJ&pgis=1.

Ministry of Information, 2007: *Make Do and Mend* (London: Sabrestorm Publishing) (Historic Booklet Series). http://books.google.co.uk/books/about/Make_Do_and_Mend.html?id=fEgAngEACAAJ&pgis=1.

Mont, O., 2008. "Innovative Approaches to Optimising Design and Use of Durable Consumer Goods", in: *International Journal of Product Development*, 6,3/4: 227–250. doi:10.1504/IJPD.2008.020395. http://www.inderscience.com/link.php?id=20395.

Mont, O.; Plepys, A., 2008: "Sustainable Consumption Progress: Should we be Proud or Alarmed?", in: *Journal of Cleaner Production*, 16,4: 531–537. doi:10.1016/j.jclepro.2007.01.009; http://linkinghub.elsevier.com/retrieve/pii/S0959652607000352.

Mugge, R., Schifferstein, H.N.J., Schoormans, J.P.L., 2010: "Product Attachment and Satisfaction: Understanding Consumers' Post-Purchase Behavior", in: *Journal of Consumer Marketing*, 27,3: 271–282. doi:10.1108/07363761011038347; http://www.emeraldinsight.com/10.1108/07363761011038347.

Oroza, E., 2009: *RIKIMBILI. Une Étude Sur La Désobéissance Technologique et Quelques Formes de Réinvention*. (Saint-Étienne: Université de Saint-Étienne).

Porritt, J., 2003: Redefining Prosperity: Resource Productivity, Economic Growth and Sustainable Development; Available at: https://research-repository.st-andrews.ac.uk/bitstream/10023/2233/1/sdc-2003-redefining-prosperity.pdf (26 May 2015).

Redström, J., 2006: "Towards User Design? On the Shift from Object to User as the Subject of Design", in: *Design Studies*, 27,2: 123–139. doi:10.1016/j.destud.2005.06.001; http://linkinghub.elsevier.com/retrieve/pii/S0142694X05000359.

Ritzer, G.; Jurgenson, N., 2010: "Production, Consumption, Prosumption: The Nature of Capitalism in the Age of the Digital 'Prosumer'", In: *Journal of Consumer Culture*, 10,1: 13–36. doi:10.1177/1469540509354673; http://joc.sagepub.com/content/10/1/13.abstract.

Rosner, D.; Bean, J., 2009: "Learning from IKEA Hacking: 'I'm Not One to Decoupage a Tabletop and Call it a Day", in: *Proceedings of the 27th International Conference on Human Factors in Computing Systems CHI '09* (New York: ACM): 419–422. doi:10.1145/1518701.1518768; http://people.ischool.berkeley.edu/~daniela/research/note1500-rosner.pdf.

Salvia, G., 2013: "Design for satisfactory and sustainable patterns of consumption and production: design for the contemporary practice of do-it-yourself" (Ph.D. thesis, Milano: Politecnico di Milano); Available at: https://www.politesi.polimi.it/handle/10589/74842 (11 June 2015).

Salvia, G.; Ostuzzi, F.; Rognoli, V.; Levi, M., 2010: "The Value of Imperfection in Sustainable Design", in: *Sustainability in Design: Now!* Bangalore, India, 1573–1589.

Sanders, E.B.; Stappers, P.J., 2008: Co-Creation and the New Landscapes of Design. in: *Co-Design*, 4,1: 5–18. http://www.tandfonline.com/doi/abs/10.1080/15710880701875068.

Schreier, M., 2006: "The Value Increment of Mass-Customized Products : An Empirical Assessment", in: *Journal of Consumer Behaviour*, 5: 317–327.

Scott, K.; Quist, J.; Bakker, C., 2009: "Co-Design, Social Practices and Sustainability Innovation: Involving Users in a Living Lab Exploratory Study on Bathing", in: *Proceedings of Joint Actions on Climate Change conference,* Aalborg, Denmark, 8–10 June 2009, 1–15. http://ordinarylifestudy.typepad.com/files/scottbakkerquistsm.pdf.

Shove, E., 2006: Towards practice oriented product design. Presented at Towards Practice Oriented Product Design, London, 6 September; Available at: http://www.lancaster.ac.uk/fass/projects/dnc/media/towards%20popd.pdf.

Shove, E.; Warde, A., 2001: "Inconspicuous Consumption: the Sociology of Consumption and the Environment", in: Dunlap, R.; Buttel, F.; Dickens, P.; Gijswijt, A. (Eds.): *Sociological Theory and the Environment: Classical Foundations, Contemporary Insight* (Plymouth: Rowman and Littlefield): 230–250.

Shove, E.; Watson, M.; Hand, M.; Ingram, J., 2007: *The Design of Everyday Life* (Oxford: Berg).

Spangenberg, J.H.; Fuad-Luke, A.; Blincoe, K., 2010: "Design for Sustainability (dfs): The Interface of Sustainable Production and Consumption", in: *Journal of Cleaner Production*, 18,15: 1485–1493. doi:10.1016/j.jclepro.2010.06.002; http://linkinghub.elsevier.com/retrieve/pii/S0959652610002143.

Stahel, W.R., 1997: "The Service Economy: 'Wealth Without Resource Consumption'?", in: *Philosophical Transactions of the Royal Society A: Mathematical, Physical and Engineering Sciences,* 355,1728: 1309–1319. doi:10.1098/rsta.1997.0058; http://rsta.royalsocietypublishing.org/cgi/doi/10.1098/rsta.1997.0058.

Thorpe, A., 2010. "Design's Role in Sustainable Consumption", in: *Design Issues,* 26,2: 3–16. http://www.mitpressjournals.org/doi/abs/10.1162/DESI_a_00001.

Toffler, A., 1980: *The Third Wave* (New York: William Morrow).

Tukker, A.; Cohen, M.J.; Hubacek, K.; Mont, O., 2010: "The Impacts of Household Consumption and Options for Change", in: *Journal of Industrial Ecology*, 14,1: 13–30. doi:10.1111/j.1530-9290.2009.00208.x; http://blackwell-synergy.com/doi/abs/10.1111/j.1530-9290.2009.00208.x.

United Nations, 2002: *Report of the World Summit on Sustainable Development* (Johannesburg: United Nations).

United Nations, 2012: *Report of the United Nations Conference on Sustainable Development* (Rio de Janeiro, Brazil: United Nations).

Van Hinte, E. (Ed.) 1997: *Eternally Yours: Visions on Product Endurance* (Rotterdam: 010 Publishers).

Van Hinte, E., 2004: *Eternally Yours: Time in Design* (Rotterdam: 010 Publishers).

Vezzoli, C.; Manzini, E., 2008: *Design for Environmental Sustainability* (London: Springer). doi:10.1007/978-1-84800-163-3; http://www.springerlink.com/index/10.1007/978-1-84800-163-3.

Von Hippel, E., 2005: *Democratizing Innovation* (Cambridge, MA: MIT Press). doi:10.1111/j.1540-5885.2006.00192_2.x.

Walker, S.; Giard, J. (Eds.) 2013: *The Handbook of Design for Sustainability* (London: Bloomsbury). http://www.bloomsbury.com/uk/the-handbook-of-design-for-sustainability-9780857858528/.

Warde, A., 2005: "Consumption and Theories of Practice", in: *Journal of Consumer Culture*, 5,2: 131–153. doi:10.1177/1469540505053090; http://joc.sagepub.com/content/5/2/131.short.

Waste and Resources Action Programme (WRAP), 2012: *Composition and Re-Use Potential of Household Bulky Furniture in the UK* (Banbury: WRAP).

Watson, M.; Shove, E., 2006: "Materialising Consumption: Products, Projects and the Dynamics of Practice", Working Paper no. 30. Cultures of Consumption and ESRC-AHRC Research Programme, Vol. 1.

Watson, M.; Shove, E., 2008: "Product, Competence, Project and Practice: DIY and the Dynamics of Craft Consumption", in: *Journal of Consumer Culture,* 8,1: 69–89. doi:10.1177/1469540507085726; http://joc.sagepub.com/cgi/doi/10.1177/1469540507085726.

WCED (World Commission on Environment and Development) 1987: *Report of the World Commission on Environment and Development: 'Our Common Future.'*; at: http://www.un-documents.net/our-common-future.pdf (26 May 2015).
Woolley, M., 2003: "Choreographing Obsolescence—Ecodesign", in: *Proceedings of the 2003 International Conference on Designing Pleasurable Products and Interfaces—DPPI '03,* Vol. 77. (New York: ACM Press). doi:10.1145/782896.782916; http://portal.acm.org/citation.cfm?doid=782896.782916.

Chapter 3
The Individual-Practice Framework: A Design Tool for Understanding Consumer Behaviour

Laura Piscicelli, Mariale Moreno, Tim Cooper and Tom Fisher

Abstract Design for behaviour change is a growing research field which aims at providing methods and tools to foster pro-environmental and pro-social action through the application of diverse theories, models and approaches from the social sciences. This chapter presents the Individual-Practice Framework, which uniquely combines insights from social psychology and social practice theory, and discusses its possible use as a design tool. The Individual-Practice Framework captures the interrelation between the individual and specific combinations of the 'material', 'meaning' and 'competence' elements of practices. The framework is proposed here as a design tool for the effective exploration and envisioning of innovative, and conceivably more sustainable, product and service solutions. The paper discusses the advantages of employing the framework as part of the design process, sets preliminary guidelines for practical application and considers possible limitations. It concludes with an assessment of the potential for adoption of the Individual-Practice Framework in participatory design workshops.

Keywords Consumer behaviour · Individual-practice framework · Participatory design · Social practice theory · Social psychology

Laura Piscicelli, Ph.D., Nottingham Trent University, Nottingham, UK; E-mail: laura.piscicelli@ntu.ac.uk.

Mariale Moreno, Ph.D., RECODE Network, Cranfield University, Bedford, UK; E-mail: m.moreno@cranfield.ac.uk.

Tim Cooper, Ph.D., Professor of Sustainable Design and Consumption and co-Director, INDEMAND Research Centre, Nottingham Trent University, Nottingham, UK; E-mail: t.h.cooper@ntu.ac.uk.

Tom Fisher, Ph.D., School of Art and Design, Nottingham Trent University, Nottingham, UK; E-mail: tom.fisher@ntu.ac.uk.

A. Genus (ed.), *Sustainable Consumption*, The Anthropocene: Politik—Economics—Society—Science 3, DOI 10.1007/978-3-319-29665-4_3

3.1 Introduction

Current models of consumption and production cannot be sustained because they result in excessive demand, manifest in a fast throughput of material and energy, and unprecedented environmental, social and economic challenges (Tukker et al. 2006; Cooper 2005; Green/Vergragt 2002; Jackson 2005a, b). The unsustainable nature of our present economic development path is linked to consumer behaviour. Understanding what motivates behaviour and how to bring about change has therefore been seen to be key to efforts and strategies to promote more sustainable patterns of consumption (Jackson 2005b).

Conceptual models of consumer behaviour and behavioural change that draw from disciplines such as economics, psychology and, to some extent, sociology have been widely used in the UK to inform policy interventions aimed at more environmentally sustainable consumption (Southerton et al. 2011). Meanwhile the design field has applied these models to propose a range of methods and tools to trigger behavioural change, an emerging research area known as 'design for behaviour change' (for a comprehensive literature review see Niedderer et al. 2014).

This chapter reviews two different disciplinary approaches to understand consumer behaviour and behavioural change: social psychological models of behaviour and social practice theory. The Individual-Practice Framework is then presented as a way to fruitfully combine both (Piscicelli et al. 2015). The two theoretical perspectives have generated two distinct design approaches: the Loughborough Model (Bhamra et al. 2011; Lilley 2009; Tang/Bhamra 2012) and practice-oriented design (Kuijer/de Jong 2012; Scott et al. 2012; Lidtke et al. 2012). These are described and contrasted in Sect. 3.3, followed in Sect. 3.4 by a discussion of how the Individual-Practice Framework could be used as an effective design tool.

3.2 Understanding Consumer Behaviour

Consumer behaviour is widely considered to be partly responsible for the impact that society has on the environment (Jackson 2005b). Understanding what motivates behaviour and how to bring about change is thus seen as key to efforts and strategies to promote more sustainable patterns of consumption. Social psychological models of behaviour and sociological theories of practice have recently attracted attention as different, if not contrasting, approaches to conceptualize pro-environmental behaviour and inform policy interventions (Darnton et al. 2011).

3.2.1 Social Psychological Models of Consumer Behaviour

Social psychological models of consumer behaviour provide frameworks for conceptualising (and predicting) behaviour by accounting for both the social influences and psychological antecedents of behaviour. The 'rational choice model', based on traditional neoclassical economic theory, is commonly acknowledged as a starting point for modelling consumer behaviour (Jackson 2005b; Darnton 2008). The model assumes that individuals make decisions between different courses of action by calculating expected costs and benefits and choosing the option that maximizes personal net benefits. Underlying this is an assumption that behaviour is a result of processes of cognitive deliberation driven largely by individual self-interest. Consumer preferences are exogenous to the model, which does not seek to explain their origins or antecedents. Accordingly, the approach has been criticized for its failure to address a variety of affective (i.e. emotional) or cognitive limitations occurring in the decision process (e.g. habits, routines, mental cues, emotional attachment to products) (Jackson 2005b).

'Adjusted' social psychological models attempt to overcome the shortcomings of the rational choice model by considering the psychological antecedents of consumer preferences or accounting for the influence of other people's attitudes on individual behaviour, most notably in the case of Ajzen and Fishbein's 'Theory of Reasoned Action' and Ajzen's 'Theory of Planned Behaviour'. These are helpful in explaining some intentional behaviours, but arguably do not provide enough insight into affective (i.e. emotional), normative (i.e. moral) and certain cognitive (e.g. habitual) dimensions of behaviour (Jackson 2005b).

By contrast, moral beliefs and normative considerations are explicitly recognized as driving (or inhibiting) pro-environmental or pro-social behaviour in other theoretical models, such as Schwartz's 'Norm Activation Theory', Stern's 'Value-Belief-Norm Theory' and Cialdini's 'Focus Theory of Normative Conduct'. While these mainly focus on cognitive processes and determinants of behaviour that are internal to the individual (e.g. values, attitudes, intentions), other models add external factors (e.g. fiscal and regulatory incentives, institutional constraints, social norms) in order to provide a more comprehensive picture. Some such examples of 'integrative theories of consumer behaviour' are Stern's '*Attitude-Behaviour-Context* (ABC) Model', Triandis's 'Theory of Interpersonal Behaviour' and Bagozzi's 'Comprehensive Model of Consumer Action'.

In particular, Stern's (2000) ABC model of pro-environmental consumer behaviour accounts for four types of causal variable: attitudinal (e.g. including values and beliefs), contextual or situational (e.g. interpersonal influences, government regulations, financial cost), personal capabilities (e.g. knowledge, skills, resources) and habits or routines. Nonetheless, even this integrated model has critics, such as Shove (2010), who argue that there are intrinsic limitations to social psychological understandings of behaviour and advocate the use of social and technological theories of practice and transitions, which they consider more holistic. More specifically, social practice theory is proposed by Shove as an alternative paradigm able to re-frame academic debate and policy approaches to behaviour change and sustainable consumption.

3.2.2 Social Practice Theory

In contrast to social psychological understandings that assume consumption is based on deliberate and rational considerations by individuals, social practice theory regards consumption as less conscious and shaped instead by habits and routines. It argues that people use (and consume) resources and products while engaging in a variety of mundane activities (Warde 2005; Mylan 2015), and thus focuses on the routine actions that people (referred to as 'practitioners' or 'carriers') perform in daily life. Driving, walking and cooking are all examples of a 'practice' with the characteristics that Reckwitz (2002: 249–250) describes: "a routinized type of behaviour which consists of several elements, interconnected to one other: forms of bodily activities, forms of mental activities, 'things' and their use, a background knowledge in the form of understanding, know-how, states of emotion and motivational knowledge. A practice [...] forms so to speak a 'block' whose existence necessarily depends on the existence and specific interconnectedness of these elements."

Shove et al. (2012: 14) group these elements into three categories—'material', 'competence' and 'meaning'—and argue that "in doing things like driving, walking or cooking, people (as practitioners) actively combine the elements of which these practices are made". Therefore, "practices emerge, persist, shift and disappear when connections between elements of these three types are made, sustained or broken" (see Fig. 3.1). Specific configurations of elements making up practices are socially and culturally shared. Being geographically and historically grounded, they vary across space and over time.

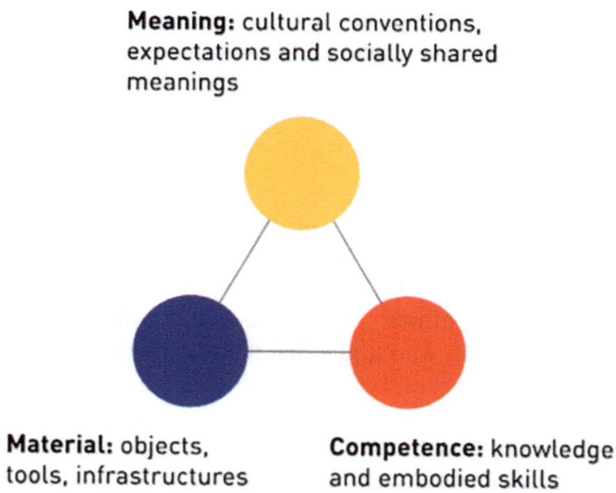

Fig. 3.1 The elements of practices. *Sources* Piscicelli et al. (2015). Reprinted from the Journal of Cleaner Production, 97, Piscicelli et al., The role of values in collaborative consumption: insights from a product-service system for lending and borrowing in the UK, 21–29, Copyright 2015, with permission from Elsevier

Social practice theory shifts the focus from individual deliberation in decision making to practices and their emergent dynamics. Rather than originating from individuals' attitudes, beliefs and other motivational factors, "behaviour is the observable expression of social phenomena (socially shared tastes and meanings, knowledge and skills, and materials and infrastructure)" (Spurling et al. 2013: 47). However, in shifting attention from the 'individual' to the 'social', social practice theory is vulnerable to critique as it reduces individuals to "more or less faithful carriers or practitioners" (Shove et al. 2012: 63) routinely reproducing "what people take to be 'normal' ways of life" (Shove 2003: 3). This prompts a series of considerations around agency (i.e. the role of the individual) and whether conceptions of 'normality' are culturally and socially shared as much as personally determined. In particular, it raises the possibility that shared understandings, social expectations and culturally constructed conventions (i.e. the 'meaning' element of practices) are mediated by and through personal traits, characteristics and preferences (Piscicelli et al. 2015).

3.2.3 The Individual-Practice Framework

Social psychological models of consumer behaviour and social practice theory appear to rest upon and support different paradigms in conceptualising behaviour. Although some reject the possibility of merging the positions and overcoming the theoretical divide (e.g. Shove 2010, 2011), academic researchers in the area of sustainable consumption increasingly advocate a dialogue between these perspectives (Boldero/Binder 2013; Darnton et al. 2011; Whitmarsh et al. 2011; Wilson/Chatterton 2011).

Along the same lines, Piscicelli et al. (2015) combined insights from social psychology and social practice theory in exploring the role of values in the context of collaborative consumption.[1] Their study investigated the possibility that personal values, located within the individual, act upon the 'meaning' element (i.e. the bundle of cultural conventions, social norms, collective assumptions and expectations) of practices, thus contributing to (or hindering) the acceptance, adoption and diffusion of more sustainable patterns of consumption.

Departing from Shove et al. (2012), the resulting framework positions the carrier of a practice (i.e. the individual) at the centre of the practice itself. In doing so, it overcomes the 'agency-structure' divide by acknowledging the existing interaction between the carrier and a specific configuration of 'material', 'competence' and 'meaning' elements. Besides connecting the elements together through the reproduction of a practice, the individual interacts with, and renegotiates, each element (Fig. 3.2). This relationship is mediated by individual traits, preferences and characteristics, such as personal values.

---

[1] An economic model based on sharing, lending, swapping, gifting, bartering or renting products and services, which prioritizes access over ownership.

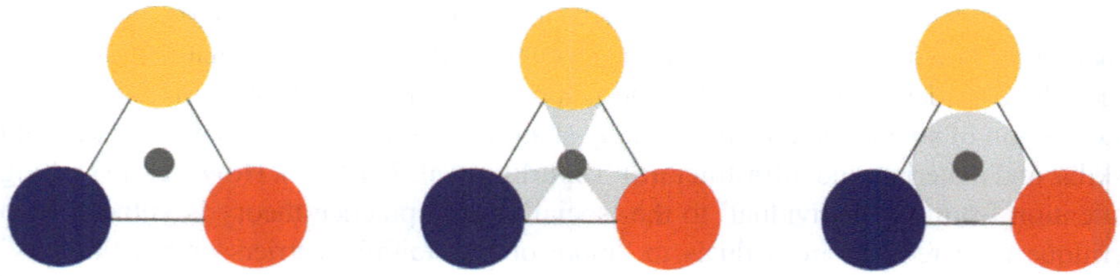

Fig. 3.2 The Individual-Practice Framework. Individual (*dark grey*) and interaction (*light grey*) with elements of practice. *Source* Piscicelli et al. (2015). Reprinted from the Journal of Cleaner Production, 97, Piscicelli et al., The role of values in collaborative consumption: insights from a product-service system for lending and borrowing in the UK, 21–29, Copyright 2015, with permission from Elsevier

3.3 Design for Behaviour Change

The potential to influence consumer behaviour and consumption patterns through design has attracted growing academic interest in recent years. A range of theories and tools has been developed in an attempt to encourage pro-environmental and social actions (Jelsma 2006; Lilley 2009; Lockton et al. 2010; Kuijer/de Jong 2012; Niedderer 2014; Scott et al. 2012; Wever et al. 2008; Zachrisson/Boks 2012; Selvefors et al. 2011). Although most focus on sustainability, due to their generic nature these 'design for behaviour change' models may be transferable to other areas as they provide a broad understanding of ways in which design can be used to influence behaviour (Niedderer et al. 2014).

Social psychological theories of behaviour and sociological theories of practice have informed the development of different design methods, strategies and tools. Two main design approaches linked to social psychology and social practice theory have so far been developed: The Loughborough Model and practice-oriented design. These are compared and contrasted to set the context for introducing the Individual-Practice framework as a design tool.

3.3.1 *The Loughborough Model*

Social psychological theories of behaviour have been widely used in recent design studies to identify antecedents of behaviour and determine how to achieve pro-environmental behaviour change. For example, in exploring how design could help to reduce the negative impacts of consumption, Lilley (2009) identified three strategies for changing user behaviour through design: Ecofeedback (McCalley/Midden 2006), Behaviour Steering (Akrich 1992; Jelsma/Knot 2002) and Persuasive Technology or Captology (Fogg 2003). Her approach, described as the 'Loughborough Model' (Wilson et al. 2010), was revisited by Bhamra et al. (2011) applying insights from the Theory of Interpersonal Behaviour (Triandis 1977) which suggests that social factors, along with attitudes, play a key role in forming habits, and highlights the importance of habits as a mediated factor for behavioural change. From this, they elaborated seven design intervention strategies: Eco-Information, Eco-choice, Eco-Feedback, Eco-Spur, Eco-Steer, Eco-technical intervention and Clever Design. These strategies are mainly focused on individual decision-making, and the possibility to promote behaviour change through design rests upon an underpinning view of users as primary agents of choice and change. The design interventions aim at purposefully affecting the interaction between the user and product/services by triggering the 'right' user reaction (Bhamra et al. 2011).

Critics have pointed out some limitations of this approach. First, behaviour-based strategies build on a number of causal factors and external drivers in order to explain and predict behavioural responses. In doing so, they take behaviours and technologies as given, thus supporting the reproduction of current patterns of consumption without fundamentally questioning them (Kuijer/de Jong 2012). Second, social psychological models focus on micro-level dynamics targeting specific behaviours in defined and somewhat stable environments. Based on these assumptions, products and services meant to change a particular behaviour are susceptible to failure because actual ways, situations and contexts of use may vary considerably (Pettersen et al. 2013). Accordingly, critics argue for a more holistic perspective and systemic level of design intervention, as provided through social practice theory (Kuijer/de Jong 2012; Pettersen et al. 2013; Scott et al. 2012).

3.3.2 *Practice-Oriented Design*

Combining science and technology studies with theories of consumption and design, Shove et al. (2007: 9) have articulated a "materialized account of the emergence, reproduction and transformation of social practice" and advanced a *Practice Oriented Product Design* (POPD) conceptual model which attributes designers a unique influence in the configuration, persistence and evolution of social practices. In their 'POPD manifesto' Shove/Watson (2006) urge designers to consider material artefacts as embedded in (and enablers of) situated and situational practices, in order to understand the relations between users, objects, meanings and skills and to identify possible areas of intervention.

This provided the basis for subsequent elaboration of 'Practice-oriented design' (Scott et al. 2012), an approach that integrates social practice theory into design processes. In taking practices as the unit of analysis, it shifts the focus from products and services to practices (e.g. 'showering' instead of 'shower heads', 'commuting' instead of 'cars'), and from design innovation in products and services to innovation in social practices of which those products and services are part. People are considered carriers and performers of practices, reproducing them through the active integration of socially shared elements. Rather than being individual-focused and choice-based, their actions are seen as routines learnt over time in spatially and temporally defined social contexts.

Changes in practices are the result of reconfigurations, in Shove's terms, of 'material', 'competence' and 'meaning' elements (Fig. 3.1). Opportunities for design arise from the possibility to modify or disrupt existing practices and establish completely new ones. The role of design, then, is to provide and enable novel elements to be integrated into novel configurations (Kuijer/de Jong 2012). However, to date only a few attempts have been made to apply a practice-oriented approach to sustainable design; these have been in the context of bathing (e.g. Scott et al. 2012), energy efficiency (e.g. Kuijer/de Jong 2012; Haines et al. 2012) and rethinking thermal comfort (Kuijer 2014).

Practice-oriented design is built around the idea of shifting the focus from the individual to the practice on the basis that this can inform the development of innovative ways of living and doing (Scott et al. 2012). However, critics argue that it is necessary to combine individual and contextual approaches to provide more holistic approaches and be able to address complex ecological and social challenges (Niedderer et al. 2014). Moreover, social practice theory reduces 'user needs' to a "malleable construct tied to norms of existing practice" (Shove el al. 2007), which disregards how individuals interact and can renegotiate each element of the practice (Piscicelli et al. 2015). Finally, although the practice is the unit of investigation in practice-oriented design, prominent scholars working in this area still integrate insights from user-centred design,[2] thus recognising, more or less explicitly, the role of individuals, as users, in the introduction and diffusion of practices. For example, practice-oriented design using co-creation methods engages users on redefining their practices (Scott et al. 2012).

3.4 The Individual-Practice Framework as a Design Tool

The above discussion highlighted some limitations of the two main design approaches to behaviour change. In particular, a focus on individual behaviour (in the Loughborough Model) or, alternatively, on the elements and dynamics of practices (in practice-oriented design), fails to capture the interaction between both. On the other hand, considering exploring this interaction through design could reveal opportunities to enable and trigger behavioural change, especially in the context of sustainability.

Using the Individual-Practice Framework as a design tool aids the designer wishing to explore the interaction between individual behaviour and the dynamics of practices. The tool is meant to be applied in the early stages of the design process proposed by Martin/Hanington (2012): 'Planning, Scoping, and Definition', during which the project parameters are explored and defined, and the 'Exploration,

[2]User-centred design is a design process and philosophy in which the designer focuses on 'users needs' in which users are involved either as informers or co-creators. Informers are seen as a subject of study to get information, and co-creators are users which actively participate in the design process (Sanders/Kwok 2007).

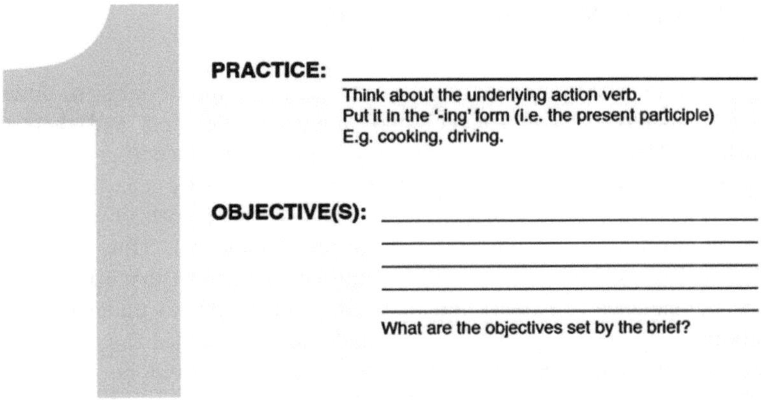

Fig. 3.3 'Practice and Objectives' card. *Source* Authors

Synthesis, and Design Implications', which is characterized by immersive research and design ethnography, leading to implications for design.[3]

The toolkit comprises four cards that are used in sequence, entitled 'Practice and Objectives', 'Material-Competence-Meaning', 'Individual' (these supporting the 'Planning, Scoping, and Definition' stage) and 'Individual-Practice' (supporting 'Exploration, Synthesis, and Design Implications'). From a theoretical point of view, the proposed order allows the designer to move progressively through four phases, from analysis of the brief to considering the 'social', accounting for the 'individual' and, finally, appreciating their (two-way) interaction.

3.4.1 Phase 1: Understanding the Brief

This phase focuses on identifying the practice within the design brief and the objectives set by the brief through using a 'Practice and Objectives' card (Fig. 3.3). Identifying the practice targeted by the brief shifts the attention from a particular product (and its associated service or system) to the relevant actions, thus providing a broader perspective. Identifying the objectives can then help designers to focus on what the brief is asking them to do.

To provide a practical example, if the brief set is to redesign a kettle, using the card the designer will be encouraged to consider the underlying action verb in its '-ing' form (i.e. boiling water for a cup of tea) and take this as a starting point for the design intervention. The final concept will thus not necessarily be a new kettle, but a (potentially innovative) way of boiling water for tea.

[3]Later stages not covered by the tool are: 'Concept Generation, and Early Prototype Iteration', 'Evaluation, Refinement, and Production' and 'Launch and Monitor' (Martin/Hanington 2012).

3.4.2 Phase 2: Exploring the Practice

Having determined the practice, the second card helps the designer to understand the related 'material', 'competence' and 'meaning' elements and their mutual relationships. The 'Material-Competence-Meaning' card (see Fig. 3.4) aids this scoping exercise. The elements of practice are identified by answering questions such as: 'What makes it possible?' to understand the objects, tools and infrastructures involved in the practice (i.e. the 'material' element); 'How do you do it?' to understand the knowledge and skills required to perform that specific practice (i.e. the 'competence' element) and 'Why do you do it?' to understand cultural conventions and social expectations that underlie the practice (i.e. the 'meaning' element). Other materials, competences and meanings could be found through answers to additional questions (e.g. 'When?', 'Where?') which would add insights about the contexts and time at which the practice takes place.

In this phase, the designer should remain open to all the possibilities within each element that can define the practice, should explore different settings (When/Where) of the practice, and should avoid narrowing the focus down to specific products or users. This exercise would help the designer to find areas of opportunity to modify and/or disrupt existing practices and establish (completely) new ones through design interventions. To explore each element of the practice, designers are encouraged to use post-it notes (that could match the colours of each element in the card to aid the task) to brainstorm ideas from their previous knowledge of the practice. To aid this process and get inspiration, the designer could also use established design tools commonly used in Phase 1 such as territory/image/concept maps (cf. Martin/Hanington 2012).

To return to the kettle example, in Phase 2 the designer lists all the objects necessary to perform the practice of boiling water to prepare tea (e.g. a kettle, teapot, hob, etc.), the skills needed (e.g. how to use a hob, the right amount of water to boil, the

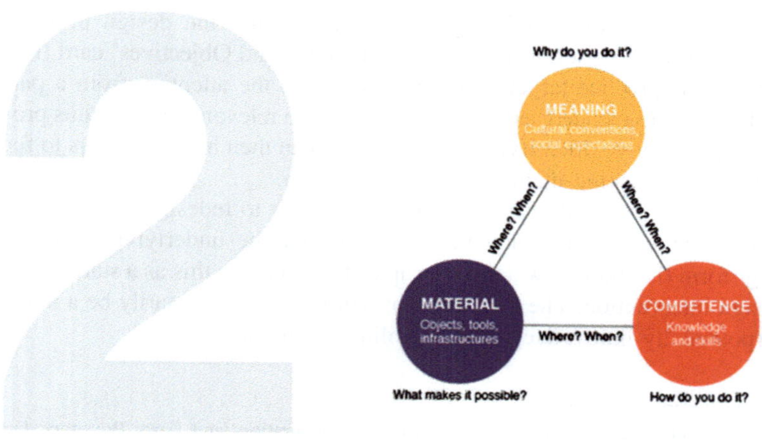

Fig. 3.4 'Material-Competence-Meaning' card. *Source* Authors

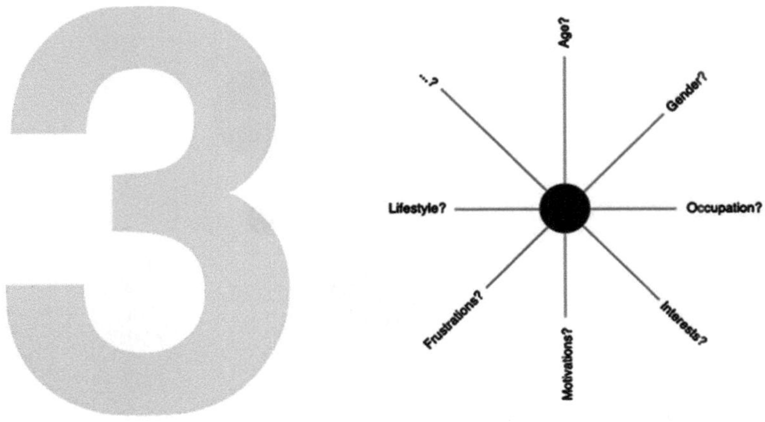

Fig. 3.5 'Individual' card. *Source* Authors

right water temperature, etc.), and the related social meanings (e.g. having a tea to relax, throwing a 'proper' afternoon tea party with friends, etc.). Boiling water for preparing tea at home will require certain materials, competences, and have a range of meanings. If the practice takes place in a different place or time, the elements will change accordingly. Boiling water while camping, for instance, will require a different set of objects and skills, and invoke different meanings. Therefore, the more options and situations considered at this stage, the more complete will be the overall picture.

3.4.3 Phase 3: Considering the Individual

Once the practice is explored, it is important to consider the potential user(s) involved—who they are demographically (e.g. through segmentation data), and their motivations, frustrations, interests and lifestyle—in order to better understand their behaviour.

The 'Individual' card (Fig. 3.5) aims at exploring user characteristics and encourages the designer to use post-it notes to brainstorm ideas about individuals that could potentially engage with the practice in question. This exercise would help designers to understand the users of the potential design intervention. In the case of boiling water for tea, the practice may be performed by older or younger people, males or females, or individuals with different cultural backgrounds, and so forth.

3.4.4 Phase 4: The Individual and the Practice

After considering separately the practice and the individual, the designer is able to identify the area(s) of opportunity to design for. Thus, before moving on to this

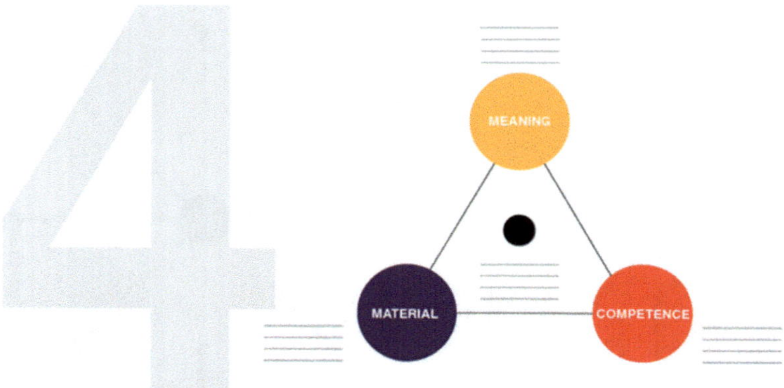

Fig. 3.6 'Individual-Practice' card. *Source* Authors

phase it is important that the designer defines the potential users of interest and a certain combination of elements of the practice to focus on.

This last phase consists of understanding the interaction between the individuals (i.e. potential users) and the practice. This phase heavily relies on immersive research and design ethnography using primary and secondary data. Techniques such as cultural probes, observations, interviews, focus groups, co-design workshops, diary studies and directed story telling amongst others (cf. Martin/Hanington 2012), could be used to collect information.

The aim of the 'Individual-Practice' card (Fig. 3.6) is to collate the research data to understand specific individuals' motives in relation to the elements of a specific practice. Thus, the designer is encouraged to use multiple cards, because for each individual the significant elements of the practice might be different. The designer also has the freedom to include one or more individuals as the 'centre' of the practice as this might influence how the practice is engaged with.

This last phase will help to narrow down the focus to a specific practice and a specific individual or group of individuals. This phase aims at helping the designer to better organize the data collected before continuing the design process with concepts generation, testing and evaluation.

In this phase of the kettle example, the designer would choose some areas of opportunities to investigate, e.g. boiling water for tea at home. The primary research will consist of, say, ethnographic observation of 'real' users performing the practice in their normal setting. One card can be used for each observation to collect data about the user (in the centre of the card) and the specific materials, competences and meanings relating to the practice.

The analysis of common or contrasting patterns could be used to group similar people in the form of 'personas', or to define 'scenarios' for further exploration. In particular, personas are built clustering common user behaviour patterns into representative profiles. This fictional character(s) can be then brought to life through scenarios, narratives that help the designer to explore the future use of a product or a service in a person's day-to-day life (cf. Martin/Hanington 2012).

To summarize, the Individual-Practice Framework can be applied as a tool to guide the designer through the phases of scoping and definition of the brief, exploring the practice, considering potential users and, finally, their mutual interaction. The tool also helps gathering and organising information during the data collection stage. It is envisaged that the framework could prove particularly effective with briefs that are quite open and flexible in terms of expected final outcomes.

3.5 Conclusions

Different models, approaches and tools have been developed to influence behavioural change through design. This paper compares two theoretical perspectives to understand consumer behaviour, social psychological models and social practice theory, and draws on two approaches, the Loughborough Model and practice-oriented design, in developing the Individual-Practice Framework. The paper presents preliminary guidelines for its application as a design tool to aid designers in the early stage of the design process.

The main benefit of the Individual-Practice Framework as a design tool is its ability to enable a deeper understanding of the interaction between individual behaviour and elements of practice: materials, competences and meanings. This could aid the designer to propose innovative interventions for behavioural change that could be applied in the form of a new product, service or system. In addition, this interaction might enable the (re-) configuration of less resource-intensive ways of living, doing and consuming, by considering challenging aspects of individual behaviour and capturing why and how people do what they do (both at individual and societal level). Outputs conceived using the tool would not necessarily be sustainable. As such, the final concept might need to be tested through other tools, such as Life Cycle Assessment, to assess its environmental impact.

Many benefits are envisaged from use of the Individual-Practice Framework tool, but it needs to be tested in an empirical setting to prove its practical value. Future research is required with practitioners in product and service design, sustainable design and business model design to test and refine the framework. The development of case studies should follow, in which the tool is applied in participatory design processes involving real users in conceptualising ideas and possible solutions.

References

Akrich, M., 1992: "The Description of Technical Objects", In: Bijker, W.E.; Law, J. (Eds.): *Shaping Technology. Building Society* (Cambridge, MA: Massachusetts Institute of Technology (MIT)): 205–224.

Bhamra, T.; Lilley, D.; Tang, T., 2011: "Design for Sustainable Behaviour: Using Products to Change Consumer Behaviour", in: *The Design Journal*, 14,4: 427–445.

Boldero, J.M.; Binder, G., 2013: "Can Psychological and Practice Theory Approaches to Environmental Sustainability be Integrated?", in: *Environment and Planning A*, 45,11: 2535–2538.

Cooper, T., 2005: "Slower Consumption: Reflections on Product Life Spans and the "Throwaway Society"", in: *Journal of Industrial Ecology*, 9(12): 51–67.

Darnton, A., 2008: *GSR Behaviour Change Knowledge Review*. Reference Report: An Overview of Behaviour Change Models and their Uses. Government Social Research. https://books.google.co.uk/books?id=uCqlBQAAQBAJ&pg=PA363&lpg=PA363&dq=civilservice.gov.uk/wpcontent/uploads/2011/09/Behaviour_change_reference_report_tcm6-9697.pdf&source=bl&ots=ZEGvPzxmZJ&sig=ZSAe9PpaAmZA2GcpATnZzzaKEHU&hl=en&sa=X&ved=0ahUKEwiwvrDcwanLAhXKnBoKHenWAkEQ6AEIITAB#v=onepage&q=civilservice.gov.uk%2Fwpcontent%2Fuploads%2F2011%2F09%2FBehaviour_change_reference_report_tcm6-9697.pdf&f=false (12 February 2015).

Darnton, A.; Verplanken, B.; White, P. et al. 2011: *Habits, Routines and Sustainable Lifestyles: A Summary Report to Defra* (London: AD Research and Analysis for Defra) http://sciencesearch.defra.gov.uk/Default.aspx?Menu=Menu&Module=More&Location=None&Completed=0&ProjectID=16189 (12 February 2015).

Fogg, B.J.; 2003: *Persuasive Technology: Using Computers to Change What We Think and Do* (San Francisco: Morgan Kaufman).

Green, K.; Vergragt, P., 2002: "Towards Sustainable Households: A Methodology for Developing Sustainable Technological and Social Innovations", in: *Futures,* 34(5): 381–400.

Haines, V.; Mitchell, V.; Mallaband, B., 2012: "Merging a Practice–Orientated Approach with an Engineering–Driven Product Development: A Case Study on Home Improvement", in: *Journal of Design Research*, 10,1: 28–49.

Jackson, T., 2005a: "Living Better by Consuming Less? Is there a "Double Dividend" in Sustainable Consumption?", in: *Journal of Industrial Ecology,* 9(1/2): 19–36.

Jackson, T., 2005b: *Motivating Sustainable Consumption: A Review of Evidence on Consumer Behaviour and Behavioural Change.* Report to the 'Sustainable Development Research Network'. http://citeseerx.ist.psu.edu/viewdoc/download?doi=10.1.1.337.433&rep=rep1&type=pdf (12 February 2015).

Jelsma, J., 2006: Designing 'Moralized' Products, in: Verbeek, P.P.; Slob, A. (Eds.): *User Behaviour and Technology Development: Shaping Sustainable Relations Between Consumers and Technologies.* (Berlin: Springer): 221–223.

Jelsma, J.; Knot, M., 2002: "Designing Environmentally Efficient Services: A 'Script' Approach", in: *Journal of Sustainable Product Design,* 2: 119–130.

Kuijer, L., 2014: *Implications of Social Practice Theory for Sustainable Design (PhD), Department of Industrial Design* (Delft: Delft University of Technology).

Kuijer, L.; de Jong, A., 2012: "Identifying Design Opportunities for Reduced Household Resource Consumption: Exploring Practices of Thermal Comfort", in: *Journal of Design Research*, 10,1: 67–85.

Liedtke, C.; Welfens, M.J.; Rohn, H.; Nordmann, J., 2012: "LIVING LAB: user-driven innovation for sustainability", in: *International Journal of Sustainability in Higher Education*, 13,2: 106–118.

Lilley, D., 2009: "Design for Sustainable Behaviour: Strategies and Perceptions", in: *Design Studies*, 30,6: 704–720.

Lockton, D.; Harrison, D.; Stanton, N.A., 2010: "The Design with Intent Method: A Design Tool for Influencing User Behaviour", in: *Applied Ergonomics*, 41,3: 382–392.

Martin, B.; Hanington, B., 2012: *Universal Methods of Design: 100 Ways to Research Complex Problems, Develop Innovative Ideas, and Design Effective Solutions* (Beverly, MA: Rockport Publishers).

McCalley, L.T.; Midden, C.J.H., 2006: "Making Energy Feedback Work", in: Verbeek, P.P.; Slob, E., (Eds.): *User Behaviour and Technology Development: Shaping Sustainable Relations Between Consumers and Technologies* (Berlin: Springer): 127–135.

Mylan, J., 2015: "Understanding the Diffusion of Sustainable Product-Service Systems: Insights from the Sociology of Consumption and Practice Theory", in: *Journal of Cleaner Production*, 97: 13–20. doi:10.1016/j.jclepro.2014.01.065.

Niedderer, K., 2014: "Mediating Mindful Social Interactions through Design", in: Ie, A.; Ngnoumen, C.T.; Langer, E. (Eds.): *The Wiley Blackwell Handbook of Mindfulness* (Chichester: Wiley): 345–366.

Niedderer, K.; Mackrill, J.; Clune, S.; Lockton, D.; Ludden, G.; Morris, A.; Cain, R.; Gardiner, E.; Gutteridge, R.; Evans, M.; Hekkert, P., 2014: *Creating Sustainable Innovation through Design for Behaviour Change*. AHRC Project Report; at: http://www.behaviourchange.eu (28 January 2015).

Pettersen, I.N.; Boks, C.; Tukker, A., 2013: "Framing the Role of Design in Transformation of Consumption Practices: Beyond the Designer–Product–User Triad", in: *International Journal of Technology Management*, 63,1: 70–103.

Piscicelli, L.; Cooper, T.; Fisher, T., 2015: "The Role of Values in Collaborative Consumption: Insights from a Product-Service System for Lending and Borrowing in the UK", in: *Journal of Cleaner Production*, 97: 21–29. doi:10.1016/j.jclepro.2014.07.032.

Reckwitz, A., 2002: "Toward a Theory of Social Practices. A Development in Culturalist Theorizing", in: *European Journal of Social Theory*, 5,20: 243–263.

Sanders, E.; Kwok, P., 2007: *Emerging Trends in Design Research*. International Association of Societies of Design Research; at: http://www.maketools.com/articles-papers/Emerging-Trends1_Sanders_Chan_07.pdf (12 February 2015).

Scott, K.; Bakker, C.; Quist, J., 2012: "Designing Change by Living Change", in: *Design Studies*, 33,3: 279–297.

Selvefors, A.; Pedersen, K.; Rahe, U., 2011: "Design for Sustainable Consumption Behaviour: Systematising the Use of Behavioural Intervention Strategies", in: *Proceedings of the Conference on Designing Pleasurable Products and Interfaces*, Milan.

Shove, E., 2003: Changing Human Behaviour and Lifestyle: A Challenge for Sustainable Consumption?; at: http://www.psi.org.uk/ehb/docs/shovechanginghumanbehaviourandlife-style-200308.pdf (16 August 2014).

Shove, E., 2010: Beyond the ABC: Climate Change Policy and Theories of Social Change. *Environment and Planning A*, 42,6: 1273–1285.

Shove, E., 2011: "On the Difference Between Chalk and Cheese: A Response to Whitmarsh et al's Comments on 'Beyond the ABC: Climate Change Policy and Theories of Social Change'", in: *Environment and Planning A*, 43,2: 262–264.

Shove, E.; Pantzar, M.; Watson, M. 2012: *The Dynamics of Social Practice: Everyday Life and How it Changes* (London: Sage)

Shove, E.; Watson, M., 2006: Practice oriented product design manifesto. Leaflet [online]; at: http://www.lancaster.ac.uk/fass/projects/dnc/wkshpjul06/popd%20manifesto.pdf (12 February 2015).

Shove, E.; Watson, M.; Hand, M.; Ingram, J., 2007: *The Design of Ev-eryday Life* (Oxford: Berg).

Southerton, D.; McMeekin, A.; Evans, D., 2011: *International Review of Behaviour Change Initiatives*. Scottish Government Social Research; at: http://www.scotland.gov.uk/Resource/Doc/340440/0112767.pdf (12 February 2015).

Spurling, N.; McMeekin, A.; Shove, E.; Southerton, D.; Welch, D., 2013: Interventions in Practice: Re-Framing Policy Approaches to Consumer Behaviour; at: http://www.sprg.ac.uk/uploads/sprg-report-sept-2013.pdf (16 August 2014).

Stern, P., 2000: "Toward a Coherent Theory of Environmentally Significant Behaviour", in: *Journal of Social Issues*, 56: 407–424.

Tang, T.; Bhamra, T., 2012: "Putting Consumers First in Design for Sustainable Behaviour: A Case Study of Reducing Environmental Impacts of Cold Appliance Use", in: *International Journal of Sustainable Engineering*, 5,4: 288–303.

Triandis, H.C., 1977: *Interpersonal Behaviour* (Monterrey, CA: Brooks/Cole Pub. Co.).

Tukker, A.; Cohen, M.J.; de Zoysa, U.; Hertwich, E.; Hofstetter, P.; Inaba, A.; Lorek, S.; Stø, E., 2006: "The Oslo Declaration on Sustainable Consumption", in: *Journal of Industrial Ecology*, 10,1/2: 9–14.

Warde, A., 2005: "Consumption and Theories of Practice", in: *Journal of Consumer Culture*, 5: 131–153.

Wever, R.; Van Kuijk, J.; Boks, C., 2008: "User-Centered Design for Sustainable Behaviour", in: *International Journal of Sustainable Engineering*, 1,1: 9–20.

Whitmarsh, L.E.; O'Neill, S.; Lorenzoni, I., 2011: "Climate Change or Social Change? Debate Within, Amongst, and Beyond Disciplines", in: *Environment and Planning A*, 43,2: 258–261.

Wilson, G.T.; Bhamra, T.A.; Lilley, D., 2010: Reducing Domestic Energy Consumption: A User-Centred Design Approach. in: Wever, R.; Quist, J.; Tukker, A.; Woudstra, J.; Boons, F.; Beute, N. (Eds.): *Knowledge collaboration and learning for sustainable innovation. Proceedings of ERSCP-EMSU 2010 Conference*, 25–29 October, Delft, 200–222.

Wilson, C.; Chatterton, T., 2011: "Multiple Models to Inform Climate Change Policy: A Pragmatic Response to the 'Beyond the ABC' Debate", in: *Environment and Planning A*, 43,12: 2781–2787.

Zachrisson, J.; Boks, C., 2012: "Exploring Behavioural Psychology to Support Design for Sustainable Behaviour Research", in: *Journal of Design Research*, 10,1: 50–66.

Chapter 4
From Print to Digital: Textual Technologies and Reading as a Sociotechnical Practice

Athena Piterou and Fred Steward

Abstract It is assumed that digital technologies contribute to sustainable consumption and production through dematerialization. Hence, digital text is seen as a way to reduce the environmental implications of printing. This chapter focuses on printed text which is published (mainly in the form of books) rather than on home or office printing. It is argued that a transition of books towards digitization involves changes not only in the technologies of book production, but also in the practices of writing and reading, and will more generally affect the ways readers interact with texts in a variety of situations. The chapter analyses the sociotechnical system of the printed paper text (focusing on printed books) and the historical co-evolution of print technologies and reading practices. The implications of digitization for textual production and consumption are then considered. The societal function of the printed paper text can be broadly defined as the development, preservation and diffusion of (usually) textual information. Yet, the concept of function is too limited in describing the multiple ways readers engage with texts: the interaction between books and readers differs according to readers' intentions and the context of the action.

Keywords Book history · Print technology · Reading practices

4.1 Introduction

Since the invention of the printing press print-on-paper has been established as the prevailing technology for the dissemination of textual information in the form of books although there are currently widespread concerns regarding its sustainability.

Athena Piterou, Ph.D., Lecturer in Innovation and Sustainability, University of Greenwich. London, UK; Email: a.piterou@gre.ac.uk.

Fred Steward, Ph.D., Professor of Innovation and Sustainability, Policy Studies Institute, University of Westminster, London, UK; E-mail: f.steward@psi.org.uk.

A. Genus (ed.), *Sustainable Consumption*, The Anthropocene: Politik—Economics—Society—Science 3, DOI 10.1007/978-3-319-29665-4_4

The main environmental impacts of books result from the loss of carbon storage capacity due to the use of wood fibre and from the energy demands of paper production, while the decomposition of books sent to landfill and book distribution/retail also cause climate impacts (BISG 2008). Print-on-paper technology is embedded in a sociotechnical system that includes industries such as publishing and bookselling, readers and technical artefacts in both spheres of production and consumption, as well as a set of rules and practices that co-ordinate the behaviour of the actors. The book in the form of the bound volume (codex) is the focal artefact of the print-on-paper system.

Steward et al. (2004) argue that radical innovation can address the sustainability problems in the print-on-paper system by the application of three generic technologies—biotechnology, nanotechnology and *information technology* (IT). The role of information technology connects to the broader discussion on the relation between digitization and the environment (Berkhout/Hertin 2004). It is suggested that IT contributes to sustainability through digitization and dematerialization of products and services (Yi/Thomas 2007). Dematerialization is promoted as a pathway towards an "ethereal economy" where the role of ideas would dominate over that of material and physical inputs (Newman/Dale 2008). The electronic book is perceived as those applications of IT that provide an alternative to print as a medium of textual dissemination and particularly textual display. Such applications are likely to have radical effects on the print-on-paper system.

The diffusion of electronic books may have the potential to reduce the environmental effects of print-on-paper yet it will require that reading practices are adapted accordingly. There is already a growing body of research which examines how electronic/digital text alters the practice of reading (see Hillesund 2010). As e-reader devices become more widely adopted and their display quality improves, more data will become available regarding impacts on both book acquisition and reading practices. In addition to these future developments, the co-evolution of printing technology and reading practices demonstrates how reading is also a material, corporeal rather than a purely mental practice. The materiality of reading practices should be considered in relation to both print and electronic books.

The chapter examines the print-on-paper regime as a sociotechnical system drawing on the concepts of sociotechnical system/regime developed in the literature on sociotechnical transitions (Geels 2002, 2004). Emphasis is placed on user practices and industry structures associated with the technology. The historical development of the print-on-paper system is presented with a focus on the co-evolution of technological changes, market development and user practices. Finally, the attributes of the book are considered in order to evaluate the significance of a shift from print to electronic text: some preliminary evidence is presented regarding the environmental impact of digital versus print formats.

4.2 The Sociotechnical Regime of the Printed Paper Text

The shift from print to digital electronic text is considered a potential transition in the field of textual communication. Transitions are defined as radical transformations in the way societal functions are fulfilled (Geels 2002). The societal function of the print-on-paper system can be generally defined as the development, preservation and diffusion of (usually) textual information (Sutherland 1996). Yet, this definition does not account for the varied impacts of print on social developments and the varied ways people have engaged with printed texts. The literature on reading purposes demonstrates how readers alter their behaviours according to their motivations and the context of the actions (Schilit et al. 1999; Brown 2001).

Sociotechnical systems are loosely defined as the linkages between the elements necessary to fulfil societal functions (Geels 2004). Sociotechnical systems usually comprise the following elements: artefacts, infrastructure, market and user practices, production system and industry structure, maintenance and distribution networks, regulation and policy, and the cultural meaning of technology (Geels 2002, 2005). Systems are reproduced by a network of human actors (organizations, social groups). Actors operate in the context of rules that enable and constrain their activities (Geels 2004).

The aspect of rules is represented in the concept of regimes, "a rule set or grammar embedded in a complex of engineering practices, production process technologies, product characteristic skills and procedures, ways of handling relevant artefacts and persons and ways of defining problems" (Rip/Kemp 1998: 3). Different dimensions of a sociotechnical regime have been identified relating to elements in the sociotechnical system: techno-scientific knowledge, technology, infrastructure, market and user practices, sectoral policy, industrial networks and the symbolic meaning of technology. These dimensions are aligned and explain the stability of sociotechnical systems.

Sociotechnical regimes serve as a framework in understanding the evolution of the print-on-paper text. We use the invention of the Guttenberg press as the starting point for the analysis although reference is made to earlier systems of textual production. The invention of movable type marks the origins of the print-on-paper system. A historical examination leads to identification of past transitions in the system. The analysis focuses on the following dimensions of the regime: technology, markets and user practices, and symbolic meaning. Questions arise regarding the effects of particular technological developments regarding print: for instance, how have print technologies been affected by pervasive technological trends such as mechanization? In addition, it is examined how the introduction of print technologies has led to changes in practices of book acquisition and reading. The development of the book market and the industry structures in publishing and bookselling are also discussed.

4.3 The Co-evolution of Printing Technologies, Industry Structures and User Practices

Print applies to a wide range of written material. Yet, this chapter focuses on printed material which is published in the form of books. Hence, research in the field of book history informs our analysis of print-on-paper as a system in transition. A short description of the book history field follows before discussing the evolution of the printed book. Book history is a relatively recent, interdisciplinary field with links to Bibliography and Social History but it is distinctive in that it emphasizes print culture and the role of books as material artefacts within that culture (Finkelstein/McCleery 2006). Book historians are interested in texts and their physical form (Finkelstein/McCleery 2005). Along with this emphasis on materiality book history scholar have argued towards a socialization of texts. McKenzie (1986) proposed that the analysis of texts should extend beyond their meaning to the circumstances of their production: meaning results through subsequent acts of interpretation in the lifecycle of texts. The field of book history was influenced by the *Annales* School of socioeconomic history so it emphasized changes in book production over long periods of time instead of focusing on detailed bibliographical points of specific editions (Darnton 1982). The focus on materiality is a common point between book history and research in sociotechnical transitions.

Darnton (1982) introduced the concept of a communication circuit (Fig. 4.1) which suggests that books should be studied through the interaction of various agents involved in their production and consumption. The circuit also includes actors mediating between the two spheres such as booksellers.

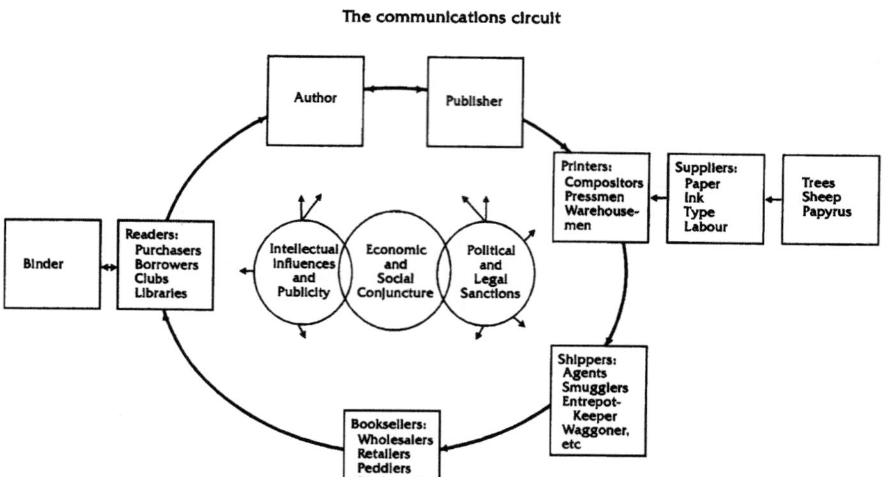

Fig. 4.1 The communication circuit. *Source* Reproduced from Darnton (1982: 68) (used with permission)

We can identify commonalities between the representation of the communication circuit and the network of actors involved in the reproduction of sociotechnical systems as defined by Geels (2002, 2004).

Adams/Barker (1993) criticized the concept of the communication circuit as overtly focused on communication processes to the detriment of studying books as artefacts: their concept of the bio-bibliographical communication circuit proposes a shift towards the lifecycle of the text. Finally, the importance of including readership studies into the history of the book has also been emphasized (see Cavallo/Chartier 1999). Addressing the practice of reading enables a better understanding of consumption debates in relation to the book.

4.3.1 Stages in the Evolution of the Book

This section outlines the main stages in the evolution of the book concentrating on the era since the invention of printing. However, reference is made to the era of manuscripts in order to identify how the printed book artefact was configured: analogies among manuscripts, print books and electronic books can then be made.

Models in the history of communication have identified three major transformations (Finkelstein/McCleery 2005) where the history of the book can be positioned:

- The movement from oral to written culture
- The movement from literacy to printing
- The current transformative phase characterized by a movement from print towards computer-generated content

A broad historical perspective over the last five thousand years identifies four major transformations in the format of books. The following formats acted as the main manifestations of the book and overlapped often for long periods: (a) clay tablets (2500 BC–AD 100); (b) the papyrus roll (2000 BC–AD 700); and (c) the codex (AD 100) (Kilgour 1998). In this categorization the electronic book is described as the fourth major transformation. Kilgour emphasizes the shape and structure of the book hence he does not include printing in these major transformations. Instead, he regards printing as transformation in the ways of reproducing the codex. Three such transformations are outlined (ibid.).

- Machine printing from cast type using muscle power (1455–1814)
- Non-human power (mechanization) driving presses and typecasting (1814–1970)
- Computer driven photocomposition and offset printing (1970–)

These stages suggest that the history of the book is characterized by long periods of stability punctuated by radical innovations. According to Kilgour (1998) these transformations were not purely technological but also required societal need for information, economic feasibility, organizational experience and the capability to link to the incumbent communication system.

Our account largely follows approximately the first two stages (Invention of the printing press to the Industrial Revolution, Industrial Revolution—late 18th Century–to late 20th century). The third stage signifies the introduction of IT in the production side of the print-on-paper system. However, increased use of IT in publishing workflows has enabled the publishing world to prepare for the introduction of electronic books.

4.3.2 From the Invention of the Printing Press to the Industrial Revolution

In popular history, printing is often presented as a single invention but it was actually an agglomeration of distinct innovations: the application of moveable metal type to printing relied on pre-existing skills relating to the screw-press, wood cutting and writing master (Finkelstein/McCleery 2005). Print can be considered a modular technology. Prior to the Guttenberg press, in the early 15th century, wood block prints depicting religious scenes were increasingly popular and can be regarded as predecessors of the printed book (Kilgour 1998). Guttenberg combined a range of technologies in the invention of printing. Printing from cast metal type used skills in metallurgy and techniques for moulding, pressing, inks and paper making. The wooden screw press had been used in paper making before and was adapted into a printing press. A further innovation was the use of oil based inks that would adhere to metal rather than water based inks used in manuscripts (ibid.).

It should be emphasized that the diffusion of print was so rapid that it can indeed be considered revolutionary (Eisenstein 1993). Other scholars have expressed ambivalence regarding whether the growth of print culture was evolutionary or revolutionary (Briggs/Burke 2005). There are difficulties in quantifying the level of manuscript production prior to printing but the introduction of print led to massive increases in output (Eisenstein 1993). The fast growth of printing during its first century has been attributed to the lack of trade structures that applied to other professions (Finkelstein/McCleery 2005), so industry structure had a role to play in the diffusion of the technology. Finkelstein/McCleery (2005) have addressed industry and market developments in the early stages of print culture. One basic discontinuity between manuscript and print culture is that books moved from collectable to tradable commodities indicating the development of a market. The location of the emergent printing industry manifests this commercialization as printing firms tended to be located in commercial centres rather than university or religious towns. In the incunabula period all processes associated to book production and selling were undertaken within the same firm. Gradually printers developed into publishing businesses separating production and sales. Yet, until the 17th century there was little distinction between publishers and booksellers. These activities began to separate in different firms as the early printers internationalized their activities. Shaw (2009) remarks that in the 16th century printers became gradually less important than booksellers and publishers, though some printers remained influential due to commercial and technical skills.

Print technology faced resistance as there were concerns that it would lead to corruption and commercialization of knowledge (Morgan 1997). Distrust towards printing was associated with the distrust towards literacy. Lower classes were suspicious of printing due to the association of writing with privilege and power (ibid.).

Technological developments in the early stages of print culture affected the practices of book consumption. Printing technology allowed for the reproduction of different types of material. It would be more accurate to refer to two distinct innovations: print for texts and engraving for images (Bowden/Robinson 2000; Eisenstein 1993). Although books were also reproduced in the manuscript system, the potential of accurately reproducing images was only made possible through printing (Eisenstein 1993). In particular, the reproduction of maps became an important activity as new worlds were discovered (ibid.).

Among early innovations in printing was the introduction of the octavo format which led to the first pocket sized editions targeted to personal ownership (Finkelstein/McCleery 2005). The earlier development of silent reading among the 14th century elites had also been a factor that led to the development of private readers (Kilgour 1998). During the 16th century there were changes in the format of printed books such as the introduction of title pages and pagination which enabled information retrieval by the use of indices while small formats such as the octavo became increasingly popular as they were more cost-effective in their use of paper (Shaw 2009).

Changes in the constitution of the reading public can be observed at the same time: by the end of the 15th century three quarters of books were in Latin, while by the end of the 16th century over half of published books were in vernacular languages (Hirsch 1967 cited in Shaw 2009). The increased proportion of books in vernacular languages reflects the rise in literacy mainly in Protestant countries. Publishers' strategies attempted to develop a popular market for print by decreasing manufacturing costs, distribution in both urban and rural areas and a choice of material that would appeal to a wide number of readers (Chartier 1999); the same texts could be put for circulation in a different format addressing readers of different social levels. For instance, the *Bibliothèque Bleue* in France was instrumental in bringing texts that had already been published in other formats to the reach of new readers (ibid.). The book trade until the late 17th century relied on the use of barter and bills of exchange as the banking system was not well adapted to the requirements of the trade (Febvre/Martin 1976). Books were valuable objects hence there was a thriving market for second-hand books often sold at auctions (ibid.)

Between the invention of the printing press and the Industrial Revolution no significant changes were observed in the technologies or business models of the print-on-paper system. Business models remained fairly stable till the early 19th century (Finkelstein/McCleery 2005). The next section describes the evolution of book production and consumption as new printing technologies were introduced during the Industrial Revolution.

4.3.3 From the Industrial Revolution (Late 18th Century) till the Late 20th Century: The Book as a Mass Medium and the Early Origins of Digitization

In the era of the Industrial Revolution significant technological changes took place in printing technology. The all metal press and the first steam-powered press were both invented at the beginning of the 19th century. The first steam-powered press was built for the Times newspaper and became known as the flatbed cylinder press. The first rotary press was invented in the United States in 1846, while in 1886 the first mechanized compositor, the Linotype linecasting machine was invented (Kilgour 1998). Developments towards mechanization originated from the periodical press and newspapers (Finkelsten/McCleery 2005). These four innovations demonstrate the effects of the pervasive technology of steam power and of mechanization on the print on paper system. Kilgour (1998) considers them direct responses to social needs for increased speed in the dissemination of information. Steam power was the core technology in the third techno-economic paradigm (Freeman/Perez 1988). This is a historical example of the application of a generic technology on the print-on-paper system. The mechanization and industrialization of book production generated substantial growth in output (Finkelstein/McCleery 2005).

By the 18th century publishing had started to become a separate industry from bookselling and printing. Formerly patrons would finance the production of books or booksellers would invest their own funds to publish a book (Kilgour 1998). Publishing became a more commercially oriented industry. Also, it became more professional as the establishment of relative societies demonstrates. The commercialization of publishing necessitated the development of an intellectual property rights regime with the invention of copyright in the 18th century: copyright established some control of the authors over their work and transferred the emphasis on texts rather than on books as assets. The very idea of copyright emerged from European print culture and required a distinction between a physical object and its content: printers with copyright grants had a monopoly benefit limited to a specific territory (Feather 2009). Towards the 19th century the book trade also benefited from improved communication and distribution networks (Finkelstein/McCleery 2005).

The need for a better educated workforce led to a rise in literacy levels which altered the profile of the readers. Still, literacy levels differed considerably between nations and regions in the 19th century (Lyons 1999). New literary forms emerged to address the growth of the potential market for books and other reading material. Urbanization also increased demand for books and other reading matter

(Finkelstein/McCleery 2005). Printers in small towns and cities were better aware of the type of books that would attract the interests of the reading public, while learnt books were still published in Latin for the elite (Kilgour 1998). Population growth was another factor that grew the potential market for books (Kilgour 1998). Gas illumination increased the time available for reading thus further promoting book consumption (ibid.).

There is evidence to suggest that there was a reading revolution towards the end of the 18th century which was remarked by contemporary commentators in different countries (Wittmann 1999). Reading practices changed from the intensive reading of a small, selective canon of text to the detailed reading of a wider range of material. New forms of organization developed to support the expansion of reading: commercial lending libraries and non-commercial lending societies (ibid.).

Lyons (1999) identified women, children and children as new groups of readers in the 19th century. Increases in leisure time meant that working classes had more time available for reading. These new readers had a high preference for cheap novels. Formerly the novel was not considered a respectable literary form but in the first quarter of the century it consolidated its position as a dominant literary form in a bourgeois society. Increased print runs provide evidence for the increasing popularity of popular fiction and its role in unifying the reading public. Publishers used new business models, such as monthly instalments, to reach this wider public. These new classes of readers were a lucrative market for the publishers but there was also some unease among the elites regarding the effects of subversive literature and the perceived quality of popular fiction. Watt (2000) also noted the extension of the reading public as one of the factors behind the rise of the novel, although he remarked that the meaning of literacy changed to refer to the understanding of the native language rather than classical languages; intermittent schooling also suggested the semi-literacy was common. Kilgour (1998) suggests that the economic crises in the latter half of the 19th century led to a decline in the production of luxury books and in increase in the production of cheaper editions.

The increase in women readers was accompanied with the secularization of their reading tastes. Cheap popular novels were mainly targeted to women along with cookery and etiquette books, and magazines. Women would often improvise their own reading collections from magazines and serialized editions rather than buy books as such. Among the middle classes women readers also had access to public libraries and gradually female readers gained more recognition (Lyons 1999). Working class readers mostly relied on public lending libraries. These institutions were perceived as a tool for social control that would integrate a section of the working class into the value system of the ruling classes, thus providing social harmony. Still, a self-educated working class emerged which placed high emphasis on reading as a tool for self-improvement (ibid.). The development of the municipal library funded through taxation and available to all was arguably the most important institutional innovation around the middle of the 19th century (Kilgour 1998).

The invention of mechanized typesetting in 1890 also resulted in increase productivity in book production while the introduction of the typewriter (1873) altered the processes of writing (Kilgour 1998). The typewriter mechanized the process of writing itself and was linked to a new group of largely female, clerical workers (Davies 2004). Offset printing was another technology enabled by computerization that was mostly developed after World War although the first offset press was invented around 1877 (ibid.). Furthermore, printing was among the first US manufacturing industries that adopted electricity with book and job printing switching to electric power in the 1920s (Goldfarb 2005).

Arguably, the most significant change at the beginning of the 20th century was associated with the rise of paperback books. Innovations in bookbinding, specifically "perfect binding", enabled the growth of the paperback market although it led to the production of lower quality, less durable books (Kilgour 1998). Low prices and increased print runs can be seen as the greatest successes of publishing in the first half of the 20th century (ibid.). It is argued that paperbacks were influential in enriching the readers' cultural experience as they frequently repackaged works that were initially addressed to a more educated audience in a format that appealed to the wider public (Rabinowitz 2014).

The origins of digitization in book production precede the development of electronic books as an alternative form of display. The impact of digitization on publishing firms can be addressed at four levels (Thompson 2005).

- Operating systems: digitization is presented as a solution to problems in the book supply chain such as the problem of returns
- Content management and manipulation (desktop publishing)
- Marketing and service provision, for instance, the use of the internet in book marketing
- Content delivery

The area of content delivery is more relevant to the development of electronic books, however the introduction of digital processes in content management and manipulation can be regarding as a precursor to the electronic book. Digitization has had an impact on book production processes (e.g. by desktop publishing) before affecting the end user's reading practices. Hence, Thompson (2005) argues that a hidden revolution has taken place in the publishing world as a result of the wider impacts of digitization.

Despite the promised links between digitization and dematerialization, it is not yet clear whether electronic books and digital reading are likely to bring environmental benefits. Evidence regarding the use of paper in offices suggested that digitization may in fact lead to increased use of paper as it enables the faster distribution of documents (Sellen/Harper 2002). A comparative lifecycle analysis of newspapers in print and electronic tablet format indicated that print newspapers had higher energy use and greenhouse gas emissions. Yet, more research is needed to evaluate the full impacts from tablet newspapers addressing the use of toxic and rare materials in the production of tablets and the effects from the disposal of the devices (Moberg et al. 2010). A comparative Life Cycle Assessment of print and electronic books showed that the environmental performance of e-readers improves as they are used more frequently and their lifecycle is extended (Moberg et al. 2011).

4.4 Attributes of the Book: Implications for Digitization

Studies in book history demonstrate that the book is a technological artefact. Landow (1996) clarifies that the printed book is a product of technology, so any movement away from print is not a shift from something natural and human towards the artificial. Still, the shift towards digitization raises the question whether the book can survive in a digital format. Even in the case of printed documents one can question how books can be distinguished from other reading matter such as periodicals (Patten 2006). Our definition of books has been shaped by technological change.

The attributes of printed books can be summarized as follows: durability, multiplicity, fixity and collectivity. The commercial character of books can be perceived as a secondary attribute since books are published through mostly commercial organizations. Durability regards the preservation of written information. Print was initially considered inadequate for preservation as paper is less durable than parchment. Yet, printed books are more durable than other methods of communication. Regarding electronic texts and durability, the paradox that electronic text is simultaneously more and less durable is noted. Digital text can be reproduced infinite times without wear-and-tear but since it can be recalled and disappear from a screen it is at the same time transitory (Chernaik et al. 1996). The printed book is more durable because it provides a completed version of texts as works, in the case of digital text there is fluidity regarding the standard version of a text (Sutherland 1996).

Books are collective because of their mass production. Unlike manuscripts printed books were not produced on demand but for a market, so they were standardized according to the needs of a typical reader (Eisenstein 1993). Printing has thus added two main qualities to the written text: multiplicity and fixity which have changed our perception of education and scholarship (Landow 1996). For instance, the availability of large number of identical copies has removed the aura of uniqueness that surrounded manuscripts and changes the ways that information is preserved (ibid.). It is doubtful whether this collectivity and uniformity can be preserved in electronic communication as electronic means allow for customization of content. While the printed book offers a sense of completion, the electronic text lacks that (Sutherland 1996). In the electronic realm fixity recedes in favour of reconfigurability and malleability of the text (Chernaik et al. 1996).

Finally printed text is distinctive regarding the user artefact interface. Unlike electronic communication no intermediaries are required (Chernaik et al. 1996). Books present texts in a sequential order and this affects the processes of understanding. The electronic text in the case of hypertext is diffuse open and multiple, with no defined sequence (ibid.). The linearity of printed text appears to reduce the agency of the reader; on the other hand sequential order is embedded in our understanding of texts. Linearity is seen as a property of narrative so it is claimed that only tool-like texts, such as dictionaries, will benefit from their transformation to hypertext format. To a degree some hypertext functions exist in print such as indices. The introduction of these ‘hypertext’ functions was connected with the standardization of texts (Eisenstein 1993). Hypertext fiction has emerged as a new genre which is specifically written to be read digitally (Mangen 2008).

4.5 Conclusion

Understanding how the co-evolution of textual production technologies and reading practices has shaped the incumbent print-on-paper sociotechnical regime can provide insights regarding the emergence of electronic book: technologies of textual reproduction are associated with changes in industry structures and reading practices. In the words of McKenzie (1986: 20) “new readers make new texts, and their meanings are a function of their new forms”. A historical perspective on the evolution of printing technologies, reading practices and the book industries demonstrates that reading is a sociotechnical practice: printed books are also technological artefacts. Regardless of the technological changes in book production, reading has always concerned the acquisition of meaning: acquiring meaning from text includes skills that can be taught but also results from individual experience (Manguel 2010). Despite the wider diffusion of texts beginning from the invention of printing and accelerated by digital technologies exploring a text fully largely remains a privileged activity (ibid.). There has already been a growing body of research regarding the practice of digital reading; however, it is difficult to evaluate whether in future digital text will retain the design format of printed books or whether new forms of texts will become more prevalent. Evidence suggests that readers engage with print and electronic texts in different ways (Mangen 2008; Hillesund 2010). Understanding how readers engage with digital documents is necessary in order to evaluate the environmental impacts of a shift towards digital reading. Although there is currently only limited evidence on the topic, there are indications that the environmental impact of digital reading is reduced when e-reader devices are used more intensively as more intensive usage lowers the impact per document (Moberg et al. 2011). Any comparison between print and electronic books should also consider the complete lifecycle effects: hence, practices associated with disposal of printed books and electronic readers will also need to be compared.

References

Adams, T.; Barker, N., 1993: “A New Model for the Study of the Book”, in: Nicolas, Barker (Ed.): *A Potencie of Life: Books in Society* (London: British Library): 5–43.

Berkhout, F.; Hertin, J., 2004: “De-materialising and Re-materialising: Digital Technologies and the Environment”, in: *Futures*, 36,8: 903–920.

BISG, 2008: *Environmental Trends and Climate Impacts Findings from the U.S. Book Industry: A research Report Commissioned by the Book Industry Study Group and the Green Press*

Initiative and Prepared by the Borealis Centre for Environment and Trade Research (New York, NY: Book Industry Study Group/Green Press Initiative).

Bowden, D.; Robinson, L., 2000: "A Distant Mirror? The Internet and the Printing Press", in: *Aslib Proceedings*, 52: 51–57.

Briggs, A.; Burke, P., 2005: *A Social History of the Media: From Gutenberg to the Internet,* 2nd edition (Cambridge: Polity).

Brown, G.J., 2001: "Beyond Print: Reading Digitally", in: *Library Hi Tech*, 19,4: 390–399.

Cavallo, G.; Chartier, R., 1999: *A History of Reading in the West* (Cambridge: Polity).

Chartier, R., 1999: "Reading Matter and "Popular" Reading: From the Renaissance to the Seventeenth Century", in: Cavallo, G.; Chartier, R. (Eds.): *A History of Reading in the West* (Cambridge: Polity): 269–285.

Chernaik, W.; Deegan, M.; Gibson, A., 1996: "Introduction", in: Chernaik, W.; Deegan, M.; Gibson, A. (Eds.): *Beyond the Book: Theory, Culture and the Politics of Hyperspace*. Office for Humanities Communication Publication, No 7, Published with the Centre of English Studies (London: University of London): 1–10.

Darnton, R., 1982: "What Is the History of Books?", in: *Daedalus*, 111,3: 65–83.

Davies, M., 2004: "Women Clerical Workers and the Typewriter: The Writing Machine", in: Kramarae, C. (Ed.): *Technology and Women's Voices* (London and New York: Routledge): 23–32.

Eisenstein, E.L., 1993: *The Printing Revolution in Early Modern Europe* (Canto edition) (Cambridge: Cambridge University Press).

Eliot, S.; Rose, J., 1999: *A Companion to the History of the Book* (Oxford: Wiley-Blackwell).

Feather, J., 2009: "Copyright and the Creation of Literary Property", in: Eliot, S.; Rose, J. (Eds.): *A Companion to the History of the Book* (Oxford: Wiley-Blackwell): 521–530.

Febvre, L.; Martin, H.-J., 1976: *The Coming of the Book* (London and New York: Verso).

Finkelstein, D.; McCleery, A., 2005: *An Introduction to Book History* (New York and London: Routledge).

Finkelstein, D.; McCleery, A., 2006: *The Book History Reader,* 2nd edition (London and New York: Routledge).

Freeman, C.; Perez, C., 1988: "Structural Crises of Adjustment, Business Cycles and Investment Behaviour", in: Dosi, G.; Freeman, C.; Nelson, R.; Silverberg, J.; Soete, L. (Eds.): *Technical Change and Economic Theory* (London: Pinter): 38–66.

Geels, F.W., 2002: "Technological Transitions as Evolutionary Reconfiguration Processes: A Multi-level Perspective and a Case-study", in: *Research Policy*, 31,8–9: 1257–1274.

Geels, F.W., 2004: "From Sectoral Systems of Innovation to Socio-Technical Systems: Insights About Dynamics and Change From Sociology and Institutional Theory", in: *Research Policy*, 33,6–7: 897–920.

Geels, F.W., 2005: "Processes and Patterns in Transitions and System Innovations: Refining the Co-evolutionary Multi-level Perspective", in: *Technological Forecasting and Social Change*, 72,6: 681–696.

Goldfarb, B., 2005: "Diffusion of General-Purpose Technologies: Understanding Patterns in the Electrification of US Manufacturing 1880–1930", in: *Industrial and Corporate Change*, 14,5: 745–773.

Hillesund, T., 2010. "Digital Reading Spaces: How Expert Readers Handle Books, the Web and Electronic Paper", in: *First Monday*, 15: 4–5.

Kilgour, F.G., 1998: *The Evolution of the Book* (New York and Oxford: Oxford University Press).

Landow, G.P., 1996: "We are Already Beyond the Book", in: Chernaik, W.; Deegan, M; Gibson, A. (Eds.): *Beyond the Book: Theory, Culture and the Politics of Hyperspace*. Office for Humanities communication publication, No 7, Published with the Centre of English Studies (London: University of London): 23–32.

Lyons, M., 1999: "New Readers in the Nineteenth Century: Women, Children, Workers", in: Cavallo, G.; Chartier, R. (Eds.): *A History of Reading in the West* (Cambridge: Polity): 313–344.

Mangen, A., 2008: "Hypertext Fiction Reading: Haptics and Immersion", in: *Journal of Research in Reading*, 31,4: 404–419.

Manguel, A., 2010: *A Reader on Reading* (New Haven and London: Yale University Press).

McKenzie, D.F., 1986: *Bibliography and the Sociology of Texts* (The Panizzi Lectures 1985) (London: British Library).

Moberg, Å.; Johansson, M.; Finnveden, G.; Jonsson, A., 2010: "Printed and Tablet E-paper Newspaper from an Environmental Perspective—A Screening Life Cycle Assessment", in: *Environmental Impact Assessment Review*, 30,3: 177–191.

Moberg, Å.; Borggren, C.; Finnveden, G. 2011: "Books from an Environmental Perspective—Part 2: E-books as an Alternative to Paper Books, in: *The International Journal of Life Cycle Assessment*, 16,3: 238–246.

Morgan, N.S., 1997: "Pen, Print, and Pentium", in: *Technological Forecasting and Social Change*, 54,1: 11–16.

Newman, L.; Dale, A., 2008: "Limits to Growth Rates in an Ethereal Economy", in: *Futures*, 40,3: 261–267.

Patten, R., 2006: "When Is a Book not a Book?", in: Finkelstein, D; McCleery, A. (Eds.): *The Book History Reader*, 2nd edition (London and New York: Routledge): 354–368.

Rabinowitz, P., 2014: *American Pulp: How Paperbacks Brought Modernism to Main Street* (New Jersey: Princeton University Press).

Rip, A.; Kemp, R., 1998: "Technological Change", in: Rayner, S.; Malone, E.L. (Eds.): *Human Choice and Climate Change*, Vol. 2 (Columbus: Batelle Press): 327–399.

Sellen, A.J.; Harper, R., 2002: *The Myth of the Paperless Office* (Cambridge, Mass, London: MIT Press).

Schilit, B.N.; Price, M.N.; Golovchinsky, G.; Tanaka, K.; Marshall, C.C., 1999: "The Reading Appliance Revolution", in: *Computer*, 32,1: 65–73.

Shaw, D.J., 2009: "The Book Trade Comes of Age: the Sixteenth century", in: Eliot, S; Rose, J. (Eds.): *A Companion to the History of the Book* (paperback edition) (London: Wiley-Blackwell): 220–231.

Steward, F.; Coles, A.-M.; McNally, R. 2004: "Technology Transition as a Process of Innovation Network Reconfiguration", Conference on Innovation Sustainability and Policy, Kloster Seeon.

Sutherland, K., 1996: "Looking and Knowing: Textual Encounters of a Postponed Kind", in: Chernaik, W.; Deegan, M; Gibson, A. (Eds.), *Beyond the Book: Theory, Culture and the Politics of Hyperspace*. Office for Humanities communication publication, No 7, Published with the Centre of English Studies (London: University of London): 11–22.

Thompson, J.B., 2005: *Books in the Digital Age: the Transformation of Academic and Higher Education Publishing in Britain and the United States* (Cambridge: Polity).

Watt, I., 2000: *The Rise of the Novel* (London: Pimlico).

Wittman, R., 1999: "Was There a Reading Revolution at the End of the 18th Century?", in: Cavallo, G; Chartier, R. (Eds.): *A History of Reading in the West* (Cambridge: Polity): 284–312.

Yi, L.; Thomas, H.R., 2007: "A Review of Research on the Environmental Impact of E-business and ICT", in: *Environment International*, 33,6: 841–849.

Chapter 5
Availability Cascades and the Sharing Economy: A Critique of Sharing Economy Narratives

Sarah Netter

Abstract As scholars search for a new concept that will provide answers on how modern societies should make sense of and resolve the social and environmental problems linked to our modes of production and consumption, the sharing economy is attracting increased attention. To better understand this emergent focus on a sharing economy and associated business and consumption models, this conceptual chapter applies cascade theory to some of the most pronounced narratives, suggesting a win-win scenario, especially as they relate to the claim of sustainability. Given academics, practitioners, and civil society's shared history of (too) rapidly embracing new concepts that enable both business opportunities and a clear conscience, this chapter proposes that the implications of the sharing economy should be critically explored before it is actively promoted as the latest best fix.

Keywords Availability cascades · Availability entrepreneurs · Cascade theory · Sharing economy

5.1 Introduction

Whether regional currencies in Bavaria, couch surfing in San Francisco, fashion libraries in Copenhagen, or car sharing in Berlin, all signs point to a paradigm shift toward a sharing economy. Ownership was yesterday; today everything seems to be a matter of access (Rifkin 2000). The sharing economy ultimately involves sharing and collaborating to meet certain needs, encompassing practically all types of products and services. Specifically, people come together to share excess resources, expand product life expectancies, and utilize capacities through access to use rather than ownership (Belk 2010; Botsman/Rogers 2010). Hence, what started out as action by a few grassroots organizations critical of the current growth-oriented economic system

---

Sarah Netter, Ph.D. Fellow, Department of Intercultural Communication and Management, Copenhagen Business School, Frederiksberg, Denmark, Email: sn.ikl@cbs.dk.

A. Genus (ed.), *Sustainable Consumption*, The Anthropocene: Politik—Economics—Society—Science 3, DOI 10.1007/978-3-319-29665-4_5

and our current modes of production and consumption now looks poised to gain a foothold with the average citizen (Grimm/Kunze 2011; Seidl/Zahrnt 2012). As a result, the concept of a sharing economy is attracting increased attention. For example, in 2010, *Time Magazine* listed it as one of the "10 ideas that will change the world" (Walsh 2011) with sustainability not always being the driver but frequently considered a positive side-effect of sharing products and services (Botsman/Rogers 2010). Such statements, together with anecdotal evidence from different industries, have significantly contributed to the hype surrounding the sharing economy, with media, academia, the business world, and civil society alike singing the praise of business models and organizations built around the idea of sharing.

There are thus good reasons to pay attention to the recent mushrooming of initiatives based on the ideas of sharing and community, a proliferation that suggests the sharing economy may be more than a simple fad. In fact, the idea might turn out to be a disruptive, even transformative force, one that will fundamentally challenge and change the way business systems work today—whether for better or for worse. As modern societies search for a new concept that will provide answers to how they should make sense of and resolve the social and environmental problems linked with our modes of production and consumption, the sharing economy is increasingly being treated as the latest craze. In fact, since Botsman/Rogers (2010) popularized the term in *What's Mine Is Yours*, the concept has gained particularly widespread media attention. The majority of these media stories issue narratives, suggesting a win-win scenario for all parties involved. Especially pronounced are claims of economic, environmental, and social sustainability. While the sharing concept might add to the solution to the problems with our current systems of production and consumption, unquestioningly adopting and actively promoting the sharing economy without understanding its pitfalls and downsides might come at a price. Changes towards a sharing economy could have severely negative implications, consequences that society currently cannot or does not want to foresee. We may, for example, not only overestimate the sharing economy's current market size and potential, i.e. creating a "sharing bubble", but more profoundly underestimate rebound effects, such as a worsening of the job and housing crisis, increasing CO_2 emissions, which might hinder sustainable development. Therefore, society needs to critically assess the dominant narratives in order to understand (a) the actual substance (i.e., market potential) of a sharing economy and (b) the sustainability implications of producing and consuming in a sharing manner.

Based on interviews with leading experts, a thorough study of the available literature, and anecdotal evidence, this conceptual chapter aims to shed light on some of the dominant narratives surrounding this rediscovery of an old phenomenon. By applying cascade theory to some of the most pronounced narratives, this chapter seeks to provide a better understanding of the emergent focus on a sharing economy, especially in its commercialized form, and readily adoption of win-win scenarios. To date, however, despite a range of examples from popular literature, scant scholarly attention has been paid to the sharing economy. Hence, the major contribution of this chapter lies in being (to the author's best knowledge) the first attempt to apply cascade theories to the emergence of the sharing economy phenomenon. This cascade framework has proven especially helpful in making sense of why certain ideas and approaches have—sometimes misleadingly—risen to popularity in society and academia while others were deemed a fad from the start (Sunstein 2001; Lemieux 2003/2004). In this way, this chapter advances our limited knowledge of the potentials and risks associated with this alternative mode of consumption.

The remainder of the chapter proceeds as follows: After introducing a sharing economy taxonomy, there is an outline of several prominent justifications for the emergence of the sharing economy. Following this the chapter takes a closer look at some of the arguably win-win narratives. Subsequently, an alternative approach is proposed which helps to explain the emergence of the sharing economy and these narratives by introducing and applying the underlying theoretical framework, i.e. availability cascades. The chapter concludes with some remarks regarding future work which should be undertaken in the area under scrutiny.

5.2 A Sharing Economy Taxonomy

In recent years, the sharing economy and its affiliated concepts collaborative consumption, peer-to-peer economy, mesh, gift economy, or solidarity economy have increasingly received attention in practice and public discourse. However, as Heinrichs (2013) notes the majority of the academic discourse still lags behind. Some streams of research have more and more begun to study sharing economy practices, especially with regard to the eco-efficiency of product-service systems for investment goods, such as cars (Hockerts 2008; Mont 2000). Such interest is not surprising considering the potential resource reductions and financial savings from, for example, decreasing the number of cars and optimizing usage. With the car sharing services provided by Citroën, Mercedes, and similar companies, the automotive industry is living proof that the sharing economy not only constitutes a social movement with disruptive potential but provides opportunities for developing business models that go beyond traditional forms and traditional relationships between producers and consumers (Bardhi/Eckhardt 2012; Botsman/Rogers 2010).

At its core, the sharing economy can be defined as people sharing underutilized assets and skills to meet certain needs, whether related to transportation, accommodation, land, skills, or other elements of everyday life. With one of the early forms of collaborative consumption relating to collaborative housing, first introduced in the 1960s in Denmark, today, different forms of collaborative consumption exist, varying not only in purpose but also in scale and maturity. According to Botsman/Rogers (2010), these different forms can be roughly organized into three subsystems: (1) product-service systems, (2) redistribution markets, and (3) collaborative lifestyles.

In a product-service system, people pay for the benefit of using a product, without having to own the product themselves. Classic examples of product-service systems are car rentals, or car or tool sharing services. Products in these systems can be privately owned by individuals or owned by companies. Sustainability aspects of product-service systems pertain primarily to decreasing the number of underutilized products. That is achieved through sharing, the utility of often infrequently used individually owned products gets optimized. Besides the obvious benefit for individuals of not having to pay the full price for owning the product, individuals are also relieved of the burdens associated with ownership, i.e. costs associated with maintenance, repair, and insurance, which can be shared among all users as well (Botsman/Rogers 2010). Redistribution markets on the other hand refer to a system in which pre-owned goods are being distributed to new owners. Sustainability aspects of redistribution markets evolve around the reduction of waste and use of resources, which would otherwise be involved in the making of new products, through the promotion of reusing and reselling instead of discarding unwanted items (ibid.). While product-service systems and redistribution markets are primarily concerned with the sharing and exchanging of physical goods, collaborative lifestyles are concerned with the exchanging and sharing of less tangible assets, such as skills, space, or time (ibid.).

These three subsystems can be further systematized. In an early attempt, Cohen (2014b) suggests a taxonomy of sharing activities, based on ownership motivation as well as ownership structure. In his taxonomy, he suggests that items up for sharing can be individually owned or conjointly owned, with the act of sharing being driven by either pecuniary or non-pecuniary motives. Although the sharing economy is typified by serialized rental of durable investment goods (e.g. Zipcar (car sharing)) as well as micro-entrepreneurship (e.g. Lyft or Uber (service sharing)), the idea is increasingly expanding to other archetypes, as well as non-durable types of products and services that offer opportunities to share excess resources and expand product life expectancy; for example, fashion items and accessories (Pedersen and Netter in press).

Plausible popular explanations for the growth of the sharing economy phenomenon range from technological advancements, to economic necessity, and subjective well-being (Botsman/Rogers 2010). Plausible alternative explanations for wider public acceptance of alternative forms of production and consumption stress a rising discontent with our throwaway economy's wastefulness (Albinsson/Perera 2012), disenchantment with the green growth agenda, and distrust of prevailing market structures (Seidl/Zahrnt 2012).

5.3 A Closer Look at Narratives

In order to contribute to slowing down the formation of a sharing bubble and preventing the implosion of what could be a positive force in the transformation of today's growth-oriented society, we need to take a closer look at the working mechanisms of this phenomenon, its narratives. In this regard, there are two major possibilities for overestimating the phenomenon and creating a sharing bubble: (a) methodological flaws, which lead to overestimating its current market size and potential and (b) overestimating the sharing economy's potential to contribute to sustainable development. This pertains especially to the more commercialized, for-profit archetypes of the sharing economy, as highlighted in Sect. 5.2. In the following paragraphs, some of the different win-win narratives, or rather elements of the sharing economy narrative will be discussed. What all of these narratives have in common are their sustainability claims, whether on the environmental, social, or economical level, or frequently constituting a combination of all three elements.

5.3.1 Overestimation of Current Market Size and Potential

In terms of statistical information, our knowledge of the sharing economy is to date rather limited. To the authors' knowledge, no representative statistical information is available of the total available market size of the sharing economy, much less by product or service category or country. That is not only due to most of the recently emerged mobile enabled sharing websites and platforms being in their infancy but also due to sharing activities historically being part of an informal system, which was not relevant to grasp statistically. Yet despite this fundamental lack of information, the sharing economy is praised by entrepreneurs, venture capitalists, consumers, and mass media alike and expected to revolutionize the economy.

A commonly used parameter for assessing the market size of the sharing economy is financial revenues. Based on this parameter, that is financial benefits, Geron (2013) predicted that the sharing economy would generate 2013 revenues worth USD 350 billion. However, this number must be assessed as a rough estimate, not only as it is based on self-reports of some large organizations. So far, no clear definition of the sharing economy exists, which makes it rather problematic, to define and delineate what kind of organizations are contributing to this development (Parsons 2014). Classic short term rentals, such as rentals of cars (e.g. Sixt, Hertz, or Avis), are for instance conceptualized by some as part of the sharing economy.

Another frequently used parameter for evaluating the potential of the sharing economy are the investments made by venture capitalists, which can be quite problematic. In the case of Airbnb for instance, as of 2014 the company has not disclosed any information on its revenues or profitability. None the less, its valuation has risen from 2.5 to 10 billion dollars within a timespan of two years (Bradshaw 2014). Furthermore, as in the case of seed funding, investment and valuation decisions by venture capitalists are made pre-revenue, that is before the start-up has even earned a single dime and managed to accomplish a positive cash flow. With approximately 75 % of start-ups failing (Gage 2012), venture capitalists need to consider how to compensate for their likely investment losses in their investment portfolio. Hence, valuations by venture capitalists as indication for the potential of the sharing economy need to be treated with great caution, as they are, especially in the early investment rounds, based on both the speculative future value of these corporations as well as a buffer to compensate for likely failing start-ups in the portfolios of the investors.

Even today, a wide variety of sharing economy activities does not involve any sort of remuneration or financial transaction. While these activities might not directly contribute to economic sustainability, indirect effects might be observed.

In the case of fashion libraries for instance, some of these organizations are operating on a free-of-charge membership base, i.e. members can borrow or take clothing out of the system without having to pay a fee (Pedersen and Netter in press). Membership of such initiatives might thus provide citizens with the opportunity to participate in elements of the social life, which are otherwise difficult to obtain, for instance by acquiring suitable outfits for job interviews. Besides these social and indirect economic effects, such forms of redistribution have the potential to reduce the amount of clothing and textiles finding their way to landfills and incineration facilities, thus having a positive environmental impact. Overall, we need to be careful of reducing the sharing economy to only those activities that are monetized or involve some sort of remuneration, when talking about its potential.

5.3.2 *Overestimation of Sustainability Potential*

In general, society has been rather quick to accept the concept of sustainable development as central to our understanding of the relationship between humans and nature without actually developing a clear definition (Bebbington 2001). This failure has created a situation in which various different definitions are accepted, depending on the academic discourse and discipline. In the public discourse, where business, policy makers, civil society, and consumers meet, business, with good reason, appears only too willing to act as an availability entrepreneur—to fill the empty shell of sustainable development with content, promote the concept, and drive the discussion. As Springett (2003) emphasizes, it is smart to 'own' the language of the debate and to fill the void with one's own definitions, terms, and concepts so as to actively silence those who might favour a stronger approach to sustainability that decouples sustainable development from economic growth.

The question, however, remains, whether we can grow into sustainability (Goodland 1995). As Daly (1977) long ago argued, further pursuing economic growth can only hinder any chances for achieving sustainable development and the survival of humankind, suggesting that growth as the motor and goal for everything is not compatible with protecting the environment and bringing about social improvement. Instead, economic growth must be seen as a major cause of today's problems and eco-efficient business-as-usual approaches as insufficient to solving them when resource-efficient product solutions are overcompensated by increased demand or usage of products and services (Schrader 2001). Thus, what are needed if environmental and social problems are to be resolved are radical structural changes in the current business and market system (Gray 2002).

While there is wide agreement on the sharing economy plausibly having the potential to revolutionize production and consumption, public and academic discourse remains more or less silent regarding plausible negative side effects, i.e. rebound effects, which could offset environmental, social and economic benefits. This might be especially true for those forms of sharing which follow the same financial and commercial logic as traditional business models and market structures, and less so for those oriented towards solidarity, aiming to disrupt the existing system towards less materialism (Stevenson 2014).

Different win-win narratives about the sharing economy exist, which frequently utilize arguments, pertaining to the phenomenon's potential to benefit both the economic, environmental, as well as social bottom line (Parsons 2014). In the following, some of the most prominent win-win narratives will be highlighted.

5.3.3 *The Environmental Win-Win Narrative*

One of the most pronounced claims of sharing economy proponents pertains to its sustainability potential. Sustainability is in these claims most frequently conceptualized as, or rather reduced to, its environmental dimensions. Almost all forms of sharing activities claim to contribute to resource efficiency by optimizing the use of underutilized assets (Cohen 2014a; Botsman/Rogers 2010). By providing access instead of relying on ownership of goods, overall consumption levels are assumed to be reduced, as the need to buy and own products is assumed to be lessened when the relevant items can be accessed elsewhere, for instance via tool-libraries or fashion libraries (Pedersen and Netter in press). Other specialized services, such as car sharing or bike sharing programs in the mobility sector, are championed for enabling energy savings, a reduction of greenhouse gas emissions, and a general reduction of overall traffic (Wogan 2013). Besides reducing resource throughput, redistribution of unwanted goods is also assumed to contribute to the reduction of the amounts of products finding their ways onto landfills and incineration facilities. Examples of redistribution range from generalist platforms, offering a wide variety of products, such as Ebay, or Yerdle, to specialized platforms, such as Vinted, or Trendsales in the case of fashion and accessories.

In terms of the positive environmental impact of sharing activities, it is important to bear in mind that we cannot simply generalize from one sharing economy archetype to another. In a similar vein, we cannot generalize from one product group or service to another. Whereas certain products inherently have long lifespans but are rarely used to their optimum during their owner's lifetime (e.g. tool kits), the lifespan of other products, such as fashion items, is far more under the control of trends and styles than the potential utility of the garments. Hence, despite its potential, a sharing economy may be unable to improve the sustainability profile of such industries as fashion. Even worse, it might actually aggravate the situation by giving consumers an opportunity for guilt free shopping, for making throw-away fashion a way of life, which will negate its sustainability claims. In addition to possibly worsening consumption through clothing acquisition and disposal, consumption by means of a sharing economy, especially in its online form, might also have negative effects by requiring increased levels of transportation for delivery and more intense use of water, energy, and chemicals for garment maintenance.

In the case of many products, the major environmental hot spots are in the use phase of the products lifespan (BSR 2009). A reduction of new products entering the system, as a consequence of sharing existing ones, might reduce the amount of resources used in production. However, these positive effects might very well be cancelled out by intensifications in the use phase. In the case of clothing, for instance, the impact portfolio will not only tip very strongly in favour of the use phase, if for example a T-shirt is being worn and washed 200 times more than what is common nowadays before it is discarded, but increase the overall environmental impact as well. Similar assumptions can be made for other contexts, which are facilitating the sharing of existing products with a heavy use phase impact, such as cars. Hence, while car sharing schemes might decrease the amount of people owning an automobile, the number of people making use of an automobile might actually increase (Martin/Shaheen 2011). Thus, the environmental impact of this intensified use might invalidate the reduction of emissions accomplished by the decrease in privately owned cars. This is especially so when these alternative mobility schemes are not only targeting and affordable for former car owners but also an audience otherwise reliant on public means of transportation, for instance students (ibid.).

Furthermore, increasing sharing activities might also undermine and cancel out regulations, which were actually put in place in order to reduce the environmental pollution of certain regions or cities. In the case of the city of San Francisco, for instance, 85 % of the city's taxi fleet consists of hybrid or CNG fuelled cars. The connected reduction of carbon emissions benefits not only the health of the city residents but also the environment. These efforts are undermined by unregulated ride sharing companies, such as Lyft or Uber (Bond-Graham 2013), which might not only have severe environmental but also social impacts, i.e. regarding the health of citizens.

5.3.4 The Employment and Empowerment Narrative

In terms of economic and social benefits, the sharing economy is said to offer employment opportunities, i.e. the ability to empower citizens economically by enabling them to capitalize their skills and resources. By means of the creation of jobs and business opportunities, with citizens being frequently conceptualized as nano- or micro-entrepreneurs, the sharing economy has the potential to contribute to the alleviation of poverty (Troncoso 2014). Popular examples range from renting out one's spare room on Airbnb, using one's car as a quasi-taxi on Lyft, or offering one's skills and services on Taskrabbit. Besides empowering citizens to make use of their skills and resources, the sharing economy is frequently presented as a democratizing and inclusive force in the economy, contributing to equity and social justice (Parsons 2014). Democratizing and inclusive, as it allows for citizens to participate in otherwise unobtainable parts of social life, whether by means of creating one's own job potpourri or finally accessing otherwise unaffordable objects. Sharing might also have a positive impact on individuals' subjective well-being, as it can contribute to rebuilding social ties, which have been lost or degraded in the age of hyper-consumption (ibid.).

Empowering citizens to create their own jobs, and monetize their skills and assets might enable financially challenged individuals to pay their bills and earn a livelihood for themselves and their families. However, in the long-term, this development might very well put the livelihoods of themselves and others at risk. Self-employment might have detrimental effects on basic working conditions, such as healthcare, insurance, or pensions. While employment in the sharing economy might help to make ends meet in the short run, it might come at the cost of not being able to afford basic protection. Besides direct effects on those employed in the sharing economy, the system as such might also have severe effects on those employed in the competing traditional industries. The hotel and taxi industries for instance are heavily regulated sectors, with many living-wage union jobs. The majority of this workforce is of immigrant origin or people of colour (Burns 2014); very vulnerable socio-demographic subgroups, whose livelihood and wellbeing might significantly be impaired by regulated industries such as the hotel or taxi industry losing their business to sharing economy organizations (Byers et al. 2013).

While one could argue that vulnerable socio-demographic sub groups could improve their situation by capitalizing on the sharing economy themselves, Edelman/Luca (2014) suggest that certain ethnic, aesthetic, as well as socio-demographic factors might pose a challenge to participating in the sharing economy. In their (ibid.) study of Airbnb landlords in New York City, they found that black hosts are facing racial discrimination, with non-black hosts being able to charge approximately 12 % more for an equivalent property, highlighting the rebound effects of seemingly routine trust building mechanisms, such as personal profiles, pictures and links to social media accounts. In a similar vein, it can be questioned whether participation in the sharing economy might be as appealing for the poorest parts of society as advertised. Even though sharing has been known to be a long standing practice among economically disadvantaged groups in society, this is by no means a welcome one. For instance in the case of clothing, reliance on hand-me-downs or redistribution markets for the acquisition of new clothing is perceived as a sign of poverty (Hamilton/Catterall 2007). The question needs to be raised whether the sharing economy is in fact merely catering to itself, "the urban, middle class and fashionably Left-leaning hipsters with a lot of 'western guilt' (Kaushik 2014).

Another issue which is infrequently discussed is matters of undermining democracy, by circumventing regulations and taxation (Parsons 2014; Burns 2014). While Airbnb and other examples of the sharing economy might empower citizens to create their own jobs and monetize underutilized assets, this rise of the sharing economy might very well contribute to the exacerbation of the job and housing crisis in many cities, none the least undermining democratic governance (Parsons 2014).

Undermining the democratic system by encouraging deregulated and precarious employment might have severe consequences, not only for those so called micro- or nano-entrepreneurs, but wider parts of the public. In the words of author Morozov (2013), the sharing economy contributes to "the erosion of full-time employment, the disappearance of healthcare and insurance benefits, the assault on unions and the transformation of workers into always-on self-employed entrepreneurs who must think like brands. The sharing economy amplifies the worst excesses of the dominant economic model: it is neoliberalism on steroids." It can be argued that these forms of employment constitute a form of illicit labor, since it happens outside the documented, taxed economy. With the public budget being strained from potential revenues (Stevenson 2014; Burns 2014), welfare expenses might very well be reduced while at the same time the numbers of those in need might very well rise. This is not only relevant with regard to the hotel industry and its sharing competition in the form of Airbnb and others, but also with regard to other highly regulated business sectors, based on collective agreements and unionized labour, such as the taxi industry.

5.3.5 The Community Narrative

Closely linked to the creation of jobs and empowerment of individuals by means of the sharing economy is the revitalization of communities, i.e. community development, as well as community resilience. As the San Francisco Sharing Economy Working Group highlights (2012), greater economic empowerment of citizens and creation of local jobs will in turn produce more local economic benefits and contribute to the communities' development. Looking at the case of Airbnb, for instance, money generated through these transactions will predominantly flow back into the very neighbourhood where the short-term rental is located. With the majority of short-term rentals being located in resident areas, i.e. outside classical tourist areas, the local economies of these neighbourhoods are assumed to profit greatly.

Besides economic vitalization, the sharing economy and especially its technological platforms are said to have vast potential of contributing to community resilience, especially in light of man-made or natural disasters (Cohen 2014a). The city of San Francisco, for instance, has initiated a partnership with a local sharing economy association, in order to prepare the city to be more resilient in times of crisis. The city of Boston experienced the fast organization of citizens, offering their homes to strangers in the response to the 2013 Boston marathon bombing (Cohen 2014a). In a similar vein, Airbnb partnered with the city's Mayor in the aftermath of Hurricane Sandy to provide free housing for those citizens affected by the disaster (Smith 2012).

However, besides potentially exacerbating the job crisis and straining the public budget, the sharing economy might also very well worsen the housing crisis. While short-term rentals have always existed as part of the informal economy, this becomes problematic when individuals start operating de facto hotels, which are neither subject to rental laws and the therewith connected obligations, nor subject to hotel regulations, for instance pertaining to the safety of the property. Instead of a government mandated price control, prices for properties in the sharing economy are dictated by demand. In cities such as San Francisco or New York, which are geographically strictly delineated by natural boundaries, rents are climbing while the housing supply diminishes. One of the reasons why these two cities constitute two of the most expensive housing markets in the USA might very well be the development of the housing market in favour of short-term rentals, which are more lucrative for landlords than year-long leases at rent-controlled prices (Monroe 2014). Propelling prices of property as a consequence of many short-term rental arrangements could further contribute to urban gentrification, where long-term tenants do not have a say or influence on the blueprint of their neighbourhoods and communities (Burns 2014).

5.4 The Sharing Economy, an Availability Cascade

In the following, an alternative explanation for the emergence of the sharing economy and its powerful win-win narratives will be presented. After providing a theoretical introduction to the underlying framework, cascade theory will be applied to the sharing economy phenomenon.

5.4.1 Introduction to Availability Cascades

Availability cascades are a variation on information cascades (Bikhchandani et al. 1992; Lemieux 2003/2004). Availability cascades were developed by Kuran and Sunstein (1999) to explain why novel ideas gain rapid prominence in popular discourse. In these cascades, information is mediated by a number of heuristics, rules of thumb, or mental shortcuts. which individuals employ in their everyday decision-making. These enable individuals to make sense of their environment and make judgments by replacing complex decisions with simpler ones. Yet, as a series of experiments have shown, the ways in which individuals receive, store, retrieve, and process information are subject to a number of systematic problems (Kuran/Sunstein 1999: 705). The most critical factor is the availability heuristic, "which involves estimating the probability of an event on the basis of how easily instances of it can be brought to mind" (Tversky and Kahneman, as cited in Kuran/Sunstein 1999: 706). Thus, in an availability cascade, individuals not only follow the lead of others thought to possess reliable information but also take the mere availability of information or examples as an indication of probability and reliability, which further reinforces the cycle. In Lemieux's (2003/2004: 20) words, "the availability of information influences individual perceptions, which in turn adds more of the same to available information", thereby reinforcing individual responses. Availability cascades, therefore, through their rising popularity in public discourse, can create social errors and mistaken beliefs that can produce mass delusion and detrimental market bubbles, as well as harmful policies and laws (Kuran/Sunstein 1999).

Another key social mechanism contributing to the development of availability cascades are reputational factors, although reputational cascades differ from informational cascades in the underlying personal motives. That is, whereas in an informational cascade, individuals subject themselves to social influence by ascribing greater knowledgeability to others; in reputational cascades, they seek social approval and avoid disapproval regardless of their own knowledge. As Kuran and Sunstein put it, "in seeking to achieve their reputational objectives, people take to speaking and acting as if they share, or at least do not reject, what they view as the dominant belief" (1999: 686–687). Additionally, "if a particular perception of an event somehow appears to have become the social norm, people seeking to build or protect their reputations will begin endorsing it through their words and deeds, regardless of their actual thoughts" (1999: 687). Because of this reputational element, availability cascades tend to be more stable than pure informational cascades because "once an availability cascade has started, few will dare to question the underlying self-righteous and apparently obvious conventional wisdom. [...] New information is much less forthcoming because nobody wants to risk his [or her] reputation by going against the trend" (Lemieux 2003/2004: 20).

This active management of availability cascades—by not only silencing deviant opinions and actions in public discourse but also creating availability campaigns aimed at triggering cascades likely to advance one's own agenda—is very much in the sphere of the social agents that Kuran/Sunstein (1999) label "availability entrepreneurs." These availability activists are willing to invest resources in advancing a certain agenda in a market of competing beliefs at the risk of economic and reputational damage. Hence, although enough individuals being receptive to any given availability cascade constitutes an important precondition for successful diffusion, the impact of information salience and vividness cannot be overestimated (Kuran/Sunstein 1999: 706).

5.4.2 Application of Cascading Theory to the Sharing Economy

As noted earlier in this chapter, plausible explanations for the emergence of the sharing economy phenomenon range from technological advancements, economic necessity, well-being, disenchantment and distrust, to resistance against the wastefulness of our throwaway society. Yet there are other possible explanations that point to a potential availability cascade rather than an actual substantive phenomenon. The cited work on informational and reputational cascades, particularly that by Sunstein (2001), provides a useful theoretical framework and factors for examining the emergence and popularity of certain approaches to sustainable development in civil society, the business community, and among academics.

One such factor is the appealing familiarity of the underlying phenomena—sharing, swapping, lending, bartering, renting. As emphasized earlier, despite some novelties such as leasing jeans or subscribing to weekly clothing deliveries, most sharing approaches are anything but new. Likewise, the acquisition and disposal of second hand clothing and the handing down, borrowing, or swapping of clothes within families or groups of friends are very familiar concepts. Therefore, when information on sharing fashion is readily available and instances easy to find, individuals see them as an indication of the behaviour's reliability and plausibility.

Familiarity, however, pertains not only to the practices of swapping, lending, bartering, and renting but also to the media, including the mobile technologies that facilitate most of these practices. Hence, the driving socio-demographic force behind the development of a sharing economy (Thompson/Weissmann 2012) is a subset of the millennial generation or generation Y born in the 1980s and 1990s, the so-called digital natives (Palfrey/Gasser 2008; Palfrey et al. 2009). This group, having "grown up immersed in a networked world, with access to ubiquitous digital technologies and the ability to learn and use them in fluent and sophisticated ways" (Vodanovich et al. 2010: 711–712), tends to trust enabling technologies and strives to push these quasi-primordial practices out of their niche existence.

Two major contributory factors to the availability cascade are salience and vividness. Powerful win-win narratives and anecdotes, such as Airbnb CEO Brian Chesky's account of not owning an apartment but travelling the world staying at Airbnb homes in beautiful locations, which make this system of production and consumption seem very appealing to those longing to free themselves of all dead weight. Similarly, when trendsetting character Carrie Bradshaw in *Sex and the City* chats with her assistant about renting an expensive handbag from Bag Borrow or Steal, formerly out-of-reach fashion items suddenly become affordable for the average citizen.

It is also significant that the majority of sharing initiatives build on social media to provide transparency by means of reference systems and instil trust between strangers, which greatly increases their visibility—and thus the availability of related information and examples. Given the importance of social approval during times of increased social media exposure and the need to actively manage online selves, reputational factors may also play their part. For instance, Cheng et al. (2002) suggest that the sharing economy dominates digital natives at a stage in their lives when finding individual identities through experimentation and play is crucial. Social media aids them in their attempts to find the identity that will provide them with the most approval while not risking their membership in social groups (McKenna/Bargh 1999).

Another crucial factor in availability cascade formation around the sharing economy phenomenon is the presence of availability entrepreneurs, who in this context are primarily founders of sharing initiatives, venture capitalists, sharing lobby organizations, or mass media proprietors. The first two, especially, are highly invested in development of this type of cascade in the hope of striking it rich with the next Airbnb-like business idea (Brincat 2013). Not only would failure mean major financial losses, but their reputations are on the line, which could be even more costly in the long run. They thus have an interest in sustaining the cascade and making the market development happen by (a) silencing critical voices via the work of their affiliated sharing lobby organizations such as the case of Peers and Airbnb in the Los Angeles neighbourhood Silverlake (Leonard 2013) and (b) striving to create appealing narratives in the mass media. Such public exposure increases the availability of information on the sharing economy and ultimately adds (often false) credibility and authority to the phenomenon through market assessment. Yet because the mass media's objective, rather than educating, is to reach the largest possible number of print runs, i.e. public attention, this latter can come at a cost for society. As Kuran/Sunstein (1999) point out, media outlets have diverse and complex objectives, but it is clear that most newspapers, magazines, and television stations seek to enlarge their 'audience'. It is also clear that this goal generally causes them to emphasize dangers over security, give some risks more exposure than others, and treat certain risks as particularly serious. The media exercise these influences by controlling the prominence with which stories are pursued, by selecting, soliciting, and shaping the quotations used in developing storylines, and by selecting the facts reported to advance editorial purposes, among other mechanisms (ibid: 719).

Without doubt, these availability entrepreneurs' efforts are landing on fertile soil. Over the last few years, consumer awareness levels have risen about such issues as problems with how we produce and consume. For instance in the case of fashion, the latest shocking incident that spurred media and public interest worldwide was the signing of the Accord on Fire and Building Safety in the aftermath of the collapse and burning of Bangladeshi garment factories. Nevertheless, even though such events certainly inspire a wish in consumers to do something good and meaningful, such altruism is not always possible despite the best intentions. Hence, even the slightest indication that an alternative like the sharing economy might be a more sustainable approach to consumption without any need for complete abstinence, these consumption forms become more salient and more readily recalled. As a result, society may end up exaggerating certain benefits and underestimating risks to the actual sustainability potential.

5.4.3 Concluding Remarks

As Sunstein (2001: 2) puts it, "the underlying forces [of cascades] can spark creativity and give new ideas a chance to prosper. Unfortunately, these same forces can also produce error and confusion". While there is reason to believe that the sharing economy and associated business and consumption models have vast potential of alleviating some of society's economic, environmental, and social challenges, there is also a legitimate risk that the hype surrounding the sharing economy might in fact constitute a false cascade. Such a cascade is based on powerful win-win narratives circling around commercialized archetypes, false assumptions or overestimations of its current market size and potential to contribute to sustainable development.

One feature that makes the sharing economy concept so particularly attractive is its variety of forms and archetypes, which "fulfils the hardened expectations on both sides of the socialist and capitalist ideological spectrum without being an ideology in itself" (Botsman/Rogers 2010: xxii). On one side of the spectrum, the hedonistic consumers and venture capitalists searching for the next Airbnb see this paradigm shift as the rise of a new business model, as new opportunities for consuming even more and capitalizing on such consumption. On the other, political consumers see the sharing economy as a social movement, as an alternative to current overconsumption patterns. This appeal to different actors, which combines feel-good elements with business opportunities, helps make this availability cascade more stable, spanning otherwise local cascade boundaries.

Within this framework, the heavy business support for the win-win rationale of the sharing economy agenda is very understandable as it provides a combination of business opportunities and a clear conscience. Similar observations have been made with regard to the development of the green growth agenda, especially in terms of the rapid acceptance of certain concepts, i.e. sustainable development and corporate social responsibility, as central to our understanding of the relationship between nature and all actors involved (Lain 2005). However, the very factors that may make the sharing economy successful could also lead to its downfall, with the sharing economy running the risk of washing out because of its myriad of interpretations and applications.

While a variety of broad and fuzzy definitions might be beneficial in the early stages of the formation of a new field, there is a risk of the most powerful players in the field hijacking the discourse in their favour. As Bebbington (2001) highlights in the case of sustainable development, its loose definition has positively contributed to the concept's dominant place in discourses worldwide. Its vagueness, however, has also led to myriad interpretations of the concept and to various parties instrumentalizing it for their own means or hijacking it for green washing.

In fact, as with sustainable development and the related CSR discourse, part of the sharing economy's success lies in its very opacity and vagueness. The discourse is carefully driven by availability entrepreneurs, especially entrepreneurs, venture capitalists, and sharing lobby organizations, who author and manage powerful win-win narratives, suggesting the sharing economy as a type of fix-all solution, one that will not only provide solutions for environmental problems and improve social issues but also further economic growth. Hence, there is a strong need for clarification.

In addition to its heavy support by availability entrepreneurs from business sectors (i.e. primarily entrepreneurs and venture capitalists) and lobbying organizations who hope to silence critical voices, this sharing economy agenda has also attracted policy makers, academics, and large parts of the civil society. However, it is questionable whether all actors actually share this win-win thinking. Nor would it be appropriate to assume that supporters of this line of thought consist only of the easily persuaded. Rather, it may be that promises of win-win scenarios make it easier to engage people in dialogue and advance certain agendas than threats of fundamental changes to our current thinking on production and consumption. It must also be acknowledged that politicians and academics are subject to the same cognitive biases and reputational forces that form the rules of the game for the average citizen. It is thus quite likely that a fair number of these actors actually have different personal opinions of what sustainability should encompass, but in circumstances where deviating from the dominant discourse can mean putting one's reputation, career, or re-election at risk, towing the party line may seem a more appealing option (Sunstein 2001). The more individuals adopt the dominant opinion and contribute to this discourse, the more the available information and the more seemingly plausible the agenda.

To date, little is known about the effectiveness and potential of sharing economy initiatives, so a clearer understanding is needed of how to proceed. In particular, more clarity is needed on which approaches deserve support, so that financing for these initiatives can be directed toward the most suitable purposes and rebound effects can be prevented or mitigated. Following the public discourse, the stories about Airbnb, Taskrabbit, Uber, and the like, one easily gets the idea that the sharing economy only consists of commercial, monetized approaches, which follow the traditional capitalistic market logic. More research is needed on the potentials and limitations of the different sharing economy archetypes, in order to assess the sharing economy's potential of transforming the current system of production and consumption and its potential to contributing to more sustainable development.

References

Albinsson, P.A.; Perera, Y.B., 2012: "Alternative Marketplaces in the 21st Century: Building Community Through Sharing Events", in: *Journal of Consumer Behaviour*, 11: 303–315.

Bardhi, F.; Eckhardt, G.M., 2012: "Access-based Consumption: The Case of Car Sharing", in: *Journal of Consumer Research*, 39,4: 881–898.

Bebbington, J., 2001: "Sustainable Development: A Review of the International Development, Business and Accounting Literature", in: *Accounting Forum*, 25,2: 128–157.

Belk, R., 2010: "Sharing", in: *Journal of Consumer Research*, 36 (February): 715–734.

Bikhchandani, S.; Hirshleifer, D.; Welch, I., 1992: "A Theory of Fads, Fashion, Custom, and Cultural Change as Informational Cascades", in: *Journal of Political Economy*, 100,5: 992–1026.

Bond-Graham, D., 2013: Uber and Lyft get a Lot of Hype—but Ridesharing is a Parasitic Business Model; at: http://www.alternet.org/labor/uber-and-lyft-get-lot-hype-ridesharing-parasitic-business-model?paging=off&current_page=1#bookmark (5 June 2014).

Botsman, R.; Rogers, R., 2010: *What's Mine is Yours: The Rise of Collaborative Consumption* (New York: Harper Business).

Bradshaw, T., 2014: Airbnb Valuation Soars to $10 bn; at: http://www.ft.com/cms/s/0/f572c31e-b03e-11e3-b0d0-00144feab7de.html#axzz421wkZ7E2 (5 June 2014).

Brincat, S., 2013: Investing in Collaborative Consumption: Venture Funding in 2012; at: http://www.triplepundit.com/2013/01/investing-collaborative-consumption-venture-funding-2012 (2 January 2014).

BSR, 2009: Apparel Industry Life Cycle Carbon Mapping; at: http://www.bsr.org/reports/BSR_Apparel_Supply_Chain_Carbon_Report.pdf (10 March 2014).

Burns, R., 2014: The 'Sharing' Hype; at: http://inthesetimes.com/article/16111/the_sharing_economy_hype (5 July 2014).

Byers, J.; Proserpio, D.; Zervas, G., 2013: "The Rise of the Sharing Economy: Estimating the Impact of Airbnb on the Hotel Industry", Boston University. School of Management Research Paper.

Cheng, L.; Farnham, S.; Stone, L., 2002: "Lessons Learned: Social Interaction in Virtual Environments", in: Tanabe, M.; Besselaar, P.V.D.; Ishida, T., (Eds.): *Digital Cities II: Computational and Sociological Approaches* (Springer: Berlin and Heidelberg): 203–218.
Cohen, M., 2014a: How to Support Boston's Sharing Economy; at: http://rappaportbriefing.net/2014/03/22/how-to-support-bostons-sharing-economy/ (2 April 2014).
Cohen, M., 2014b: The Sharing Economy Redux; at: http://ssppjournal.blogspot.dk/2014/05/the-sharing-economy-redux.html (15 May 2014).
Daly, H., 1977: *Steady-State Economics* (San Francisco, CA: W.H. Freeman).
Edelman, B.; Luca, M., 2014: "Digital Discrimination: The Case of Airbnb.com", Harvard Business School Working Paper, 14–054.
Gage, D., 2012: The Venture Capital Secret: 3 out of 4 Start-ups Fail; at: http://www.wsj.com/articles/SB10000872396390443720204578004980476429190 (3 March 2014).
Geron, T., 2013: Airbnb and the Unstoppable Rise of the Share Economy; at: http://www.forbes.com/sites/tomiogeron/2013/01/23/airbnb-and-the-unstoppable-rise-of-the-share-economy (26 October 2013).
Goodland, R., 1995: "The Concept of Environmental Sustainability", in: *Annual Review of Ecology and Systematics*, 26: 1–24.
Gray, R., 2002: "Of Messiness, Systems and Sustainability: Towards a more Social and Environmental Finance and Accounting", in: *British Accounting Review*, 34: 357–386.
Grimm, F.; Kunze, A., 2011: Meins ist Deins [What's Mine is Yours] 3.0; at: http://enorm-magazin.de/files/downloads/leseprobe/leseprobe_2-11.pdf (26 October 2013).
Hamilton, K.L.; Catterall, M., 2006: "Keeping up Appearances: Low-Income Consumers' Strategies Aimed at Disguising Poverty. Asia-Pacific Advances in Consumer Research Volume 7", in: Craig Lees, M.; Davis, T.; Gregory, G., (Eds.): (Sydney, Australia: Association for Consumer Research): 184–189.
Heinrichs, H., 2013: "Sharing Economy: A Potential New Pathway to Sustainability", in: *Gaia*, 22,4: 228–231.
Hockerts, K., 2008: "Property Rights as a Predictor for the Eco-Efficiency of Product-Service Systems", Unpublished working paper, Copenhagen Business School Center for Corporate Social Responsibility.
Kaushik, P., 2014: Rise of the Sharing Economy: Will Indian Consumers Embrace the New Concept? at. http://www.businessinsider.in/Rise-of-The-Sharing-Economy-Will-IndianConsumers-Embrace-The-New-Concept/articleshow/36874578.cms (15 July 2014).
Kuran, T.; Sunstein, C.R., 1999: "Availability Cascades and Risk Regulation", in: *Stanford Law Review*, 51,4: 683–768.
Lain, M., 2005: "Meanings of the Term 'Sustainable Development' in Finnish Corporate Disclosures", in: *Accounting Forum*, 29: 395–413.
Lemieux, P., 2003/2004: "Following the Herd", in: *Regulation*, 26,4: 16–21.
Leonard, A., 2013: The Sharing Economy Muscles up; at: http://www.salon.com/2013/09/17/the_sharing_economy_muscles_up/ (13 March 2013).
Martin, E.W.; Shaheen, S.A., 2011: "Greenhouse Gas Emission Impacts of Car-sharing in North America", in: *IEEE Transactions on Intelligent Transportation Systems*, 12,4: 1074–1086.
Matten, D.; Crane, A., 2005: "Corporate Citizenship: Toward an Extended Theoretical Conceptualization", in: *Academy of Management Review*, 30: 166–179.
McKenna, K.Y.A.; Bargh, J.A., 1999: Causes and Consequences of Social Interaction on the Internet: A Conceptual Framework", in: *Media Psychology*, 1,3: 249–269.
Mont, O., 2000: *Product-Service Systems* (Stockholm: Swedish Environmental Protection Agency).
Monroe, R., 2014: More Guests, Empty Houses; at: http://www.slate.com/articles/business/moneybox/2014/02/airbnb_gentrification_how_the_sharing_economy_drives_up_housing_prices.html (15 June 2014).
Morozov, E., 2013: The 'Sharing Economy' Undermines Workers' Rights; at: http://evgenymorozov.tumblr.com/post/64038831400/the-sharing-economy-undermines-workers-rights-my (6 May 2014).

Parsons, A., 2014: The Sharing Economy: A Short Introduction to Its Political Evolution; at: http://www.sharing.org/information-centre/articles/sharing-economy-short-introduction-its-political-evolution (25 March 2014).

Palfrey, J.; Gasser, U., 2008: *Born Digital: Understanding the First Generation of Digital Natives* (New York: Basic Books).

Palfrey, J., Gasser, U., Simun, M.; Barnes, R.F., 2009: "Youth, Creativity, and Copyright in the Digital Age", in: *International Journal of Learning*, 1,2: 79–97.

Pedersen, E.R.G.; Netter, S., in press: "Collaborative Consumption: Business Model Opportunities and Barriers for Fashion Libraries", in: *Journal of Fashion Marketing and Management*.

Rifkin, J., 2000: *The Age of Access: The New Culture of Hypercapitalism, where All of Life is a Paid-for Experience* (New York: J.P. Tarcher/Putnam).

San Francisco Sharing Economy Working Group (2012). Mayor Lee, President Chiu, Supervisors Farrell, Kim and Wiener Announce Nation's First "Sharing Economy" Working Group to Support Innovative New Economy, Confront Emerging Issues; at: http://www.shareable.net/blog/san-francisco-announces-sharing-economy-working-group (10 June 2014).

Schrader, U., 2001: *Konsumentenakzeptanz Eigentumsersetzender Dienstleistungen. Konzeption und Empirische Analyse [Consumer acceptance of ownership replacing services. Conception and empirical analysis] (own translation)* (Frankfurt am Main: Peter Lang Verlag).

Seidl, I.; Zahrnt, A., 2012: "Postwachstumsgesellschaft: Verortung Innerhalb Aktueller Wachstumskritischer Diskussionen [Post-growth society: Localization within Current Growth Critical Discussions] (Own Translation)", in: *Ethik und Gesellschaft*, 1: 1–22.

Smith, G., 2012: Airbnb Partners with New York to Provide Free Housing for Sandy Victims; at: http://www.huffingtonpost.com/2012/11/07/airbnb-new-york-sandy-housing_n_2089883.html (10 January 2014).

Springett, D., 2003: "Business Conceptions of Sustainable Development: A Perception from Critical Theory", in: *Business Strategy and the Environment*, 12,2: 71–86.

Stevenson, H., 2014: Sharing and Caring: the Answer to Our Economic and Environmental Woes? at: http://speri.dept.shef.ac.uk/2014/05/29/sharing-caring-answer-economic-environmental-woes/ (5 June 2014).

Sunstein, C.R., 2001: "Academic Fads and Fashions (with Special Reference to Law)", Working Paper No. 118 (2D Series), John M. Olin Law and Economics, The Chicago Working Paper Series.

Thompson, D.; Weissmann, J., 2012: The Cheapest Generation: Why Millennials Aren't Buying Cars or Houses, and What that Means for the Economy; at: http://www.theatlantic.com/magazine/archive/2012/09/the-cheapest-generation/309060/ (15 May 2014).

Troncoso, S., 2014: Job Creation and the Sharing Economy; at. http://www.resilience.org/stories/2014-05-09/job-creation-and-the-sharing-economy (5 June 5 2014.

Vodanovich, S., Sundaram, D.; Myers, M., 2010: "Research Commentary: Digital Natives and Ubiquitous Information Systems", in: *Information Systems Research*, 21,4: 711–723.

Walsh, B., 2011: 10 Ideas that will Change the World. Time, March, 2011, at: http://www.time.com/time/specials/packages/article/0,28804,2059521_2059717_2059710,00.html (26 October 2013).

Wogan, J.B., 2013: How Will the Sharing Economy Change the Way Cities Function?; at: http://www.governing.com/topics/urban/gov-how-sharing-economy-will-change-cities.html (6 January 2014).

Chapter 6
Communicating Sustainability: The Case of Slow-Fashion Micro-organizations

Claudia E. Henninger, Panayiota J. Alevizou, Caroline J. Oates and Ranis Cheng

Abstract This chapter analyses how micro-organizations operating in the UK's slow-fashion industry communicate online with their target audiences and promote sustainability utilising the RACE Framework. It focuses on the challenges these companies are facing, as well as aspects these organizations are handling well within their online communication. Furthermore, it outlines current events, issues, and challenges faced in the slow-fashion industry before presenting a brief literature review on online communication. A case study approach provides the basis for analysis by following and extending the RACE Framework. The concluding remarks highlight key implications and highlights potential areas of further study.

Keywords Micro-organizations · Online communication · RACE framework · Slow-fashion · Sustainability · Sustainable fashion

6.1 Introduction

Sustainability is a complex concept (Steger et al. 2007), defined as meeting the needs of current and future generations without limiting their ability to prosper (UN 2011). Sustainability concerns translate into the fashion industry, which calls for "alternative business models for a sustainable fashion industry" (Gould 2013). The Brundtland Commission laid the foundations for initial projects that focused on assessing the natural environment and scarce resources (Belz/Peattie 2012). It was

Claudia E. Henninger (Ph.D., University Teacher in Marketing), University of Sheffield, Sheffield, UK, Email: c.e.henninger@sheffield.ac.uk.

Panayiota J. Alevizou, (Ph.D., Lecturer in Marketing), University of Sheffield, Sheffield, UK, Email: p.j.alevizou@sheffield.ac.uk.

Caroline J. Oates, (Ph.D., Senior Lecturer in Marketing), University of Sheffield, Sheffield, UK, Email: c.j.oates@sheffield.ac.uk.

Ranis Cheng, (Ph.D., Lecturer in Marketing), University of Sheffield, Sheffield, UK, Email: r.cheng@sheffield.ac.uk.

A. Genus (ed.), *Sustainable Consumption*, The Anthropocene: Politik—Economics—Society—Science 3, DOI 10.1007/978-3-319-29665-4_6

suggested that "the major cause of the continued deterioration of the global environment is the unsustainable pattern of consumption and production" (UN 1992: 4.3). This is a key challenge that the fashion industry needs to tackle, where issues surrounding *sustainable consumption and production* (SCP) have received increased attention in recent years and are seen as a top global priority (Coles 2013).

The fashion industry is highly competitive (EC 2012; Martin 2013) and in the past "has alas often turned a blind eye toward its environmental and social impacts and an overall sustainable vision for the industry is still lacking" (Martin 2013: 1). Thus, more consumption is perceived as "always better for business" (Martin 2013: 25), which contradicts the approach of producing 'more with less' and encouraging mindfulness in purchasing behaviour (Gardetti/Torres 2013). However, the fashion industry is changing with key players in the sector advocating slowed down production cycles and mindful fashion consumption (DFI 2014). Although sustainable fashion similarly to any other type of fashion encourages purchasing behaviour and consumption beyond utilitarian needs, it is argued that contrary to fast-fashion sustainable or slow-fashion seeks to achieve this in accordance with the Brundtland Commission's definition (WCED 1987), by emphasising environmentally friendly production (Eder-Hansen et al. 2012). To explain, slow-fashion organizations produce collections bi-annually, whilst fast-fashion companies create 20 fashion lines per annum (BSR 2012). In this regard, "today's mainstream fashion industry relies on globalized, mass production" (Dickson et al. 2011), whereas slow-fashion organizations manufacture smaller batch sizes with, in their opinion, higher quality, and thus move away from quantity to quality (Dickson et al. 2011). This implies that the production process itself becomes a unique selling point, as consumers, ideally, purchase garments that are not only 'limited editions', but also of higher quality.

A key challenge is to produce more garments and accessories with less, in terms of the overall environmental impact of the individual fashion lines and their ecological footprint (Princen 2005). Researchers such as McDonagh (1998) and Salvioni/Bosetti (2014) argue that whilst it is vital to change production processes and work towards sustainable development goals, these aspects need to be communicated to a wider audience. New technologies such as online communication channels and e-marketing have not only the potential to reach these wider audiences, but also to extend traditional communication channels by establishing a platform that facilitates a two-way communication process (Gilmore et al. 2007). Online communication is much more than simply sending a message to potential audiences, rather it facilitates a dialogue between an organization and its stakeholders, which can be in real time, customized and personalized (Gilmore et al. 2007). This chapter explores online sustainable communication, by investigating:

(1) How micro-organizations operating in the UK's slow-fashion industry communicate online with their target audiences;
(2) How these micro-organizations communicate sustainability through their communication strategies.

Past sustainability and businesses research, whilst instructive, predominantly focused on large organizations (Baden et al. 2011; Fassin et al. 2011) and only more recently included *small- and medium-sized enterprises* (SMEs) (Hussey/Eagan 2007), which exclude micro-organizations (Halme/Korpela 2013). The whole of marketing communications in framing sustainable consumption and production lacks research (McDonagh/Prothero 2014).

6.2 Sustainable/Slow-Fashion: An Overview

The rise of sustainable fashion and more generally the increasing demand for green products (Niinimäki 2010; Niinimäki/Hass 2011) is accompanied by the emergence of green marketing (Belz/Peatti 2012), which aims to promote products and services that are more environmentally friendly than their counterparts (Polonsky 1994; AMA 2012) and is apparent within various industry sectors, including the fashion industry (Sheth et al. 2011). However, green marketing has been heavily criticized within an academic context (Peattie/Cran 2005), in terms of failing to achieve its original aims (Rettie et al. 2012).

This highlights the point that although, "rethinking business for resource and environmental constraints creates significant opportunity, […] there are also risks and costs associated with inaction" (WEF 2012: 2). Consumers often seem to distrust 'green' or 'sustainable' products, as they believe these claims are deceptive and misleading (Bonini/Oppenheim 2008). This links to a criticism brought forward by Kilbourne et al. (1997) stating that green marketing focuses only on symptoms rather than the problem's causes. Similarly, Peattie/Crane (2005) indicate a bridge between current lifestyle and marketing needs to be built for "a future of sustainable marketing based around more sustainable production and consumption" (p. 366). This implies that in order to create more awareness for sustainability it is vital to develop communication strategies that not only inform consumers about available product and/or service options, but also educate them about environmental issues (Prothero et al. 1997).

The above comments underline the importance of marketing communications and the ability of organizations to emphasize their core values, philosophy, and ethos, as well as the distinctive sustainable characteristics of their products. Thus, it is not enough to simply satisfy the demand for sustainable consumption, but rather their key benefits and values need to be broadcasted (Salvioni/Bosetti 2014). Marketing communications is characterized as a process that shares knowledge, information, and meaning and may be between individuals and/or organizations (Leydesdorff 2001). Sustainable communication takes this definition further in that it emphasizes "ecological issues of sustainable development" (McDonagh 1998: 592) in the dialogue between an organization and its stakeholders. In this manner, sustainable communication is a key practice that seeks to move society from hyper-towards sustainable consumption (McDonagh 1998). With the emergence of technology online communication has developed as a key contributor to driving sustainability within organizations (Reilly/Hynan 2014). Research indicates that the benefits of online communication for SMEs are low cost and wide reach (Heggestuen/Danova 2013). However, a drawback of digital communication for micro-businesses is the time factor (Connell 2014). To explain, micro-organizations may struggle to implement new technology and thus, only keep pace with consumer demands (Connell 2014).

Simultaneously to the emergence of green marketing, e-marketing increased in popularity (Fader/Winer 2012), which has changed the overall marketing environment (Low 2000). For micro-organizations, which employ fewer than 10 workers (Europa 2007), depend on their *owner-manager* (O/M), and have limited financial resources (EC 2013), the rise of e-marketing provided an effective, cost efficient opportunity to communicate with their stakeholders (Chaffey/Ellis-Chadwick 2012). Today, online communications are part of a daily business routine (Leeflang et al. 2014). However, e-marketing (Chaffey/Ellis-Chadwick 2012), whilst seen as affordable, bears various challenges, such as keeping up with continuous technological innovations, implementation time, and customer preference (Chaffey/Ellis-Chadwick 2012).

Marketing communications is the medium that enables micro-organizations to create a dialogue with their stakeholders and inform them about their products and/or services and any company related news (Gabrielli/Balboni 2010). In this chapter, the focus is solely on digital/online communication utilized by micro-organizations, which face challenges integrating all their online communication channels (Keller 2001), in terms of coherence (Gabrielli/Balboni 2010) and frequency (Ryan/Jones 2012). For slow-fashion micro-organizations utilising effective communication strategies are vital to stay competitive.

In summary, this chapter seeks to address a gap in the literature, by investigating digital sustainable communication and its role in framing SCP (Kolandai-Matchett 2009; McDonagh/Prothero 2014). Furthermore, the chapter investigates the RACE framework of online communication and explores how micro-organizations make sense of their digital channels.

6.3 RACE Framework

RACE focuses on analysing the effectiveness of using online media and incorporates four elements:

(1) *R*each investigates the actual media platforms and analyses in how far organizations create awareness for their brands across various communication channels (Chaffey/Bosomworth 2012).
(2) *A*ct encourages a dialogue between stakeholders and organizations, thereby actively stimulating the exchange of ideas, information, and knowledge (Chaffey 2013).

Table 6.1 Summary of data from 'RACE' project

	Organization 1	Organization 2	Organization 3	Organization 4
Type	Non-customer facing	Non-customer facing	Customer facing	Customer facing
Minimum/maximum duration of interviews	13:33–57:22 min	10–60 min	7:51–45:35 min	10:52–34:10 min
Semiotics (SE)	✓ • Website • Facebook • Blog • Newsletter • Email	✓ • Website • Facebook • Newsletter • Email	✓ • Website • Facebook	✓ • Website • Facebook
Twitter feed (TF) analysis	✓	✓	✓	✓

Note In text, citations are abbreviated as follows: Organization 1 Employee interview 4: Org1EI4. All employee names used within this chapter are pseudonyms

(3) *C*onvert implies that companies should convince their audience to buy into the brands and their underlying values (Chaffey 2013).

(4) *E*ngage, seeks to create a long-term relationship and, ideally, leads to consumer loyalty (Chaffey/Ellis-Chadwick 2012).

Whilst it is acknowledge that this framework is simplistic in nature, it provides a basis for investigations of online communication channels used by, in this case, micro-organizations and allows for interpretations to be made.

A case study approach fits this research, as the online communication strategies and the messages that, ideally, communicate sustainability are investigated within the boundaries of individual micro-organizations (Yin 2003). Case study research allows for a broader understanding (Punch 2005) of the individual companies and an in-depth analysis of the stakeholders' perceptions and thus, is appropriate to be used. Findings are supported through the extensive, comparative case study approach, utilising various methodological tools: semi-structured interviews, semiotics, and social media analysis (see Table 6.1).

6.3.1 Organizations 1, 2, 3 and 4

Organization 1, a women's wear provider, established in 2007, employs one full-time and four part-time workers, and manufactures upcycled and recycled fashion collections, which are sold globally. It is non-customer facing and has varied distribution networks, including, but not limited to online direct sales, marketplace websites, and third party stores.

Organization 2 produces children's wear, was founded in 2002, and employs 10 full-time seamstresses. Products are predominantly exported to China, Taiwan, and

Singapore. Their main method of distribution is through their own website or on a business-to-business basis. Organization 2 also is non-customer facing.

Organizations 3 and 4 are co-operatives, established in 2012. Contrary to Organization 4, which specializes in women's and children's wear, Organization 3 caters for a broad audience, offering children's, women's, and men's wear. Both are customer facing and located in a city centre.

The following sections present key findings of this research focusing on online communication channels.

6.3.2 Reach

The case companies utilize a variety of online channels to create close links with their target audiences. Each organization has their own website, which provides an overview of their core values and information on their products and/or services. Compared to the co-operatives, Organizations 1 and 2 provide more details on their individual creations, thereby strongly emphasising their products' attributes and production techniques. Organization 2 does not capitalize on all their materials used within the production process. Although they incorporate genuine Italian leather (Org2O/M2I29), this is not advertised within the product specifications (website). By contrast, Organizations 3 and 4 provide a general overview of what the companies are: cooperatives that showcase local designers. The limited information can be explained as each designer in the co-operatives has their own set of values and production techniques. Thus, creating a website that provides information on each individual collection, which may also change overtime (Org3ES), is not feasible to maintain (Org3EI11).

Organizations 1 and 2 have blogs linked to their official websites that are dedicated to current events, news within the industry and company, and projects. Additionally, all participants have social media accounts, which in the cases of Organizations 1 and 2 are linked to their websites and blogs. Organization 3 and 4's social media accounts are not featured on the official website, which indicates that their audiences are not guided to these accounts through an icon. In Organization 3, individual designers link themselves to the official Twitter account by using the @-sign, which connects tweets to both news feeds, those of the designers and Organization 3. Organization 4's account is seldom used and not linked to the designers. Lastly, Organizations 1 and 2 distribute e-newsletters and e-mails, which recap on key events, advertise sale items, product launches, and upcoming events. Table 6.2 provides a summary of the purpose of the individual channels used.

In summary, all participants utilize various online channels. Two out of four companies actively seek to integrate their communication channels, in terms of providing social media icons on their official websites. Although the co-operatives have the same opportunity, they currently do not fully utilize their 'reach' potential.

Table 6.2 Purpose of channels

	Organization 1	Organization 2	Organization 3	Organization 4
Website	–Values –Creations –Product attributes –Production techniques –Material –Provides social media account link	–Values –Creations –Product attributes –Production techniques –Material –Provides social media account link	–General information –Address	–General information –Address
Blog	–Current events –Industry/company news –Achievements	–Current events –Industry/company news –Achievements	N/A	N/A
Twitter	–Link to website –Official account –Used regularly	–Official account –Used regularly	–Official account –Not regularly used –Employees link themselves to account	–Official account –Seldom used
Facebook	–Link to website –Official account –Used regularly	–Official account –Used regularly	–Official account –Not regularly used	–Official account –Seldom used
Newsletter	–Recap on events –Advertise sales/ new product launch –Event updates	–Recap on events –Advertise sales/ new product launch –Event updates	N/A	N/A
Emails	–Recap on events –Advertise sales/ new product launch –Event updates	–Recap on events –Advertise sales/ new product launch –Event updates	N/A	N/A

Source The authors

6.3.3 *Act*

The analysis indicated that all participants utilize online communication tools to update their stakeholders on current events and claim to encourage a dialogue that allows for suggestions and feedback.

O/M1 insists that her internal communication is 'constant' (Org1EI4), which is supported by employee Anna, who works from a remote location. She mentions that she talks to O/M1 "twice a day" (Org1EI4), keeping up-to-date with what is going on in the studio "through email, phone […] [or] online resources like Dropbox, [and] Google calendar" (Org1EI4). Whilst Anna visits Organization 1 regularly, her main method of communication is through online channels (Org1EI4; ES). A key challenge Organization 1 faces is the fact that Anna is in charge of the online updates, but works remotely.

Organization 1 utilizes digital channels to promote their brand to external stakeholders, thereby re-emphasising their values. Anna highlights that they changed their digital strategy:

We [...] [get] people [consumers] online more involved in us and what we do and how. [...] Because people are interested in that sort of thing, people like to know [...] what they [are] buying [...] has that personality to it (Org1EI4).

Anna informs their audience by posting 'studio updates', which contain news on collections, projects, and events. Social media and semiotic analysis indicate high online presence through approximately four daily 'visible tweets', which incorporate their website and/or pictures. Contrary to Anna's comment followers are neither updated regularly on 'studio events' nor do they seem to engage with them. The analysis indicates that 'studio updates' are only sporadic: within a five months period only three 'studio events' were recorded (Org1TF). Moreover, these 'studio updates' did not receive any third party responses, compared to other tweets about sales and industry news, which were re-tweeted and 'favourited' multiple times each (Org1TF).

Organization 2 is also vocal online, posting event updates, facilitating discussions, and responding to queries from consumers, customers, and suppliers (Org2O/MI39). O/M2 mentions that they utilize online channels predominantly to stay connected with their stockists, as these channels allow overcoming challenges with time differences and long-distances, long-term relationships (Org2O/MI37). In the same manner, O/M2 utilizes these channels to gain feedback from end-consumers (Org2O/MI39), which was previously encouraged by providing incentives, such as product giveaways or 15 %-off vouchers. However, since stopping these giveaways end-consumer responses dropped dramatically (Org2TF): rather than receiving 60 pictures each month of end-consumers wearing their products, they now only occasional get pictures and/or written feedback (Org2O/MI39).

Organization 3 has a public and a secret Facebook profile and one Twitter account to communicate with their various online communities. The 'secret' group connects the designers, O/M3, and employees to discuss issues and rotas. To explain, Ciara highlights that:

The official [...] page [allows] us to communicate with [...] customers. [...] We also have [...] a hidden group [...] that we can [...] send messages [to people] if they are out of stock or if a customer [...] [wants a different] size (Org3EI1).

Data indicated that participants use the 'secret' group seldom and prefer to be contacted through their personal accounts (Org3ES). The designers highlight that checking multiple accounts takes too much time and is inconvenient (Org3EII1).

Organization 4 rarely uses online communication. O/M4 states: "Facebook is hard enough, [...] but Twitter is beyond me" (Org4O/MI20). By contrast, employees emphasize that they have frequent discussions on their secret group: "everyone is really friendly [...] we talk to each other [...] and I have [not] met most of them, but on Facebook we [have] [...] spoken [a lot]" (Org4EI22). Moreover, they utilize digital channels to change shifts, discuss new products, and learn about events (Org4EI24).

Data indicate that the organizations communicate with various target audiences, providing them with (in their opinion) news worthy information, updates on the company, and incentives, whilst receiving, ideally, feedback and suggestions. The analysis highlights that especially Organizations 1 and 2 post information on issues in the fashion industry, as well as opinion pieces on, for example, their belief that 'Black Friday' promotes hyper-consumption, whilst they are against it and thus, opt-out of participation (Organization 1 website). Both companies also blog about either their newest workshops that allow participants to keep wearing their old clothes, by creating 'new' upcycled version of them, or how old, discarded items can be donated. These actions indirectly promote sustainable consumption, as the idea behind these 'projects' is to make people think about the end-of-life treatment of their garments. Organizations 3 and 4's online channels do not provide evidence of communicating and/or encouraging stakeholders to participate in sustainable consumption. Rather, Organization 3 continuously highlights that their Twitter users should 'come and buy' their products (Org3TF).

6.3.4 Convert

The majority of participants indicate that they seek to promote their core values through digital channels and encourage stakeholders to buy into their brand. O/M1 emphasizes that although she actively promotes how she produces fashion, not all stakeholders understand what it means to be a 'sustainable fashion brand':

[T]here is only so much I can do, but […] [people] still come in and say they [have] bought […] something new from [Highstreet]. […] It [is a] really difficult […] position to be in, I do [not want to] be too preachy (Org1O/M1I2).

This statement shows that whilst O/M1 talks about sustainable fashion, she is not persistent and/or pushy about advocating sustainable fashion production and consumption.

Furthermore, O/M1 emphasizes in an interview that online channels reach a broad audience, which makes them lucrative. O/M1 associates herself with hashtags that link her brand with sustainable fashion and sustainability: "Time for [Organization1]'s back to school [and] end of summer sale! […] #sustfash" (Org1TF) or "Learning from the past with our new Make, Do and Mend feature […] #sustfash #fashion #sustainability" (Org1TF). This observation is noteworthy, as O/M1 mentions that she does not promote sustainability openly, as she believes this could limit her audience only to those, who are interested in sustainable fashion. She states that

[Y]ou could go on our website and not know that you are on a sustainable brand's website. You might just [think] you are on a brand website. […] How much do we wanna say we [are] an ethical brand and how much do we want people to just to buy into the brand and then find out that it [is] sustainably produced (Org1O/M1I2).

However, the website clearly mentions that Organization 1 is a 'sustainable brand with an irregular twist' (website). Although O/M1 indicates that she wants her customers to "buy their first piece of ethical fashion without knowing" (Org1O/M1I2), she labels herself on the website as 'sustainable', which contradicts the previous statement. Similarly, using hashtags, such as #sustfash, risks challenges, as Organization 1 predominantly tweets promotional posts. This contrasts starkly with the tweets associated with #sustfash, which focus on blogs, news, and articles surrounding the topic of sustainable fashion. Moreover, the majority of 'Tweeters' who are using this hashtag are either fellow fashion designers or organizations involved in fashion and thus, may not necessarily benefit the company. Thus, it can be said that there are two issues: firstly, although O/M1 communicates that her company produces sustainable fashion, she does not actively convert her audience to take part and/or buy into her way of producing. Secondly, O/M1 seems to be confused about what communicating values and promotions entail.

Organization 2 emphasizes their values, highlighting the 'local', 'British Made', and 'home-grown' aspect of the business (Org2TF): "Made in the UK—[Organization2]" or "Bubble London Homegrown showcases labels that are designed and manufactured in the UK. Come and see [Organization2] [...]. We [are] completely Homegrown!". O/M2 does not utilize hashtags, which could potentially expose the brand to a broader audience and attract new customers.

O/M2 mentions they use their online channels to communicate and build relationships with their external stakeholders, however, this is not apparent from their Twitter feed. No communication is initiated using the @-sign, nor are followers tagged in posts. Similarly, tweets posted by Organization 2 do not incorporate their official website, which could be seen as problematic, as potential customers are not guided to the original resource. However, both social media accounts are featured on the website. Similarly to Organization 1, Organization 2 does not seem to have a 'convert' approach. Their online communication is not pushing an agenda on why their audience should buy into and/or change to their brand.

Organization 3 utilizes a 'hard sales' approach online and does not clearly communicate its core values. Within this co-operative multiple workers have access to the main account and tweet approximately ten times a day. A majority of the messages are not related to the business' attributes or characteristics, but rather focus on sales promotions (Org3TF1): "There [is] still time to buy those last minute gifts! Get down to @[Organization3] lots of lovely, quirky, one-off pieces!! #buylocal" or "We sell art and craft from up and coming UK designer-makers! Our micro-boutique can be found @[Organization3] #BuyBritishBrands". Similarly to O/M1, O/M3 highlights that she does not want to promote sustainability, as she believes this might make potential customers shy away, as they could believe sustainable fashion is not for them (Org3OM3I 7). On the other hand, Organization 3's shop window reads 'A local store for local people', which could be seen as contradicting the discussion with O/M3. A shop window sign that specifies a target audience as 'local people' could also imply the loss of potential customers, who do not associate themselves with the city.

As previously indicated, Organization 4 is not vocal on any digital channel, but rather utilizes them as reminder tools, indicating when the next 'Knit and Natter' group takes place. A further observation is that the tweets posted have no punctuation, which, at times, makes it difficult to understand the meaning of what is being communicated.

In summary, this section indicates that none of the companies seem to have high knowledge of social media and thus, simply use it as a tool that communicates a message. Whilst Organization 2 promotes essential details that make up 'sustainable' fashion, it fails to convert the audience to buy into their values. Both Organizations 3 and 4 have low levels of social media knowledge and decoding aspects of sustainable fashion. O/M1 furthermore is not only contradicting herself, but also seems to be confused about the actual target audience for their communication.

6.3.5 Engage

Organization 1 uses digital channels to engage with their end-consumers, the community, and customers (agents/distributers). O/M1 emphasizes that they are regularly posting polls on Facebook and Twitter to gain feedback from their end-consumers about what materials, styles, and garments they liked best (Org1O/MI2). This data is utilized and considered when creating new collections. Moreover, their blog allows anyone to comment on their posts. The analysis indicated that the majority of blog posts remain unnoticed, in that there are no third party comments attached.

Organization 2 utilized incentives to gain feedback from end-consumers and receive candid photographs. However, without giveaways the response rate has dropped dramatically. O/M2 mentions that she lately feels that she has a monologue rather than a dialogue on her social media accounts, as no one is replying or retweeting any posts. The only example that showed active engagement between O/M2 and a customer was through an email exchange. A customer pointed out issues with their packaging material, which was taken into account. O/M2 reviewed the suggestion, decided that the feedback was valuable and feasible, and together with the customer created a new packaging material that fulfilled both their needs.

Due to their communications strategies, which seem to be either a hard sales approach or non-existent, Organizations 3 and 4 do not show any online engagement with their audience.

In summary, data emphasized that none of the case study organizations has established an online dialogue with their stakeholders. Whilst Organization 2 provides one example of successful collaboration between them and an external party, there is no evidence of engaging the online community in promoting sustainability.

6.4 Discussion

The analysis highlights various challenges faced by micro-organizations that provide the basis for modifying and extending the initial RACE framework. Although online communication is described as far reaching (Heggestuen/Danova 2013), it was also pointed out that SMEs lack time and knowledge to implement the newest technologies (Connell 2014). This research suggests an extension of the RACE framework by including two further components: '**t**rack' and '**s**ynergy' and thus, creating *T*RACE*S*. 'TRACES' is tailored to micro-organizations, which lack knowledge of online communication and resources, and provides them with a framework of how to tackle and engage with online communication.

'*T*rack' is seen as the first step towards building an online strategy. Organizations need to carefully review their options in terms of not only their availability, but also their fit with the companies' mission, as well as their target audiences' preferences. To reiterate this further, a metaphor that can be used is that of a runner, before starting the RACE, which in this case refers to the actual implementation of online communication strategies, needs to not only go to the track, but also understand how this track affects their performance. Thus, *t*rack is the initial stage that lays out the direction the organization is headed in terms of choosing their best available communication platform options that, ideally, compliment their mission and values, as well as their target audience.

Chaffey/Bosomworth (2012) define '**r**each' as the tool that analysis the awareness raised across multiple online platforms. In other words, it encourages organizations to think about not only how far their chosen online communication channels will take them, but also where they will take them. Whilst issues surrounding sustainable development and sustainability could be communicated to a wider audience (McDonagh 1998; Salvioni/Bosetti 2014) by utilising online communication channels (Gilmore et al. 2007), data indicated that the organizations lacked knowledge in terms of which channels enable them to communicate their message, as well as what needs to be communicated. To explain, it has been suggested from the findings that participants found it challenging to actually understand the purpose of the individual platforms, their potential, and how they can be utilised to promote not only their business, but also their core values and ideas. The analysis highlighted that whilst a link was created from the organization's website to their social media accounts, there was no link from these platforms back to the website. This implies that these organizations knowingly or unknowingly limit their potential to reach an even wider audience, simply by missing the opportunity to link all their online channels. In the same manner, data indicated that these micro-companies seem to also utilise the individual communication channels to target different stakeholders. The choice of channels could be described as random in that the O/Ms set up accounts for any online channel available without taking into consideration whether these platforms cater for the needs of their target audience or they can operate them.

This links to the next component of the RACE framework '**a**ct', which is set out to encourage a two-way communication process that facilitates the exchange of ideas, information, and knowledge (Chaffey 2013). The data highlighted that the exchange of ideas and knowledge is stronger between internal stakeholders and the organizations, which is facilitated pre dominantly through Facebook or Twitter accounts or tools such as Dropbox and Google calendar. On the other hand, only limited exchange was observed with external stakeholders. To explain, data suggest that external 'communication' is predominantly one-sided, with limited knowledge exchange. Neither of the tweets, blog posts, or Facebook entries seem to encourage an active dialogue with stakeholders. Moreover, it becomes apparent that the majority of messages are sales or operation focused and do not emphasise on the companies' core values, mission, or philosophy. This poses various questions: How can stakeholders gain the full picture of the organization and what it stands for, if the values, their production processes, and sustainability goals are not coherently communicated? Data show that the O/Ms shy away from labelling themselves as 'sustainable', due to wanting to be inclusive. This implies that it is up to the audience to create a unified jigsaw puzzle out of the information that can be pieced together from various channels. A second question links to the use of hashtags and why they are used. In the case of the case companies they can best be described as silent, as they are neither promoting their companies' values, nor do they add any value in terms of information.

This links to '**c**onvert', which seeks to encourage brand buy-in and, ideally, creates brand loyalty (Chaffey 2013). From the analysis it becomes apparent that various messages are broadcast through a variety of channels, however, none of them broadcast clearly what the organizations stands for, what its values are, and why they believe that sustainability is a key issue. This finding poses a further question: Do these organizations know who they are and how they fit in within a concept that has been defined as complex (Steger et al. 2007)? Specifically, the use of silent hashtags implies that on the one hand companies seek to associate themselves with sustainability, whilst on the other hand they lack knowledge not only of the concept, but also of the use of these tools. In a similar manner, the majority of participants used a hard sales approach promoting, in a way, hyper-consumption, which contradicts their core values of mindfulness. Data also indicated that the O/Ms seemed to be more successful in communicating their values in person, which implies that online channels that allow for a one-on-one customised approach might be more appropriate for them. Whilst the companies utilized a variety of online tools, it remains unclear how many people they reached, as well as what message is actually communicated.

'*E*ngage' seeks to create long-term relationships and loyalty (Chaffey/Ellis-Chadwick 2012). This part of the RACE framework seemed to be most important for the participants, as all participants highlighted that they seek to create long-term relationships with their stakeholders and brand loyalty by utilising online channels. Whilst the analysis indicated that the O/Ms incorporate feedback this is situational and not a continuous engagement. An explanation for the lack of engagement could be the fact the O/Ms, who are the sole risk takers (EC 2013) lack not only the time to fully embrace the potential of online communication channels, but also the knowledge, resources, and skills to implement them successfully.

The second addition to the RACE model is 'synergy', which provides the overall roundup to the model. Synergy is not only concerned with the overall fit of the channels and the organization, but also with the integration of the various channels utilised, and the overall messages communicated. Thus, it can be said that synergy seeks to add value to the overall process by creating a tight fit between the channels, the organization, and their stakeholders.

6.5 Conclusion

This chapter has laid out the challenges micro-organization face in terms of communicating sustainability to a broader audience. It was emphasised that rather than focusing on RACE, which emphasises the actual application of online channels, the TRACES approach enables these companies to gain a full understanding of the possibilities and opportunities available to them. It is acknowledged that this research has various limitations: firstly, it focuses on only four companies based in a niche market, the slow-fashion industry. Secondly, this research was time constrained, with online channels being monitored for a period of up to five months each. And lastly, the customers' viewpoint was not taken into consideration. Thus, for future research it is suggested to on the one hand look at a holistic, longitudinal approach that incorporates the view of the consumers, and on the other hand, see whether TRACES applies to other micro-organizations operating within a different industry.

References

AMA (American Marketing Association), 2012: Dictionary, AMA; at: http://www.marketingpower.com/_layouts/Dictionary.aspx?dLetter=G (1 August 2012).

Baden, D.; Harwood, I.; Woodward, D., 2011: "The Effects of Procurement Policies on Downstream CSR Activity: Content Analytic Insights into the Views and Actions of SME Owner–Manager", in: *International Small Business Journal*, 29: 259–277; doi:10.1177/0266242610375770.

Belz, F.-M.; Peattie, K., 2012: *Sustainability Marketing: A Global Perspective* (Chichester: John Wiley).

Bonini, S.; Oppenheim, J., 2008: "Cultivating the Green Consumer", in: *Stanford Social Innovation Review*, 6: 56–61.

BSR (Business of a Better World), 2012: Sustainable Fashion Design: Oxymoron No more?, BSR; at: http://www.bsr.org/reports/BSR_Sustainable_Fashion_Design.pdf (5 July 2013).

Chaffey, D., 2013: Introducing RACE: A Practical Framework to Improve Your Digital Marketing, Smart Insights; at: http://www.smartinsights.com/digital-marketing-strategy/race-a-practical-framework-to-improve-your-digital-marketing/ (23 September 2014).

Chaffey, D.; Bosomworth, D., 2012: Digital Marketing Strategy, Smart Insights; at: http://www.smartinsights.com/wp-content/uploads/2012/10/digital-marketing-plan-template-smart-insights.pdf (23 September 2014).

Chaffey, D.; Ellis-Chadwick, F., 2012: *Digital Marketing: Strategy, Implementation and Practice*, 5th edition (Harlow: Pearson).

Coles, N., 2013: International Review of Consumer Oriented Environmental Projects and Initiatives: Encouraging Sustainable Consumption Patterns, CSCP; at: http://www.scp-centre.org/projects/basic-projects-data/62-international-review.html (20 November 2014).

Connell, J., 2014: Realising the Potential: Micro Businesses' Experience of Communications Services, Consumer Communication Panel; at: http://www.communicationsconsumerpanel.org.uk/downloads/panel-micro-business-report-final.pdf (25 January 2015).

DFI (Danish Fashion Institute), 2014: Copenhagen Fashion Summit: The World's Largest Event on Sustainability in Fashion, Copenhagen Fashion Summit; at: http://www.copenhagenfashionsummit.com/ (20 November 2014).

Dickson, M.; Cataldi, C.; Grover, C., 2011: The Slow Fashion Movement, not Just a Label; at: https://www.notjustalabel.com/editorial/slow-fashion-movement (20 November 2014).

EC (European Commission), 2012: Policies to Encourage Sustainable Consumption, EC; at: http://ec.europa.eu/environment/eussd/pdf/report_22082012.pdf (20 November 2014).

EC (European Commission), 2013: Craft and Micro-enterprises, Europa; at: http://ec.europa.eu/enterprise/policies/sme/promoting-entrepreneurship/crafts-micro-enterprises/index_en.htm (24 January 2015).

Eder-Hansen, J.; Kryger, J.; Morris, J.; Sisco, C., 2012: The NICE Consumer: Research Summary and Discussion Paper, BSR; at: http://www.bsr.org/reports/BSR_NICE_Consumer_Discussion_Paper.pdf (5 July 2013).

Europa, 2007: Definition of Micro, Small and Medium-Sized Enterprises, Europa; at: http://europa.eu/legislation_summaries/enterprise/business_environment/n26026_en.htm (24 January 2014).

Fader, P.S.; Winer, R.S., 2012: "Introduction to the Special Issue on the Emergence and Impact of User-Generated Content", in: *Marketing Science*, 31,3: 369–371; doi:10.1287/mksc.1120.0715.

Fassin, Y.; Van Rossem, A.; Buelens, M., 2011: "Small-Business Owner–Managers Perceptions of Business Ethics and CSR-Related Concepts", in: *Journal of Business Ethics*, 98: 425–453; doi:10.1007/s10551-010-0586-y.

Gabrielli, V.; Balboni, B., 2010: "SME Practice Towards Integrated Marketing Communications", in: *Marketing Intelligence and Planning*, 28,3: 275–290; doi:10.1108/02634501011041426.

Gardetti, M.A.; Torres, A.L., 2013: *Sustainability in Fashion and Textiles: Values, Design, Production and Consumption* (Sheffield: Greenleaf Publishing).

Gilmore, A.; Gallagher, D.; Henry, S., 2007: "E-marketing and SMEs: Operational Lessons for the Future", in: *European Business Review*, 19,3: 234–247; doi:10.1108/09555340710746482.

Gould, H., 2013: "Alternative Business Models for a Sustainable Fashion Industry", *Guardian*; at: http://www.theguardian.com/sustainable-business/sustainable-fashion-blog/alternative-business-models-live-chat (20 December 2014).

Halme, M.; Korpela, M., (2013: "Responsible Innovation Toward Sustainable Development in Small and Medium-Sized Enterprises: A Resource Perspective", in: *Business Strategy and the Environment*, 23,8: 547–566; doi:10.1002/bse.1801.

Heggestuen, J.; Danova, T., 2013: Brand Presence: How to Choose Where to Be on Social Media, Without Breaking Your Budget, Business Insider; at: http://www.businessinsider.com/top-social-media-brand-strategies-2013-10?IR=T (20 December 2014).

Hussey, D.M.; Eagan, P.D., 2007: "Using Structural Equation Modelling to Test Environmental Performance in Small and Medium-Sized Manufacturers: Can SEM Help SMEs?", in: *Journal of Cleaner Production*, 15,4: 303–312.

Keller, K.L., 2001: "Mastering the Marketing Communications Mix: Micro and Macro Perspective on Integrated Marketing Communication Programs", in: *Journal of Marketing Management*, 17,7/8: 819–847; doi:10.1362/026725701323366836.

Killbourne, W.; McDonagh, P.; Prothero, A., 1997: "Sustainable Consumption and the Quality of Life: A Macromarketing Challenge to the Dominant Social Paradigm", in: *Journal of Macromarketing*, 17,1: 4–24; doi:10.1177/027614679701700103.

Kolandai-Matchett, K., 2009: "Mediated Communication of 'Sustainable Consumption' in the Alternative Media: A Case Study Exploring a Message Framing Strategy", in: *International Journal of Consumer Studies*, 33: 113–125; doi:10.1111/j.1470-6431.2009.00754.x.
Leeflang, P.S.H.; Verhoef, P.C.; Dahlström, P.; Freundt, T., 2014: "Challenges and Solutions for Marketing in a Digital Era", in: *European Management Journal*, 32,1: 1–12; doi:10.1016/j.emj.2013.12.001.
Leyesdorff, L., 2001: *A Sociological Theory of Communication: The Self-organization of the Knowledge Based Society* (Boca Raton: Universal Publishers).
Low, G.S., 2000: "Correlates of Integrated Marketing Communications", in: *Journal of Advertising Research*, 40,3: 27–39.
Martin, M., 2013: Creating Sustainable Apparel Value Chains: A Primer on Industry Transformation, Impact Economy; at: http://www.impacteconomy.com/en/primer2.php (20 November 2014).
McDonagh, P., 1998: "Towards a Theory of Sustainable Communication in Risk Society: Relating Issues of Sustainability to Marketing Communications", in: *Journal of Marketing Management*, 14: 591–622; doi:10.1362/026725798784867699.
McDonagh, P.; Prothero, A., 2014: "Sustainability Marketing Research: Past, Present and Future", in: *Journal of Marketing Management*, 30,11/12: 1186–1219; doi:10.1080/0267257X.2014.943263.
Niinimäki, K., 2010: "Eco-clothing, Consumer Identity and Ideology", in: *Sustainable Development*, 18,3: 150–162; doi:10.1002/sd.455.
Niinimäki, K.; Hassi, L., 2011: "Emerging Design Strategies in Sustainable Production and Consumption of Textiles and Clothing", in: *Journal of Cleaner Production*, 19: 1876–1883; doi:10.1016/j.jclepro.2011.04.02.
Peattie, K.; Crane, A., 2005: "Green Marketing: Legend, Myth, Farce or Prophesy?", in: *Qualitative Market Research: An International Journal*, 8,4: 357–370; doi:10.1108/13522750510619733.
Polonsky, M.J., 1994: "A Stakeholder Theory Approach to Designing Environmental Marketing Strategy", in: *Journal of Business and Industrial Marketing*, 10,3: 29–46.
Princen, T., 2005: *The Logic of Sufficiency* (Cambridge, MA: MIT Press).
Prothero, A.; Peattie, K.; McDonagh, P., 1997: "Communicating Greener Strategies: A Study of On-pack Communications", in: *Business Strategy and the Environment*, 6,2: 74–82; doi:10.1002/(SICI)1099-0836(199705)6:2<74::AID-BSE93>3.0.CO;2-4.
Punch, K.F., 2005: *Introduction to Social Research: Quantitative and Qualitative Approaches*, 2nd edition (London: Sage).
Reilly, A.H.; Hynan, K.A., 2014: "Corporate Communication, Sustainability, and Social Media: It's not Easy (Really) Being Green", in: *Business Horizons*, 57: 747–758; doi:10.1016/j.bushor.2014.07.008.
Rettie, R.; Burchell, K.; Riley, D., 2012: "Normalising Green Behaviours: A New Approach to Sustainability Marketing", in: *Journal of Marketing Management*, 28,3/4: 420–444; doi:10.1080/0267257X.2012.658840.
Ryan, D.; Jones, C., 2012: *Understanding Digital Marketing: Marketing Strategies for Engaging the Digital Generation*, 2nd edition (London: Kogan Page).
Salvioni, D.M.; Bosetti, L., 2014: "Sustainable Development and Corporate Communication in Global Markets", in: *Emerging Issues in Management*, 1: 1–19; doi:10.4468/2014.1.03salvioni.bosetti.
Sheth, J.N.; Sethia, N.K.; Srinivas, S., 2011: "Mindful Consumption: A Customer-Centric Approach to Sustainability", in: *Journal of the Academy of Marketing Science*, 39,1: 21–39; doi:10.1007/s11747-010-0216-3.
Steger, U.; Ionescu-Somers, A.; Salzmann, O., 2007: "The Economic Foundations of Corporate Sustainability", in: *Corporate Governance*, 7,2: 162–177; doi:10.1108/14720700710739804.
UN (United Nations), 1992: Programme for Action for Sustainable Development, UN; at: http://sustainabledevelopment.un.org/content/documents/Agenda21.pdf (2 January 2011).

UN (United Nations), 2011: *Report of the World Commission on Environment and Development: Our Common Future*, UN Documents; at: http://www.un-documents.net/wced-ocf.htm (2 January 2011).

WCED, 1987: *Our Common Future* (The Brundtland Report), World Commission on Environment and Development (Oxford: Oxford University Press).

WEF (World Economic Forum), 2012: More with Less: Scaling Sustainable Consumption and Resource Efficiency, WEF; at: http://www.weforum.org/reports/more-less-scaling-sustainable-consumption-and-resource-efficiency (20 November 2014).

Yin, R.K., 2003: *Case Study Research: Design and Method*, 3rd edition (Thousand Oaks, CA: Sage).

Chapter 7
Steering Sustainable Food Consumption in Japan: Trust, Relationships, and the Ties that Bind

Steven R. McGreevy and Motoki Akitsu

Abstract For many consumers serious about sustainability, reconnecting with the backstories that permeate our food involves creating closer relationships with the people, products, and places involved in its provisioning and highlights the importance of trusting relationships. Forming trusting relationships can be a difficult process as personal, social, and cultural factors play a role in fostering or suppressing trust, ultimately affecting long-term prospects for sustainable food consumption. Answering the call for inquiries on the link between agency and culture, this chapter focuses on the cultural factors that are unique to consumers, farmers, and groups involved with sustainable food consumption activities in Japan. Drawing on examples from the literature, cases from our previous research, and cross-cultural survey data we examine the ways in which objects, symbols, and relationships are employed by various actors in the creation or erosion of trust, assurance, and commitment. We pay particular attention to how the culturally pertinent factors of in-group trust and assurance, monitoring and sanctioning, and the emphasis on long-term personal relationships and commitments play out in helping or hindering the diffusion and maintenance of organic *teikei* food cooperatives and *chisan-chisho* (local production for local consumption) activities. Additional studies on the ways trust and food consumption practices are shaped by cultural factors are needed in other countries to better understand and facilitate a culturally sensitive steering of sustainable consumption.

Keywords Agency · Cooperatives · Food consumption · Local production · National culture · Trust

---

Steven. R. McGreevy, Ph.D., Assistant Professor, Research Institute for Humanity and Nature, Center for Research Development title, function, Research Institute for Humanity and Nature, Kyoto, Japan; e-mail: srmcgreevy@chikyu.ac.jp.

Motoki Akitsu, Ph.D., Professor of Philosophy of Agricultural Science, Graduate School of Agriculture, Kyoto University, Kyoto, Japan; e-mail: akitsu@kais.kyoto-u.ac.jp.

A. Genus (ed.), *Sustainable Consumption*, The Anthropocene: Politik—Economics—Society—Science 3, DOI 10.1007/978-3-319-29665-4_7

7.1 Introduction

A common observation from many interested in the sustainability of food consumption is that there is a series of 'disconnections' between upstream and downstream processes and actors composing food and agricultural systems—as consumers, we are unaware of the backstories that permeate our food. For many consumers serious about the sustainability and safety of their food, reconnecting with these backstories involves *creating closer relationships* with the people, products, and places involved in the provisioning of food. This intimacy is sown between consumers and farmers, between consumers and place, and amongst neighbourhood groups. *Community-supported agriculture* (CSA), direct sales from local farmers, and various "local-production for local-consumption" activities are some pertinent examples of the kinds of intimate arrangements under discussion. In all of these cases, the complexity of food provisioning systems is dealt with by reducing the physical distance and number of intermediaries separating one from their food, and by investing in personal relationships with various actors. As in any relationship, closeness necessitates active participation from those involved, which can lead to the formation of trust and sense of commitment. Nevertheless, forming these ties can be a difficult process as personal, social, and cultural factors play a role in fostering or suppressing trust, ultimately affecting long-term prospects for sustainable food consumption.

In this chapter, we are concerned with cultural factors that help and hinder the formation of trust in relationships among consumers, farmers, and groups involved with sustainable food consumption activities in Japan. This research speaks to the need for a cultural perspective to socio-environmental inquiry into sustainable consumption practices, called for by Spaargaren to further develop the "agency-culture debate" (2011). While this may be seen as a (partial) return to the socio-psychological roots of sustainable consumption research (e.g. Jackson 2005), we contend that sustainable transitions necessitate sensitivity to cultural uniqueness when steering or rolling out new consumption practices from the niche to regime level (Geels/Schot 2007). This is particularly the case when it comes to practices in the food domain, since food practices are intensely cultural, infused with ritual and history, and at the same time very intimate, often shared with family and friends on a daily basis. Social scientific inquiries into trust and food consumption have tended to focus on "system trust" and the ways consumers interpret labels, new technologies, and food scandals, not on "personal trust" formed between people or groups (Brom 2000; Sassatelli/Scott 2001).

Japan offers a unique case to explore cultural notions in the practices of sustainable food consumption for a number of reasons. First of all, it has a history of strong consumer-farmer collaboration in the formation of sustainable agriculture and food delivery partnerships—in fact, Japan is home of the original CSA, called *teikei*, some of which are over forty years old (Hatano 2008). Second, it can be argued that no other country has undergone the degree of agrifood related change as Japan over the last fifty years, including the rationalization, contraction, and looming extinction of agricultural production and the massive influx of food calories and culture from abroad—much of this change is heading in an unsustainable direction, with already low self-sufficiency rates set to decline further[1]. Lastly, Japanese culture has been described as a "collectivist society" with strong norms toward maintaining social and group cohesion and a hypersensitivity to context (Hofstede 2001). Examination of the ways in which trust is created, activated, and lost in sustainable food consumption activities in such a strongly collectivist society provides a basis with which studies in more individualist societies can compare.

We situate our inquiry on the practice of "food procurement" by drawing on examples from the literature, cases from our previous research, and cross-cultural survey data. Particular focus will be on the ways objects, symbols, and relationships are employed by various actors in the creation or erosion of trust, assurance, and commitment. Specifically, elements of overlapping activities and campaigns related to sustainable food consumption common to Japan are examined: organic *teikei* food cooperatives and *chisan-chisho* (local production for local consumption). After introducing these activities, a review of literature pertaining to trust is undertaken.

7.2 *Teikei,* Organic Agriculture, and Food Cooperatives

Following a post-WWII period of intensive agricultural modernization, agriculture-related soil and water pollution, and multiple food safety scares, the Japanese *teikei* and organic farming movement emerged together. In 1971, a group of consumers (mainly mothers and families seeking chemical-free milk), agricultural researchers, and farmers formed the *Japan Organic Agriculture Association* (JOAA). In JOAA's statement of purpose penned in 1971, modern agricultural production techniques are questioned to cause farm work-related illnesses, reductions in biodiversity, polluted waterways, and soil degradation. The same document calls for developing alternative technologies based on traditional farming methods, and establishes a platform to share these new organic methods (JOAA 1971). But the real emphasis for JOAA, at that time, was (1) how farmers could survive economically if they did not play by the market-driven rules of expansion and industrialization and (2) the 'duty' of consumers to understand and support farmers working in their community's best interest, not solely in the interest of turning a profit. It is from this focus that *teikei* was conceived.

[1]Japan currently imports about 60 % of its food calories, the highest percentage of any other industrialized country and making it first in national food mileage (MAFF 2013; Tanaka 2003). Ageing, rural depopulation, and economic marginalization have affected domestic production significantly.

Teikei, which translates roughly as 'partnership,' are formalized associations between organic farmers and consumers where produce is distributed through joint efforts based on reciprocal trust relationships (Masugata 2008). In 1978, JOAA published ten principles by which *teikei* groups should operate, including mutual assistance emphasising a relationship of friendly reciprocity, face-to-face relationships to enhance cooperation, principles on mutual consultation and negotiation of prices, and the purchasing and distribution of all produce on the consumer side (JOAA 1993). In essence, farmers and consumers form an agreement, farmers cultivate and harvest their crops with some help from consumers, and consumers distribute the produce amongst themselves. While very similar to *Community Supported Agriculture* (CSA) schemes, *teikei* may be unique in that prices for produce are negotiated collectively and there is an emphasis on year-round and long-term commitment to the partnership beyond any one growing season's group of subscribers. *Teikei* in Japan number in the thousands and membership ranges widely from as low as 20–30 consumer households with a single farmer, to as many as thousands or hundreds of households with an organized group of farmers (Hill/Kubota 2007).

Hatano (1998) classifies *teikei* dependent upon whether farmers and consumers are organized into formal groups, the most common types being *organized farmers and organized consumers* (OF–OC) and *non-organized farmers and non-organized consumers* (NF–NC). OF–OC is the oldest type, very popular during the 1970s, but is now losing popularity among younger families, while NF–NC *teikei* are gaining in popularity (Hatano 2008; Akitsu/Aminaka 2010). The reasons behind these shifts in popularity will be discussed later in the chapter.

Another way organic food is commonly purchased is through various consumer cooperatives (co-ops) that number in the hundreds. The Seikatsu Club is composed of an association of 32 consumer cooperatives in 21 prefectures, representing over 340,000 members in 2011 (Seikatsu Club 2014). The cooperative works with farmers and farmer groups to develop products, purchase, deliver, and also monitor the quality and safety of food. Consumer members are divided into *han* (groups) to order food in bulk that is delivered once a week. Co-ops occasionally host educational events and field trips to visit producers and food processors.

7.3 *Chisan-Chisho*-Local Production for Local Consumption

A relatively recent development from the perspective of sustainable food consumption in Japan is *chisan-chisho,* or "local production for local consumption". Beginning in the 1990s, both MAFF and *Japanese Agricultural Cooperative* (JAC), which represents over 9,430,000 members, started promoting the concept of *chisan-chisho* with differing aims. For MAFF, *chisan-chisho* was incorporated into its general policy of improving food self-sufficiency and boosting domestic production. JAC promoted *chisan-chisho* as a new branding scheme to increase sales and win-back consumers after JAC-associated corporations were found falsifying food labels during the early 2000s. A recent report on the status of *chisan-chisho* throughout the country indicates that 70 % of prefectures and 30 % of all cities and towns in Japan are either enacting a *chisan-chisho* plan or are formulating a plan for the near future (MAFF 2014). Kimura and Nishiyama contend that the *chisan-chisho* movement makes five local food claims: (1) "restore the trustworthiness and safety of food," (2) be a positive for the local economy and "improve the deteriorating conditions of Japanese agriculture and farming communities," (3) preserve the environment by reducing the ecological footprint of food, (4) support the maintenance of "traditional food culture" from the threat of "westernized food," and (5) improve health (2008: 54).

One way to measure the successful development of *chisan-chisho* is by the spread of *chokubaijyo,* or "direct sale/farmers markets." According to a survey conducted by MAFF in 2004, there were 2,982 *sanchi chokubaijyo* (direct sale markets of locally produced goods) throughout Japan—a similar survey five years later in 2009 revealed a 564 % increase to 16,816 (MAFF 2004, 2011). Markets are largely managed by producer groups (~64 %) and by JAC (~11 %), and sales are mostly composed of fresh vegetables and fruit (46.4 %) (ibid.). Markets tend to be located in peri-urban and suburban areas, closer to population centres, and 30 % of customers visiting rural area markets are tourists from outside the prefecture, confirming that locally produced goods are for the most part consumed locally (Urban-rural Exchange Promotion Organization 2007).

7.4 Trust, Assurance, Commitment, and Culture

For consumers, trust plays an essential role in reducing uncertainty in a complex world. Luhmann sees trust as a kind of modern day currency by which society functions and has argued for two kinds of trust: system and personal (1979). System trust refers to trust we place in the abstract functioning of systems and technical expertise, what Giddens (1990: 88) would call "faceless commitments," and is crucial in today's complex modern society. Personal trust, on the other hand, is created between people in face-to-face relationships. When considering food, we predominately place our trust in the systems that regulate the amount of agricultural chemicals that can be used during cultivation, hygienic standards during processing, methods of traceability, and certification of certain production practices. System trust erodes when food scandals and health scares occur. Coff's (2006: 147) examination of the ethics of food tracing concluded that "on the food market, personal and system trust go together" and that "in the case of food it is clear that system trust, or distrust, can be enhanced by personal contact with representatives of the food production companies" or the farmers themselves.

Toshio Yamagishi, a social psychologist and behavioural theorist, takes a functional approach to conceptualising trust and makes important distinctions. Yamagishi is concerned with how trust functions and affects interactions in the formation of relationships between people and groups. One important distinction is between *trust and assurance*: trust is the "expectation of goodwill and benign intent," while assurance is the "expectation of benign behaviour for reasons other than goodwill of the partner" (Yamagishi/Yamagishi 1994: 132). In other words, "trust is based on the inference of the interaction partner's personal traits and intentions, whereas assurance is based on the knowledge of the incentive structure surrounding the relationship" (ibid). The difference between trust and assurance is more easily understood when we factor in *social uncertainty and commitment formation*—all four notions are dynamically interrelated. While "trust provides a solution to the problems caused by social uncertainty," Yamagishi argues that in situations of high social uncertainty, "the simplest and most readily available solution… would be to form committed relations with specific partners" (ibid: 131, 134). Agreement to form mutually committed relations reduces uncertainty, provides assurance, and reduces the need for trust. Leaving committed relations when better opportunities arise requires trusting that the new partner is not dishonest or exploitative. Yamagishi redefines trust here "as a bias in the processing of imperfect information about… (a) partner's intentions" (Yamagishi/Yamagishi 1994: 136). With no assurance, or guarantee in the incentive structure surrounding the new relationship, we have no other choice but to ignore the social uncertainty and hope the new partner has benign intentions. It is here that we see how in-group/out-group norms become critical in the decision to trust. In the end, "commitment may actually reduce the level of trust in outsiders, and as a result, those who mostly stay in the security of committed relations experience higher subjective social uncertainty… (leading to)… a vicious circle of distrust of outsiders" (ibid: 137). This is referred to as Yamagishi's "emancipation theory of trust" (Ferrin/Gillespie 2010).

With Yamagishi's approach in mind, we turn to cross-cultural social-psychological studies of trust to explore the different ways trust, assurance, and commitment manifest and are mobilized in different cultures, with particular emphasis on Japan. There have been a number of attempts at surveying cross-national and cultural differences in trust. Trust has found its way into more general analyses of values and cultural difference. For example, "The World Values Survey," is an attempt at mapping cultural values at large (World Values Survey 2010). Within the survey, trust is factored into how different nations score on a scale of survival versus self-expression values—Japan was found to be a highly trusting society, holding strong values of self-expression (ibid).

Contrastingly, Ferrin and Gillespie conducted a review of fifty-six social-psychological studies of trust differences across national-societal cultures and found "evidence of cross-cultural differences, particularly on generalized trust, and also evidence of trust universals across cultures" (2010: 42). They also found that trust "operates as a variform universal… (meaning that) the general principle of trust holds across cultures, although some of its specific manifestations differ across cultures" (ibid: 72). Specifically, they state "there is repeated strong evidence suggesting that the level of generalized trust[2] is higher in American society than in Japanese society" (ibid: 50). These findings introduce the idea of 'collectivist' and 'individualist' societies[3] and how trust is uniquely mobilized in each, the main difference being the degree to which individuals invest energy in groups. Where the cultural pattern is collectivist, groups (including family and friends) are critical to individuals. In individualist societies, individuals have flexible arrangements with groups and may 'belong' to many groups if it benefits them to do so. Another general rule for collectivist and individualist societies is the degree to which uncertainty is tolerated. Hofstede's (2001) work with cultural dimensions theory revealed that Japan is has a very low tolerance level for social uncertainty, while that of the US is quite high.

Returning to Yamagishi's emancipation theory of trust, we see that groups in Japan are an important arena for trust and assurance—in-group and out-group boundaries are distinct, and generalized trust for outsiders is low. In other words, "Japanese feel a greater sense of security within established and stable relationships but are more distrustful of people outside of such relationships" (Ferrin/Gillespie 2010: 51). This in-group security is based less on the trust of group members (in the form of friendship or camaraderie) than it is on the assurance that they will behave benignly because of their commitment to the group and desire for low social uncertainty. More than trust, Japanese seek assurance in their relationships. Yamagishi summarizes best by saying "members of collectivist culture provide mutual assurance in committed relations" (Yamagishi/Yamagishi 1994: 162).

Social-psychological experiments reveal that there are a few different mechanisms by which trust and assurance can be secured in group relations. Yamagishi found that when compared to Americans, Japanese are more likely to cooperate to achieve group goals when there are clear methods for *mutual monitoring and sanctioning*, and more distrusting when there are not (Yamagishi 1988). The ability to monitor each other and a means to enforce compliance when behaviour is contrary to the groups' interest gives the assurance one needs to invest fully.[4] In Japanese society, sanctions are more likely conceived as shame or embarrassment borne not only by individuals, but also by the groups with which they are associated. Another unique characteristic for Japanese is that *long-term, personal relationships* and networks are highly valued, particularly when one must deal with persons from out-of-group—a direct or indirect personal connection is seen as a more attractive way to assess one's trustworthiness. Takahashi et al. (2008) tested students from China, Taiwan, and Japan, and found that in a modified trust game, Japanese devoted themselves to networking with a few partners over the longer-term, where Chinese and Taiwanese were more ranging in their social

[2]Generalized trust in this sense refers to the expectation of goodwill and benign intent as defined by Yamagishi/Yamagishi (1994).

[3]See Triandis (1995) for a deeper investigation of individualism and collectivism.

[4]In the more individualist society of the Netherlands, Dutch researchers saw the presence of a sanctioning system undermine trust, and the removal of the system increase trust (Mulder et al. 2006).

dealings. Kuwabara et al. (2007) confirmed this tendency in an experiment with American and Japanese participants.

7.5 Procuring Sustainable Food and Trust in Japan

What are the implications of the proceeding cultural social-psychological research for practices of food procurement in Japan? Using these findings as a lens, we now offer examples of relevant objects, symbols, and relationships at work among consumers, farmers, and organizations in sustainable food consumption activities in Japan. We pay particular attention to how the culturally pertinent factors of *in-group trust and assurance, monitoring and sanctioning, and the emphasis on long-term personal relationships and commitments* play out in helping or hindering the diffusion and maintenance of sustainable food consumption.

7.5.1 Teikei and Consumer Cooperative Activities

By no means an exhaustive summary of *teikei* operations in Japan, Akitsu/Aminaka (2010) offer an examination of six different *teikei* arrangements to determine how direct relationships between farmers and consumers are created, maintained, and fall apart. Three of the *teikei* were formally organized into farmer and consumer groups (OF–OC type) of varying membership, one small (five farmers and 305 consumer households), one medium-sized (59 farming households and an unknown number of consumers), and the last was a partnership between 482 farming households and a large consumer cooperative of 310,000 households. The remaining three arrangements were of the non-organized variety (NF–NC type), with similar memberships (1 household on 3 ha supplying 150 households; 1 household on 1.2 ha supplying 50 households; a single farmer on 2 ha supplying 80 households). The organized *teikei* offered three ways to create and maintain trust between the farmer and consumer groups: ordering and price-fixing meetings, inspections, food-related events, and direct face-to-face interaction.

For the small and medium-sized *teikei*, a meeting between farmers and consumers is held twice annually before planting and harvest to determine the cultivation plans and pricing. Growing conditions, estimated yield, last year's prices, and market prices inform negotiations. Farmers are not allowed to use chemical fertilisers or pesticides at any time and must submit a report of their farming practices with data on soil inputs. Farmers and consumers do their best to come to agreement on a price that respects farmers labour requirements and livelihood, and the consumer pocket books. To ensure farmers a fixed income, consumers purchase the entire volume of produce ordered—there are no refunds if produce is of sub-standard quality. These meetings are an important learning experience for both groups: consumers can learn about the intricacies and difficulties of farm work and cultivation, and farmers receive feedback on the produce they grow and how eating preferences change. The meetings also create a sense of community and mutual respect.

For the very large organized group of farmers and consumer cooperative, the size of the groups affects the way in which the meeting is held. Farmer union and cooperative representatives meet to determine the price of products before harvest—prices are largely determined by calculations of the average cost of production. Rice is one of the most central crops to a farmer's annual income and represents a significant cost for consumer households. For this reason, if the difference of price agreed upon at the meeting and the market price for rice increases to 10 %, an additional meeting is held to re-negotiate the price—this assures that farmers can usually sell at a premium and consumers are never spending far above the market price. When prices are determined, the 482 farmers are divided into teams and attend meetings directly with consumer groups to make face-to-face contact and hear the concerns of consumers. Here again, the consumer cooperative agrees to purchase the entire volume of produce grown by the farmers union. With 482 farming households, the rules governing the use of chemical pesticides and herbicides are a bit more flexible: weed-killer is allowed once a year and pesticides are allowed twice a year only if necessary.

By agreed upon rules or by farmer request, consumer groups inspect farmer fields and farm operations. This can either take place formally, which is often the case for the larger organized *teikei*, but it can also take place at seasonal events in a more informal manner. For formal checks, cooperative representatives and a selected group of consumer members inspect farms for cleanliness, soil conditions, food storage and delivery conditions, and evidence of agricultural chemical use. The standards are initially set by the consumer group and negotiated from there. Even though the consumer members are not experts on farm operations, everyone agrees that their presence in the investigation is necessary. Written farm records are also examined. An informant from a particular *teikei* described a situation where a farmer refused to submit his farm records, stating, "Why do you doubt me so much?" The farmer was later dropped from the *teikei*.

The relationships created in *teikei* can be quite old (in this case of organized groups 39, 28, and 22 years) and closeness is created at food related events and multiple occasions for face-to-face interaction. *Teikei* sponsored events are diverse in form and the number and frequency of the events is varied. Within the consumer groups themselves, cooking-classes, nutritional lectures, and speaking events are common. Between the consumer and farmer groups, farm visits and on-farm experiences to plant or harvest crops are typical. Some events are held annually without fail, such as a fall harvest festival where *teikei* food is shared amongst consumers and farmers. In addition to these group-oriented events, *teikei* products are ordered by teams of consumers, or *han,* on a weekly basis and delivered to a set, neighbourhood location. Members in these groups, then, must meet one another every week and can converse between themselves and with either a farmer or delivery person with extensive knowledge of the farming operations. Food is unloaded from delivery trucks in bulk and divided amongst the members together—this way, the contents of each household's order are generally known by all and ordering advice and suggestions are shared.

In *teikei* of the non-organized variety, trusting relationships between farmers and consumers are more difficult to create and maintain as there are not the opportunities for direct interaction that the organized *teikei* offer. Prices are not negotiated together and inspections are not conducted. Consumers are unorganized and do not usually meet each other, except for the occasional farmer-sponsored event. However, farmers in these *teikei* often deliver orders in-person, and appeal to consumers with their personalities and character. Personalized notes are often included in vegetable boxes and consumers are encouraged to send feedback on the quality of the products, cultivation requests, and prices through pre-stamped postal sheets. Weekly newsletters, daily email, and use of social media are other ways the farmers maintain open lines of communication with consumers. Of the three non-organized *teikei* observed, consumers from each *teikei* cited the personality, attitude, and character of the farmer as a reason why they are trustworthy.

Of the types of *teikei* observed here, Hatano (2008) finds trends indicating that organized *teikei* arrangements are losing their popularity, while non-organized *teikei* are increasing in number. He observes many long-standing organized *teikei* (established 28 years ago or earlier) in Hyogo prefecture losing three quarters of their membership on average over a period of eleven years (1996–2007) (ibid.). In the Kanto area (the region around Tokyo), a new federation of cooperatives called The Pal System has seen growth in membership, while the long-established Seikatsu Club has stagnated. The Pal System lacks the *han* or group system of ordering food together and we speculate that the time gained and labour avoided in dealing with a *han* may be a reason for the increased popularity.

7.5.2 Chisan-Chisho: Farmer's Faces

With over 16,816 direct sale/farmers markets in Japan in 2009, the move to buying local products is well underway (MAFF 2011). While freshness and price are the main reasons drawing consumers to these markets, there are unique tools used in the marketing of local produce that breed trust.

A common sight in many of these markets, as well as supermarkets with *chisan-chisho* corners, are displays and labelling with photos of and detailed information on farmers. Shelves may be dedicated to a certain farmer, their produce arrayed under their prominently displayed photograph, information as to the farm size and farming practices, and the farmer's name is printed on each label of produce (see Fig. 7.1). While it is not altogether uncommon to see photos of farmers on in-store displays anywhere in the world, the degree to which farmer's faces are seen on displays in Japan is noteworthy and with good reason: Japanese consumers respond positively, indicating a high degree of trust, when a photo of a farmer's face is associated with food.

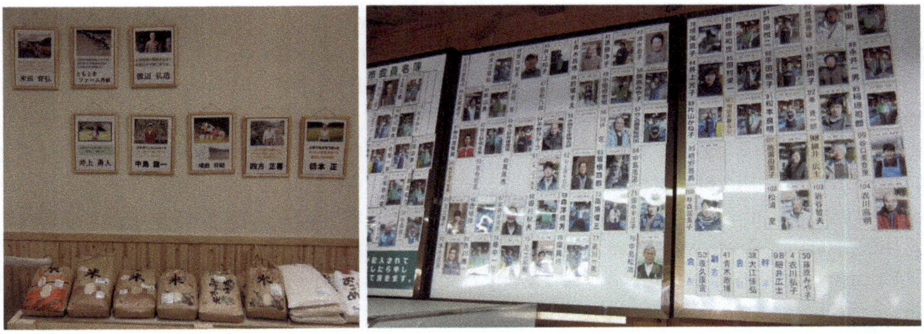

Fig. 7.1 In-store display of agriculture produce with photographs of farmer faces. *Source* Authors

In a five country, cross-cultural survey (n = 5825, 31.9 % return rate) on food risk and trust that asked parents of elementary school students the degree to which they trusted certain food-related bodies, actors, or labelling, Japanese consumers were far more likely to trust agricultural produce with a photograph of a farmer's face somewhere on or near it than their Western counterparts (see Fig. 7.2).

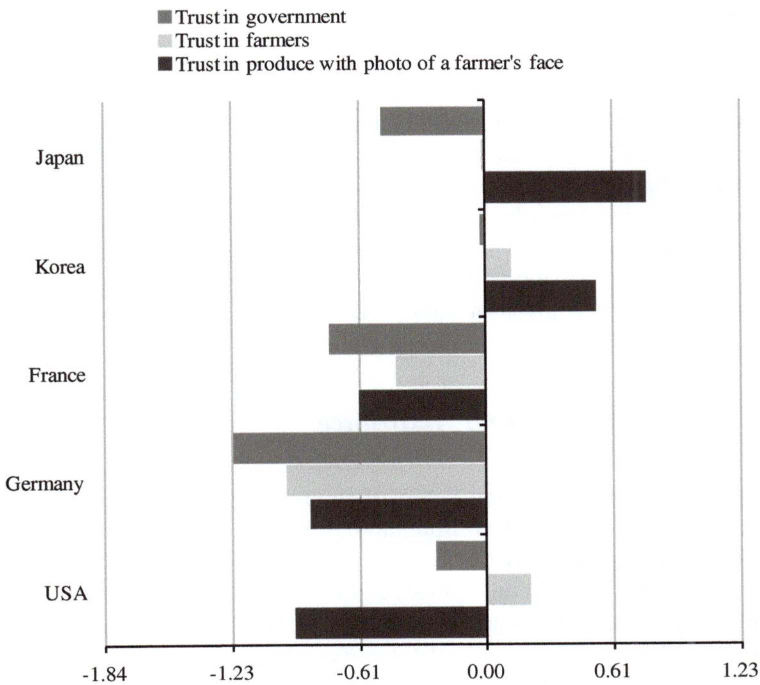

Fig. 7.2 Degree of consumer trust in farmers, government, and produce with a photo of a farmer's face (n = 5825, 31.9 % average return rate amongst the five countries; values indicate deviation from the compiled average score). *Source* Authors

What makes 'farmer-photo' produce so trustworthy in the eyes of Japanese consumers? We speculate that it is a mixture of factors. First of all, from the farmer's perspective, there is a risk in identifying oneself so completely with their products—product quality is quickly associated with a farmer's 'brand' and a decline in quality could bring sanctions in the form of a loss in business. At the same time, however farmers agree to display their faces prominently with the awareness of the possibility of sanctions, and this assures consumers of the quality of the product. In a way, the farmer is saying, "This is me, these are my products, I'm completely open with you." Local consumers are also only a few degrees of separation from their local producers, which brings an additional immediacy for feedback to further solidify the farmer's position as trustworthy producer. Consumers from outside the local area (tourists) are also sensitive to this local dynamic of monitoring and potential sanctioning, which, in turn, assures them of the quality of the produce. The increasing numbers of direct sale/farmer's markets and evidence of local consumers frequenting such markets would indicate that the *chisan-chisho* message of trustworthy food resonates within communities (Urban-rural Exchange Promotion Organization 2007).

7.6 Discussion

The diffusion and maintenance of sustainable food consumption in Japan is shaped by the ways in which trust is mediated between and within various groups of actors. With a focus on the ways in which consumer agency is influenced by cultural factors and following Spaargaren's (2011) suggestion to investigate the objects, symbols, and relationships of situated consumption practices, we found a number of examples related to the sustainable procurement of food in Japan that highlight cultural uniqueness. A summary of trust-related activities for sustainable food procurement in Japan is given in Table 7.1.

7.6.1 In-Group Trust and Assurance

We found evidence of a strong sense of in-group trust and assurance in each example of sustainable food consumption. Certain rules in *teikei* partnerships emphasized in-group trust and the need for assurance to reduce social uncertainty—the 10 % differential in price rule for rice and the rule that consumers must purchase all produce from farmers. Since assurance is about the incentive structure surrounding a relationship, we can see that these rules provide a guarantee that neither the consumer nor producer will have an unfair advantage over the other. The price

Table 7.1 Summary of trust-related activities for sustainable food procurement in Japan

	Teikei, Co-ops	*Chisan-Chisho,* farmer's faces
In-group trust and assurance	Price negotiation meeting • 10 % differential in price rule • Consumers must purchase all rule	Local consumers identify with local producer
Monitoring and sanctioning	Inspections by consumers (largely symbolic)	Complete transparency • Farmer/Farm data
	Lack of transparency punished (farm records)	Prospect of immediate community sanctions
Long-term personal relationships and commitments	Events	
	Face-to face-interaction	
	Han system	
	Communication • Personalized notes, daily email	

Source Authors

of rice is linked with fluctuations in market prices and is therefore reasonable and transparent for consumers, and farmers are saved the anxiety of not knowing whether their produce will be purchased or not. The impressive growth of *chisan-chisho* in Japan would indicate a strong degree of in-group trust, as local consumers rally around their neighbourhood producers.

7.6.2 Monitoring and Sanctioning

The presence or lack of a system for monitoring and sanctioning was a significant indicator for trust in both examples. In *teikei,* farm inspections were conducted by consumers despite the fact that they were not experts and both sides were well aware that the inspections themselves were more or less symbolic. The exercise itself builds a relationship of openness and trust. However, as we saw in the case of a farmer not agreeing to submit farm records, refusing to be completely open was not tolerated. For the farmer's face labelling, the sense of complete transparency was very evident. The farmers were on display for all to see and judge. This openness to a system of passive monitoring served as evidence that the farmer was trustworthy. If a certain farmer's produce was of low quality, consumers are assured that he or she will suffer, at a minimum, local sanctions from community members.

7.6.3 Long-Term Personal Relationships and Commitments

The formation of long-term personal relationships and commitments in securing and eroding trust was also evident in both examples. *Teikei* and consumer cooperatives offer plenty of opportunities to build personal relationships with other consumers and with farmers as well. Weekly gatherings and occasional events bring people together in a face-to-face setting. In organized *teikei* and coops, the *han* system can be a venue for fostering deeper relationships between neighbours. In non-organized *teikei*, farmers make a special effort to communicate with personalized messages and by daily emails with their membership, building a sense of closeness to foster long-term relationships.

Of course, beyond these culturally relevant examples, we must emphasize that we concur with Ferrin and Gillespie's (2010: 72) conclusion that trust is a variform universal, meaning "the general principle of trust holds across cultures, although some of its specific manifestations differ across cultures". The preference of in-group trust and assurance, monitoring and sanctions, and long-term personal relationships are not unique to Japan alone and arguments can be made for other societies and cultures being partial to these factors in the creation of trust. We maintain that in the case of Japan, these notions are of particular significance and that special sensitivity to them is necessary when tasked with steering sustainable food consumption.

Additionally, we are not arguing that cultural particularities are the *only* thing influencing the procuring of sustainable food in Japan—economic, demographic, and other social factors are important in the emergence and maintenance of certain practices. Hatano's (2008) work on the decline of *teikei* is evidence of decreased potency of in-group strength, but also confirms that other contexts, such as economic and demographic factors are also important in the maintenance of certain practices. Specifically, he offers five reasons for the stagnation of *teikei* in Japan: (1) Loss of active civil society and presence of social movements, (2) loss of consumer cooking skills and motivation, (3) emergence of an organic market, (4) lack of future vision and ability to adapt to the times, (5) women entering the work force. Japan's society is rapidly ageing and many of the founding and original members of *teikei* are now no longer very active. The majority of *teikei* and consumer cooperative members have traditionally been women—the increase in women working outside of the home has reduced the amount of time available to spend volunteering for *teikei* activities and restricted household flexibility in receiving organic produce at set times and places. Hatano brings up a relevant point in that "*teikei* groups have failed to support the wider participation of women in society—much like many organizations in Japan" (ibid: 32).

7.7 Conclusion

In this chapter we explored the importance of cultural factors in the creation and maintenance of trust for sustainable food procurement practices in Japan. However, in today's increasingly globalized world, cultural exclusivity is weakening and Japan is no exception. The kinds of cultural uniqueness identified here are typical of a collectivist society and, while they remain relevant as factors that shape consumption practices, collectivism as a whole in Japan today is on the wane. In 1994, Yamagishi noticed, "the prominence and the stability of networks of committed relations in Japanese society and business are currently being challenged by the internationalization of the economy and society" (1994: 163). In the twenty years since, we can only imagine that this trend has intensified. A social shift from an emphasis on mutual assurance to one of greater general trust throughout society is sure to have its troubles along the way.

In Japan, *okami,* or authority figures, are expected to behave properly and in the best interest of the people, but cannot be inherently trusted to do so. This sentiment is in line with collectivist notions of trust: authority figures are out-group, unable to be monitored effectively, and out-of-reach of any form of sanctioning. However, the lack of a strong civil society gives bodies of authority the leeway to exercise a paternalistic form of power over the welfare of society. Contemporary Japanese society has generally accepted this paternalism, until certain events or scandals motivate the public to re-embrace a collectivist attitude.

A similar story is emerging in the mainstreaming of sustainability issues related to food consumption in Japan. The decline of *teikei* and supermarkets' co-opting of *chisan-chisho* marketing tools are some examples of how food processing companies and retailers are beginning to set the agenda for what constitutes sustainable food. Consumers are, for the most part, accepting of what food corporations deem best. Food safety is another area that consumers were leaving to companies to manage until the Fukushima Daiichi nuclear disasters of 2011 motivated a strong public response. A relevant question is for how long will the public be engaged with sustainability and safety issues before authority figures reassert their claims of legitimacy?

We maintain that sustainable food consumption will necessitate a continuous society-wide diligence and greater fostering of trusting relationships between food chain actors. It is for these reasons that cultural factors influencing the formation of trusting "ties that bind" will continue to play a role in the spread of sustainable food consumption practices in society at large. A deeper inquiry into the ways practices are shaped by cultural factors in other countries is needed to further develop the debate on agency and culture.

References

Akitsu, M.; Aminaka, N., 2010: "The Development of Farmer-Consumer Direct Relationships in Japan: Focusing on the Trade of Organic Produce", Paper Presented at 4th Asian Rural Sociology Association (ARSA) International Conference, Legazpi City, Philippines, September 2010.

Brom, F.W., 2000: "Food, Consumer Concerns, and Trust: Food Ethics for a Globalizing Market", in: *Agricultural and Environmental Ethics,* 12,2: 127–139.

Cabinet Secretariat, Japan, 2013: *Nourinsuisanbutsu he no eikyou shisan no keisan houhou ni tsuite* [Preliminary Calculations on Influence on Agriculture, Fisheries, and Forestry Products and Calculation Methods] (in Japanese); at: http://www.cas.go.jp/jp/tpp/pdf/2013/3/130315_nourinsuisan-2.pdf (12 September 2014).

Coff, C., 2006: *The Taste for Ethics: An Ethic of Food Consumption* (Dordrecht: Springer).

Ferrin D.L.; Gillespie N., 2010: "Trust Differences Across National-Societal Cultures: Much to Do, or Much a Do About Nothing?", in: Saunders M.N.K. et al. (Eds.): *Organizational Trust: A Cultural Perspective* (Cambridge: Cambridge University Press): 42–86.

Geels, F.; Schot, J., 2007: "Typology of Sociotechnical Transition Pathways", in: *Research Policy,* 36,3: 399–417.

Giddens, A., 1990: *The Consequences of Modernity* (Cambridge: Polity Press).

Hatano, T., 1998: *Yukinogyou no Keizaigaku: Sansho Teikei no Netowa-ku* [Economy of Organic Agriculture: Teikei Networks] (In Japanese) (Tokyo: Nihonkeizaihyoronsha).

Hatano, T., 2008: "The organic agriculture movement (*teikei*) and Factors Leading to its Decline in Japan (in Japanese)", in: *Nougyou Shokuryo Keizai Kenkyu* (*Journal of Rural and Food Economics*), 54,2: 21–34.

Hill, C.; Kubota, H., 2007: "Thirty-Five Years of Japanese Teikei", in: Henderson, E.; Van En, R. (Eds.): *Sharing the Harvest: A Citizen's Guide to Community Supported Agriculture* (White River Junction, VT: Chelsea Green Publishing): 267–271.

Hofstede, G., 2001: *Culture's Consequences: Comparing Values, Behaviours, Institutions, and Organizations Across Nations*, 2nd edition (Thousand Oaks, CA: Sage).

Jackson, T., 2005: Motivating Sustainable Consumption. Report for the Sustainable Development Research Network; at: http://citeseerx.ist.psu.edu/viewdoc/download?doi=10.1.1.337.433&rep=rep1&type=pdf (16 September 2014).

Japan Organic Agriculture Association (JOAA), 1971: Statement of Purpose; at: http://www.joaa.net/english/index-eng.htm (16 September 2014).

Japan Organic Agriculture Association (JOAA), 1993: Teikei system, the Producer-Consumer Co-partnership and the Movement of the Japan Organic Agriculture Association—Country Report for the first IFOAM Asian Conference; at: http://www.joaa.net/english/teikei.htm#ch5-1 (15 September 2014).

Kimura, A.H.; Nishiyama, M., 2008: "The *Chisan-Chisho* Movement: Japanese Local Food Movement and Its Challenges", in: *Agriculture and Human Values*, 25,1: 49–64.

Kuwabara, K.; Willer, R.; Macy, M.W.; Mashima, R.; Terai, S.; Yamagishi, T., 2007: "Culture, Identity, and Structure in Social Exchange: A Web-Based Trust Experiment in the United States and Japan", in: *Social Psychology Quarterly,* 70: 461–479.

Luhmann, N., 1979: *Trust and Power: Two Works by Niklas Luhmann* (Brisbane: John Wiley).

Masugata, T., 2008: *Yukinogyo Undo to Teikei no Netowa-ku* [Movement of Organic Agriculture and Teikei Networks] (in Japanese) (Tokyo: Shinyosha).

Ministry of Agriculture, Forestry, and Fisheries (MAFF), 2004: *Heisei 16 nendo nousanbutsu chisan chisho nado jittai chousa* [Investigation into the Conditions of Agricultural Product Local Production for Local Consumption for the Year 2004] (in Japanese) (Tokyo: MAFF); at: http://www.e-stat.go.jp/SG1/estat/eStatTopPortal.do (20 September 2014).

Ministry of Agriculture, Forestry, and Fisheries (MAFF), 2011: *Sanchi chokubaijyo chousa kekka no kaiyou— Nousanbutsu chisan chishou nado jitai chousa Heisei 21 nendo kekka* [Investigation Results of Direct Sale Markets of Locally Produced Goods—Factual

Investigation into Locally Produced, Locally Consumed Agricultural Products for 2009] (in Japanese) (Tokyo: MAFF); at: http://www.maff.go.jp/j/tokei/pdf/tisan_tyokubai_09.pdf (20 September 2014).

Ministry of Agriculture, Forestry, and Fisheries (MAFF), 2013: *FY2012 Annual Report on Food, Agriculture, and Rural Areas in Japan, Summary* (Tokyo: MAFF).

Ministry of Agriculture, Forestry, and Fisheries (MAFF), 2014: *Chisan-chisho no suishin nit tsuite* [On the Progress of Chisan-Chisho] (in Japanese); at: http://www.maff.go.jp/j/shokusan/gizyutu/tisan_tisyo/pdf/chisan26_8.pdf (19 September 2014).

Mulder, L.B.; van Dijk, E.; De Cremer, D.; Wilke, H.A.M., 2006: "Undermining Trust and Cooperation: The Paradox of Sanctioning Systems in Social Dilemmas", in: *Journal of Experimental Social Psychology*, 42: 147–162.

Sassatelli, R.; Scott, A., 2001: "Novel Food, New Markets and Trust Regimes—Responses to the Erosion of Consumers' Confidence in Austria, Italy and the UK", in: *European Societies*, 3,2: 213–244.

Seikatsu Club, 2014: About the Seikatsu Club Consumers' Cooperative Union; at: http://seikatsuclub.coop/about/rengo_about_e.html (20 September 2014).

Spaargaren, G., 2011: "Theories of Practices: Agency, Technology, and Culture. Exploring the Relevance of Practice Theories for the Governance of Sustainable Consumption Practices in the New World-Order", in: *Global Environmental Change*, 21: 813–822.

Takahashi, C.; Yamagishi, T.; Liu, J.H.; Wang, F.; Lin, Y.; Yu, S., 2008: "The Intercultural Trust Paradigm: Studying Joint Cultural Interaction and Social Exchange in Real Time Over the Internet", in: *International Journal of Intercultural Relations*, 32: 215–228.

Tanaka, T., 2003: "Shokuryo no souyunyuuryou kyori fu-do maire-ji to sono kankyou ni oyobosu fuka ni kansuru kousatsu [An Investigation of Imported Food Volume, Distance, and Associated Environmental Burden] (in Japanese)", in: *Nourinsuisan Seisaku Kenkyuu* (Journal of Agricultural Policy Research), 5: 45–59.

Triandis, H.C., 1995: *Individualism and Collectivism* (Boulder, CO: Westview Press).

Urban-rural Exchange Promotion Organization, 2007: Nousanbutsu chokubaijyo no unei naiyo nikansuru zenkoku chousa no gaiyo [Summary Report of National Survey on Operation of Farmers Markets] (in Japanese) (Tokyo: Urban-rural Exchange Promotion Organization).

World Values Survey, 2010: World values survey wave 6 2010–2014 Official Aggregate v.20140429. World Values Survey Association. Aggregate File Producer: Asep/JDS, Madrid SPAIN; at: www.worldvaluessurvey.org (16 September 2014).

Yamagishi, T., 1988: "The Provision of a Sanctioning System in the United States and Japan", in: *Social Psychology Quarterly*, 51: 265–271.

Yamagishi, T.; Yamagishi, M., 1994: "Trust and Commitment in the United States and Japan", in: *Motivation and Emotion*, 18,2: 129–166.

Chapter 8
The Potential for Sustainable Production and Consumption in a Technological Society

Anne-Marie Coles

Abstract The French philosopher Jacques Ellul articulated the concept of the technological society in 1954 to describe the deeply interwoven relationship between social, cultural, economic, political and technical factors that exists in mature industrial societies. Some commentators have seen a continuing role for this concept pertinent to understanding the broad social dynamics of technological change. This chapter draws on current commentary to investigate the implications for change in existing processes of production and consumption through sustainable innovation. It reviews current thinking in the social studies of technology to identify the ways in which discourses of sustainable innovation might not transform socio-technical systems in the manner conceived by proponents. It identifies how technical characteristics relating to sustainable performance of a particular artefact could fail to transfer from artefact to system or from innovation to widespread adoption and use. In conclusion, it is suggested that calls for sustainable innovation represent part of the 'business as usual' operations of a technological society.

Keywords Boundary spanning · Discourse · Jacques Ellul · Social change · Sustainable innovation · Technological change · Technological society

8.1 Introduction

With the publication of 'A Technological Society' in France in 1954, the philosopher Jacques Ellul launched a critique on what he considered to be social dependence on the process of continual technological innovation (Ellul 1954, 1964). For Ellul, the reification of technology had resulted in a society permeated with the dominant values of rationality and efficiency (for a given stage of development) encapsulated in techniques which intertwined social and technical

Anne-Marie Coles, Ph.D., Senior Lecturer in Strategic Management, University of Greenwich, London, UK; Email: A.Coles@gre.ac.uk.

A. Genus (ed.), *Sustainable Consumption*, The Anthropocene: Politik—Economics—Society—Science 3, DOI 10.1007/978-3-319-29665-4_8

processes. He considered this social organization to be fundamentally disempowering to the individual, not least through the gap it constructed between production and consumption. For Ellul, modern techniques had invaded every field of human activity, squeezing out ethical decisions, which had been replaced with superficial notions of choice (Ellul 1964; Davies 1997). Ellul felt that, in their daily lives, people experienced the effects of innovation, while having little influence over its development. However, what is often perceived as Ellul's technologically determinist stance, the implied universalism of his world view and belief in subjugation of social life to the demands of technological mores has arguably led to scholarly disinterest in his philosophical position. This raises the question as to whether there are aspects of Ellul's thought which are enduring and continue to provide insights for current research. Certainly, some authors have continued to find his commentary prescient in explaining the interrelations between technology and society (Agbemabiese/Byrne 2005; Kovalsky/Haluza-DeLay 2011; Winner 1978). This article will draw on Ellul's contestation that innovation will always be considered as the primary solution to social problems arising from technology-in-use. In particular, it will identify social discourses which propose that new iterations of technology can be used to solve problems related to environmental sustainability. In identifying strictly technological responses to environmental problems, it is possible to observe Ellul's thesis in action. Reviewing current concepts relating to the nature of artefact construction and systemic use can help to explain why Ellul felt that relying on strictly technical solutions are, over time, an insufficient solution to social problems.

Ellul's analytical approach favours a deep level of reflection on the 'lived experience' in an advanced technological society, close to one of Kline's 'persistent' definitions of technology as embedded heterogeneous knowledge (Ellul 1964; Kline 1985; see also Afuah 2003; Coombs/Hull 1998; Freeman/Soete 1997; Narayanan 2001; Feenberg 1999). As Mitcham (1994) notes Ellul's concern is not with documenting processes of innovation but with understanding how social orientation is achieved to fundamentally facilitate these processes. For Ellul, as techniques founded on the values of rationality and efficiency become pervasive throughout social, economic and political life, these in turn start to define individual subjective experience.[1] Human moral, spiritual and cultural activities take a secondary place (Ellul 1984; Son 2004). As Roden (2011: 2) indicates, Ellul sees 'human subjectivity mediated by technical infrastructure', as he decries the loss of alternative political visions that could result in a human-centred rather than technology-centred social organization. For Ellul the separation of the activity of production from that of consumption is an inevitable feature of a society predicated on efficiency and dependent on innovation to solve social problems. This process demands that individuals and societies adapt themselves to technological systems, so that these systems become 'naturalized' (Ellul 1980; Kovalsky/Haluza-DeLay

[1]Ellul suggests that there are 7 characteristics of technological society: rationality; artificiality; automation of technical choice; self-augmentation; monism; universalism; autonomy.

2011). Furthermore, for Ellul, innovation has become self-augmenting and technology has become 'autonomous' (Ellul 1964; Roden 2011). By this he means development and diffusion of new artefacts, methods or techniques are not reducible to a single method of social governance but are shaped by the heterogeneous nature of socio-technical interactions through which innovation paths are created. Such dynamic interactions inevitably result in unplanned and unexpected social consequences (Ellul 1964, 1980, 1990; see also Vanderberg 2004).

The wide acceptance and little social critique relating to the idea of social progress through innovation form the crux of a 'technological ideology' through which social and technical relations are maintained (Garrison 2010). For Ellul, the ideology of the technological society is total and self-reinforcing, as 'all opposing acts and ideas finish up being put in the service of the technological system and finding their place in it. The technological system encompasses all things totally, ineluctably, and invincibly' (Ellul 1989: 180). Garrison (2010) points out that for Ellul there is a reduction of possibility to think 'outside' the technological sphere which creates a taken for granted social system. This gives rise to the belief that all problems created by technologies are essentially technical in nature and can be corrected through innovation, producing the reaction of 'faith in future technology as a saving force'.

8.2 Investigating the Technological Society

Ellul conceptualizes the technological society as a legitimate focus for academic study, and identifies ethical issues involved in development and use of new technologies. He refocuses attention towards the politics of innovation, in particular by raising a problem of democratic public participation in technology-related decision making (Garrison 2010; Genus/Coles 2005; Goudreau 2003; Moore 1998; Thomson 2000). Furthermore, Ellul's work elaborates on the difficult relationship between innovation, risk and uncertainty. Although the totality of Ellul's views, which left no room for human resistance or agency, has become rather unfashionable there have been some attempts to revisit his core ideas. This work has demonstrated that social subjugation to the principles of rationality and efficiency can be investigated through contingent and contextual analysis of socio-technical processes. Through controversy, negotiation and resistance individuals can influence the direction of development, speed of adoption and mode of operation of the technical. In addition, it is possible to reveal boundaries and limits to the technological society. Moore (2001), for example, echoes Ellul when referring to the embedding of new technology as comprising multiple social procedures, a point reinforced by Maley (2004) whose concern is to identify how knowledge becomes socially accepted in 'technological, liberal democratic societies'. Agbemabiese/Byrne (2005) draw on Ellul's writing in their investigation of the failure to transfer industrialized energy models to an emerging economy such as Ghana. From these perspectives it seems that aspects of Ellul's thought remain pertinent to current socio-technical analysis, although with its original universal perspective tempered by the recognition of socio-economic limitations.

Ellul's thought has been subsequently extended and modified. Rose (2003: 154) considers his approach to be limited by a macro-view of society, overlooking the role played by individual agency in local resistances to technocratic rule. These responses, she claims, are the 'everyday practices that would contest the hegemony of technology and its celebrants'. For Scott-Ruse (2005) technologies are 'culturally embedded', imbued with meanings gained from the contingency of development, which, in turn, creates barriers to their transfer between social contexts. Furthermore, the idea of a totally encompassing ideology which would make articulation of alternative technologies or values impossible has been questioned. Kozinets (2008) demonstrates that different, yet overlapping ideals, some reinforcing and others conflicting mesh together to construct the general perception of a universal technological ideology. This more complex understanding identifies gaps and fissures in ideological discourse where alternative views can be articulated and explains how these may still become adopted and incorporated into the dominant ideological perspective. Such reflexive commentary also provides an opportunity to reflect on the interrelationship between production and consumption indicating where opportunities for consumers to influence the process of change can arise. A particular issue concerns the acceptance of technologies which express alternative values to those dominant in the technological society. Ellul's ideas indicate that unpalatable values will be modified before the technology becomes widely socially embedded, explaining the resistance to certain types of alternative technologies that arise outside the established means of production. Harris et al. (2003), Winston (1998) and Prabhaker (2000) identify such processes in the development of the internet.[2] For example, a profound challenge to existing business operations was made by the introduction of fairly traded goods. Initially championed by a broad coalition of advocates, such goods have subsequently been regulated to a trading niche by multi-national corporations involved in the food sector (Coles/Harris 2006; Nicholls/Opal 2005). Such instances support Ellul's thesis regarding the power of dominant ideological perspectives to control the emergence of socio-technical initiatives (see also Coles/Yan 2010).[3]

A description of the technological society therefore, is one in which there are complex socio-technical configurations comprising multiple and inter-dependent technical systems (Grundmann 1999; Summerton 1999). However, Ellul's writing

[2]Studies of internet development demonstrate how this technology emerged from interaction between sites of innovation with vastly different objectives. Initially, blending military technology with a public service ethic embedded the values of free exchange of information and communication into the evolving technology. Commercial interests have had to contend with these values in order to shape the internet to their own needs.

[3]These authors point out that some contradictions can be tolerated, as in the ambiguous position of traditional Chinese medicine within the wider bio-medical establishment. Chinese herbal remedies are both borrowed by the pharmaceutical industry for research, while therapeutic claims for traditional medicine are rejected.

is also sympathetic to the idea that it is these complex interactive relationships that give rise to problems (see also Hobday 1998; Rycroft 2002).[4] Far from conceiving technology development as independent of social goals and driven solely by internal technical imperatives, Ellul identifies the scale of innovation to be such that no individual or single organization is in control of its development. He also recognizes that specific configurations of the social and technical give rise to contingencies in innovation, sending developments in unexpected directions (Ellul 1980). These themes indicate that there is a synergy between Ellul's thought and the more recent study of socio-technical complexity, which considers how social boundaries are drawn around innovations to exclude and disempower certain groups (Cilliers 2005; Hearn et al. 2003; Hirsh/Gillespie 2001; Levidow 2001; Tsoi et al. 2008). Consumers of technology are considered to form such a group, being remote from centres of production and excluded from the dominant social discourses regarding the desirable characteristics of sustainable innovation. In addition, both embedded socio-technical uncertainties and emergence of unexpected phenomena arising from such complex interactions contribute to the ultimate failure of using technical solutions to solve social problems (Byrne 2005; Garud et al. 2010; Nowotny 2005; Urry 2005). This chapter considers how sustainability characteristics may initially become attached to an innovation as a social or technical discourse, and how these can change as artefact becomes systemically embedded. Such analysis demonstrates how Ellul's analysis can be considered an outcome of the complex, dynamic and unpredictable interactivity between technology and society.

The chapter aims to offer a reflective commentary on what appears to be a growing social consensus that environmental sustainability is dependent on a new iteration of technology, achieved through changes that are radical in their knowledge requirements. Such change requires a concentrated collaborative effort through both government policies and business innovation, together with large scale financial investment. It appears that innovation has become the primary solution to environmental problems, marginalising earlier ideas that sustainable development requires radical social change. By implication this necessitates modification of production processes rather than individual behaviour. A new iteration of technology is exactly the response that Ellul's approach predicts from a technological society. The chapter will specifically consider three of the implications for innovation that arise from Ellul's thesis:

- The emergence of dominant discourses that support the development of new technologies as a response to environmental problems. The chapter will attempt to illustrate Kozinets (2008) point that dominant technological discourses emerge from a broad social consensus. Both policy and academic discourses

[4]These authors support Ellul's approach by claiming that innovation has become a more complex process, as a result of internationalization and increasingly innovation requiring a greater interaction of the innovating firm with external collaborators.

have arisen that provide support for radical innovation in mitigating environmental problems.
- Fragmentation between the production of innovation, and its social use. New technologies not only have to exhibit sustainable characteristics during production, but must also be able to transfer those characteristics to the technical systems in which they are used (Kline 1985). This chapter will consider how the conceptualization of sustainable technical function might not transfer to the context in which the technology is used.
- The two proceeding points help to elucidate the way in which novel innovation is developed and used under conditions of uncertainty and risk. Here it is suggested that these conditions contribute to the fact that new technologies that are introduced to solve environmental problems can also become problematic themselves.

8.3 New Iterations of Technology and Sustainable Innovation

Social critique of environmental problems began as a response to modern socio-technical behaviour linked to industrial use of large scale technologies (Carson 1962; Commoner 1971). Initially protagonists promoted the idea that technical development could become local, democratic and more 'people centred' stressing the necessity of social and behavioural change (Carter 2001; Dobson 2003; Torgerson 2000). Although the widespread use of technology was initially regarded as the source of environmental problems, paradoxically innovation is now widely proposed for their solution. The shift represents incorporation of environmental goals to reproduce the status quo rather than for radical democratic change (Jamison 2001a; Smith 2003, 2006). This belief in radical innovation as the means to improve environmental sustainability is the response Ellul predicts from entrenched interest groups. Increasingly overlapping, but supportive discourses, from both policy and academic areas can be identified which articulate this position. As Jameson (2001b: 41) states, 'the dominant or hegemonic culture seeks to incorporate environmental concerns into its established modes of operation'. For example, a number of commentators have suggested that investment in radical innovation has become the primary policy objective for the European Union's sustainable development agenda (Low/Ward 1998; Connelly/Smith 1999; McCormick 2001). Cohen points out the prime position of innovation in national policies, which require a 'firm commitment to science and a preference to address environmental problems in technological terms' (Cohen 2000: 77; see also Rydin 2010). This view is expressed by the British Prime Minister, David Cameron in February 2013, as he stated,

> Together we can make Britain a global showcase for green innovation and energy efficiency. Together we can do the right thing for our planet and, just as important, do the right thing for our economy too. With your help on this energy efficient mission we can make sure that now, and in years to come, Britain is open for business, winning in the global race, and doing it in a way that is green too (Cameron 2013).

Others have noted a growing support from academic discourses promoting sustainable innovation for continued economic growth (Fisher/Freudenberg 2001; Freeman 1996; Milanese/Buhrs 2007; Schot 1992). In the academic literature, a convergence between two conceptual approaches to sustainable development: ecological modernization and strategic niche management has been noted. Both of these discourses point to a primary focus on radical innovation as the means to achieve social transition to sustainability (Berkout et al. 2004; Kemp et al. 1998; Smith/Kern 2007). In this chapter, it is argued that the prospect of failure results from the difficulty in attributing sustainability characteristics to novel technologies and in maintaining such characteristics over time. It is not clear whether sustainability will be materially bounded by the artefact or demonstrated through dynamic processes of adoption, implementation and use (that is at the point of production or during consumption). This chapter adopts the premise that technological solutions to the perceived environmental crisis are nothing more than the mundane response of the technological society to the emergence of social problems. Such thinking adheres to Ellul's own assessment that there is continual social support for innovation, which is always proposed to solve problems caused by previous technologies.

8.4 Production: Environmental Sustainability Bounded by the Artefact

For firms that are involved in developing new technologies, improved environmental impact will be embodied by the artefact. To achieve this function, firms will attempt to strategically incorporate sustainability goals into the process of innovation from the production side. Milanese/Buhrs (2007) claim this activity demonstrates that strong ecological discourse can become transformed into a weaker aim of meeting achievable technical objectives. However, the challenge of attaining sustainable development from artefact functioning is not one that can be easily incorporated into development processes due to difficulties involved in trying to establish agreed meanings for environmental sustainability. This problem can be influenced through the creation of broad social discourses promoting expectations of sustainability arising from the technical function of a new technology. These can be used to encourage continued financial support for the development process, as expectations of future technical performance provide dynamism and momentum for innovation (Brown/Michael 2003). Thus a "mobilization of the future" gathers resources for current technical developments (Milne 2012). For Lampel (2001) innovation discourses are actively used by practitioners to manage project boundaries. They are a means to communicate the importance of the project to non-experts and to maintain a supportive context for the innovation by communicating expected environmental goals if necessary. An outcome is that environmental sustainability can quite easily become a general expectation when expressed as a future goal for technological performance but without means to evaluate its success (see Hedgecoe/Martin 2003 on the hype disappointment cycle). In fact, sustainability has become part of the expectation building process, particularly for large innovating firms eager to project a positive environmental image about key developments (Peters/Coles 2006). For example the concept of the 'hydrogen society' has been articulated as an expectation of future environmental sustainability specifically supportive of investment into fuel cell development (Hoffman 2001). Bringing together discourses related to the broad socio-economic consensus for innovation together with those that support specific technologies illustrate how Ellul's concept of the technological ideology is constructed to favour investment in innovation. It also serves to marginalize alternative approaches.

Social discourses provide a supportive context for firms' innovation practices however, in practical terms the complex issue of sustainability must be reduced to functional technical goals in order to become part of the innovation process. One example is the way in which the complex challenges of global climate change can be redefined as the need to reduce anthropomorphic carbon emissions. Expressed in technical language, reduction of carbon emissions can become incorporated instrumentally into innovation processes as a sustainability goal (Coles/Peters 2003; Jamison 1998; see also Foray/Grubler 1996; Genus/Coles 2006; Van der Sluijs et al. 1998). However, Ellul would suggest that this necessary reductionism is the process through which a new iteration of technology will be offered as solution to a social problem, but which also contains potential for failure. The reasons can be investigated through recent theoretical understandings of artefact construction. The recognition that technologies embody heterogeneous and contingent knowledge indicates how issues of environmental sustainability may become part of innovation process. However, sustainability factors must compete with other priorities in operational function as improved environmental performance may only be one of many desirable characteristics demonstrated by the technology (Hinnells 1993; Skea 1994; Wallace 1995). New technologies can be regarded as stable embodiments of social, technical and material knowledge (Kroes 2001; Latour 2000). Understanding the factors involved in their constitution can therefore provide a basis for conceptualising sustainability as a characteristic of artefact functioning (Agazzi 1998; Koch 2000; Rosenberg 1983; Shapere 1998). Sustainability goals may be incorporated as technical criteria. However, materials used in construction of the technology may have issues that are not necessarily compatible with technical function (Van Lente 2000). For example the fuel cell is a radical innovation which is expected to provide a contribution to sustainability, but the use of non-renewable platinum in its construction could in the future become an issue for sustainable resourcing.

In addition to material constitution and technical function, technologies have a social role. Operational characteristics are not only configured into artefact function but also need to be expressed in the social world for which the technology is intended. In order to realize potential for sustainability, artefacts must both become widely adopted and also demonstrate sustainable characteristics during use. Akrich's (1992) concept of artefact scripting explains how assumptions about the social role of technologies are contained within the object itself (see De Laat 2000). Van Lente (2000) sees scripting as a means to encapsulate discourses and expectations regarding future socio-technical relations (see also Koch 2000, 2001). A social script therefore acts as an interface between artefact and the system into which it will become incorporated, influencing sustainability assessments. Artefact design comprises one of the factors which span the boundary between manufacture and use, and between artefact sustainability and sustainability of the socio-technical context for which it is intended. If such improvements accrue from this new systemic configuration, it is necessary to consider the factors that influence artefact functioning in this socio-technical context. However, technologies that are developed to exhibit sustainability features may have to display more than one social script, if they are intended to demonstrate multiple functions. Photo-voltaic panels, for example, can become part of a micro-generation unit and can also become interconnected with the National Grid. In these cases a single social role could become more difficult to inscribe, particularly if new innovations, (such as grid interconnectors in this case) are necessary before all the social functions can be realized.

8.5 Consumption: Sustainability as a Boundary Spanning Characteristic

Ellul (1964) identifies the technological society as comprising interrelated social-technical networks which are constantly changed through the adoption and use of new technologies. Here, environmental sustainability will be identifiable in the operation of a system rather than as a characteristic of an individual artefact. Sustainability characteristics therefore must be able to cross the boundary between artefact and system if they are to make a significant impact in practice. This raises issues related to the conceptualization of particular socio-technical contexts, the situated nature of inherent sustainability factors, and how these will be identified and evaluated in use. The idea of technical systems (Hughes 1983), and more latterly, socio-technical regimes (Geels 2002, 2004; Kemp 1994; Kemp et al. 2001) both describe interrelation between the heterogeneous mix of social and technical factors which perform particular social functions. Socio-technical systems are built by, and become socially embedded, through the actions of a coalition of committed social actors, although the processes by which sustainability might become embedded in such systems are very poorly understood (Collingridge 1992; Coutard 1999; Genus 1997). As sustainability is not dependent ultimately on the specifications of any one component, technologies that display sustainable characteristics in the ways discussed above may not actually perform sustainably when incorporated into a technical system. For example, wind turbines exhibit the ability to produce renewable energy, but a single turbine will have a minor impact if it becomes part of a system which is still dominated by the use of fossil fuels. Sustainable energy depends on changing the balance of generation by the whole system not on the individual performance of one artefact.

Concern about risks and uncertainties associated with the use of novel technologies are not routinely integrated into the assessment of their sustainability. Risks arise because although new technologies display certain embodied functional knowledge they have not become established in use. Even though an object has been manufactured with a particular social fit unexpected effects may still occur in the functioning of the overall system over time. Collingridge (1980, 1989, 1990, 1992) emphasizes the risks inherent in decisions made over implementation of radical and untried technologies. He points to the discrepancy between the technical knowledge and competence necessary to develop a new technology and the corresponding uncertainties and unanticipated consequences that can arise during use (see Conway 1995). Collingridge's model suggests that there is a decreasing possibility that unexpected consequences from innovation will occur, so over time the risky nature of the technology is reduced. Potential risks are offset by increasing knowledge about the technology-in-use; however, risks can never be completely eliminated. One reason for this is that adverse conditions might only become clear over the longer term or with the scale of implementation. Uncertainties associated with use of radical technologies, have been shown to present a challenge to its sustainability, as unintended environmental damage is a possible but unwanted outcome of technology adoption and diffusion (Braun/Wield 1994). For example, it is in part the cumulative effect over time of automobile ownership that makes carbon dioxide emissions a problem, indicating that environmental risks can continue to emerge despite the fact that knowledge about the functioning of the technology has built up over time.

8.6 Sustainability and Socio-technical Practice

The preceding analysis attempts to explain how new iterations of technology may fail to achieve outcomes expected of them. It is clear that some of the discourses initially supportive of an innovation do not necessarily transfer to the context in which the technology is used, while uncertainties over artefact performance provide the potential for unexpected outcomes to emerge. In a similar view to that suggested by Rose (2003) who argues for local and contingent investigations of the technological society, Koch (2000) claims that technology needs to be understood contextually. Both the role of specific actors in shaping technology can be identified as well as the role the artefact plays in the process of change. For Koch, technologies are an embodiment of both human action and social discourse, communicating between innovators and technology users. Therefore the combined action of both individual and artefact agency contributes to its sustainability, so only through use can environmental impacts be evaluated over the longer term. The potential for sustainable performance, therefore, can be scripted into the artefact through the intentions of technology developers. However, sustainability can only be realized through its use in a particular socio-technical context, for example, a car being driven for an hour will emit more pollutants than one standing in a garage for the same period. In terms of identifying the environmental impact of socio-technical systems, this discussion is significant because it suggests that whatever type of sustainable performance is expected to accrue from innovation, this can only be evaluated over time. It explains why technologies which were not designed to be environmentally unsustainable, such as the automobile or aeroplane become so over time through establishing a pattern of use. Conversely, other technologies become associated with a beneficial environmental impact even though this was not part of their initial rationale (for example, railways, bicycles and windmills). Changing human agency in terms of widespread diffusion of these technologies has given rise to changing evaluation of their social impact. In this view environmental sustainability cannot entirely be scripted into an artefact, not can its future system functionality be entirely predictable because evaluation of sustainable performance will emerge as part of established socio-technical practice.

This discussion draws on Ellul's idea of the characteristics of the technological society, which conceives of innovation as a solution to social problems, yet finds the solutions fall short of expectation. The tendency to incorporate environmentally sustainable functions by reducing them to technical objectives demonstrates the limitations of dealing with complex social issues through new iterations of technology. Uncertainties and flexibilities are both bounded by the artefact and interactively created during diffusion, indicating that the development of sustainable technologies is not completely reducible to a pre-determined plan. The fact that unintended environmental harm can result from the interaction between socio-technical systems and the natural environment points not only to the fact that new phenomena can emerge from socially embedding new technologies but also that uncertainties play a significant role in the process. The success of achieving sustainability from the introduction of new technologies is hampered by the prospect of unplanned and unexpected effects. Future sustainability depends on present complex interactions which have both predictable and non-predictable aspects. This implies that environmental sustainability is, at least in part, an emergent characteristic of human-technology interactions which is not completely reducible to the interactions between individual actors, nor has a completely predictable outcome. Over time, not only does the pattern of diffusion and use of a technology change, but the social and cultural understanding of sustainability also changes, raising difficulties for capturing definitive objectives in innovation processes. This chapter has suggested that environmental sustainability is not a characteristic that can be completed fixed by a technological artefact or by its social function. As sustainability partly constitutes socio-technical practice, it can be conceptualized as an emergent property of complex and dynamic socio-technical configurations.

8.7 Conclusion

This discussion raises issues related to the understanding of how innovation will contribute to resolution of the current environmental crisis. For Ellul, solving socio-technical problems with a new iteration of innovation is a 'business as usual' operation of the technological society. A review of the theoretical analysis relating to the construction of technological artefacts and systems has served to illustrate how technologies can fall short of their functional promise. Development and use of new technologies is a complex activity which is partly founded on discursive practices relating not only to technical knowledge but also to social use and material suitability. A particular iteration of a technology may become stabilized in use but will also continue to develop and change as innovation processes continue. Also, supporters of innovation may raise expectations about a new technology which serve to normalize its development but do not necessarily become embodied by the innovation and can be abandoned or modified as the technology is incorporated as part of a larger system. The instability of these discourses is one aspect which explains why the expected attributes of an innovation may not become apparent during diffusion. The interrelation between experience in use and uncertainty forms part of the complex context in which technologies become socially embedded. Interactions over time can give rise to the emergence of unexpected effects which could not have been predicted during innovation. These basic characteristics of innovation help to elucidate the complex socio-technical practices to which Ellul's analysis of the technological society can be applied. The non-predictable emergence of new effects is the basis on which technologies give rise to new social problems and comprises the gap between expectation and performance that leads to the call for the next iteration of technology.

References

Akrich, M., 1992: "The De-scription of Technical Objects," in: Bijker, W.E.; Law, J., (Eds.): *Shaping Technology/Building Society* (Cambridge MA: MIT Press): 205–224.

Afuah, A., 2003: *Innovation Management: Strategies, Implementation and Profits* (Oxford: Oxford University Press).

Agbemabiese, L.; Byrne, J., 2005: "Commodification of Ghana's Volta River: An Example of Ellul's Autonomy of Technique", in: *Bulletin of Science Technology and Society*, 25: 17–25.

Agazzi, E., 1998: "From Technique to Technology: The Role of Modern Science", in: *Techne*, 4,2: 1–9.

Berkout, F.; Smith, A.; Stirling, A., 2004: Socio-technical Regimes and Transition Contexts. In: Elzen, B.; Geels, F.W.; Green, K. (Eds.): *System Innovation and the Transition to Sustainability: Theory, Evidence and Policy* (Cheltenham: Edward Elgar): 48–75.

Braun, E.; Wield, D., 1994: "Regulation as a Means for the Social Control of Technology", in: *Technology Analysis and Strategic Management*, 6,3: 259–272.

Brown, N.; Michael, M., 2003: "A Sociology of Expectations: Retrospecting Prospects and Prospecting Retrospects", in: *Technology Analysis and Strategic Management*, 15,1: 3–18.

Byrne, D., 2005: "Complexity, Configurations and Cases", in: *Theory, Culture and Society*, 22,5: 95–111.
Cameron, D., 2013: Green Economy. Speech Address at the Launch of the DECC's Energy Efficiency Mission; at: http://www.businessgreen.com/bg/opinion/2241323/camerons-green-economy-speech-in-full (8 July 2014).
Carter, N., 2007: *The Politics of the Environment* (Cambridge: Cambridge University Press).
Carson, R., 1962: *Silent Spring* (Boston: Houghton Mifflin).
Cillers, P., 2005: "Complexity, Deconstruction and Relativism", in: *Theory Culture and Society*, 22: 255–267.
Cohen, M.J., 2000: "Ecological Modernisation, Environmental Knowledge and National Character: A Preliminary Analysis of the Netherlands", in: *Environmental Politics*, Special Edition, 9,1: 77–106.
Coles, A-M.; Harris, L., 2006: "Ethical Consumers and E-commerce: The Emergence and Growth of Fair Trade in the UK", in: *Journal of Research for Consumers*, 10; at: http://www.jrconsumers.com/.
Coles, A-M.; Peters, S.R., 2003: "Sustainable Development, Global Innovation and Advanced Technologies: The Case of Fuel Cells", in: *International Journal of Environmental Technology and Management*, 3,3/4: 278–289.
Coles, A-M.; Yan, L., 2010: "Transnational Entrepreneurship in Action: Traditional Chinese Medicine in the UK", in: *Proceedings of the 33 Institute of Small Business and Entrepreneurship Conference, London, 2–4 November.*
Collingridge, D., 1980: *The Social Control of Technology* (London: Frances Pinter).
Collingridge, D., 1989: "Incremental Decision Making in Technological Innovation: What Role for Science?" in: *Science, Technology and Human Values*, 14,2: 141–162.
Collingridge, D., 1990: "Technology Organizations and Incrementalism: The Space Shuttle", in: *Technology Analysis and Strategic Management*", 2,2: 181–200.
Collingridge, D., 1992: *The Management of Scale: Big Organisations, Big Decisions, Big Mistakes* (London: Routledge).
Commoner, B., 1971: *The Closing Circle: Nature, Man and Technology* (New York: Knopf).
Connelly, J.; Smith, G., 1999: *Politics and the Environment: From Theory to Practice* (London: Routledge).
Conway, S., 1995: "Informal Boundary Spanning: Communication in the Innovation Process", in: *Technology Analysis and Strategic Management*, 7(3): 327–342.
Coombs, R.; Hull, R., 1998: "Knowledge Management Practices and Path Dependency in Innovation", in: *Research Policy*, 27: 237–253.
Coutard, O., 1999: "Introduction: The Evolving Forms of Governance of Large Technical Systems", in: Coutard, O. (Ed.): *The Governance of Large Technical Systems* (London: Routledge).
Davies, P.W.F., 1997: "Technology and Business Ethics Theory", in: *Business Ethics: A European Review*, 6,2: 76–80.
De Laat, B., 2000: "Scripts for the Future: Using Innovation Studies to Design Foresight Tools", in: Brown, N.; Rappert, B.; Webster, A. (Eds.): *Contested Futures: A Sociology of Prospective Techno-science* (Aldershot: Ashgate).
Dobson, A., 2003: *Citizenship and the Environment* (Oxford: Oxford University Press).
Ellul, J., 1954: *La Technique ou L'enjeu du Siècle* (Paris: Armand Colin).
Ellul, J., 1964: *The Technological Society* (New York: Vintage Books).
Ellul, J., 1980: *The Technological System* (New York: Continuum).
Ellul, J., 1984: *Money and Power* (Downers Grove, IL: Inter-Varsity Christian Fellowship).
Ellul, J., 1989: *What I Believe* (Grand Rapids, MI: Eerdmans).
Ellul, J., 1990: *The Technological Bluff* (Grand Rapids, MI: Eerdmans).
Feenberg, A., 1999: *Questioning Technology* (London: Routledge).
Fisher, D.; Freudenburg, W., 2001: "Ecological Modernisation and its Critics: Assessing the Past and Looking Toward the Future", in: *Society and Natural Resources*, 14: 701–709.

Foray, D.; Grubler, A., 1996: "Technology and the Environment: An Overview", in: *Technological Forecasting and Social Change*, 53,3: 1–13.
Freeman, C., 1996: "The Greening of Technology and Models of Innovation", in: *Technological Forecasting and Social Change*, 53,3: 27–39.
Freeman C.; Soete, L., 1997: *The Economics of Industrial Innovation* (London: Pinter).
Garrison, K., 2010: "Perpetuating the Technological Ideology: An Ellulian Critique of Feenberg's Democratized Rationalization", in: *Bulletin of Science Technology and Society*, 30: 195–204.
Garud, R.; Kumaraswamy, A.; Karnøe, P., 2010: "Path Dependence or Path Creation?", in: *Journal of Management Studies*, 47,4: 760–774.
Geels, F.W., 2002: "Technological Transitions as evolutionary Reconfiguration Processes: A Multi-level Perspective and a Case Study", in: *Research Policy*, 31: 1257–1274.
Geels, F.W., 2004: From Sectoral Systems of Innovation to Socio-technical Systems: Insights about Dynamics and Change from Sociology and Institutional Theory. *Research Policy*, 33: 897–920.
Genus, A., 1997: "Unstructuring Incompetence: Problems of Contracting, Trust and the Development of the Channel Tunnel", in: *Technology Analysis and Strategic Management*, 9,4: 419–436.
Genus, A.; Coles, A.-M., 2006: "Firm Strategies for Risk Management in Innovation", in: *International Journal of Innovation Management*, 10,2: 1–14.
Genus, A.; Coles, A-M., 2005: "On Constructive Technology Assessment and Limitations on Public Participation in Technology Assessment", in: *Technology Analysis and Strategic Management*, 17,4: 433–443.
Goudreau, K.A., 2003: "Habermas on Purposive-Rational Action: A Contribution to the Understanding of Ellul's Technique", in: *Bulletin of Science Technology and Society*, 23: 174–179.
Grundmann, R., 1999: "On Control and Shifting Boundaries: Modern Society in the Web of Systems and Networks," in: Coutard, O. (Ed.): *The Governance of Large Technical Systems* (London: Routledge): 239–257.
Harris, L.; Coles, A.-M.; Davies, R., 2003: "Emerging Ethical Perspectives of E-commerce", in: *Journal of Information, Communication and Ethics in Society*, 1,1: 39–48.
Hearn, G.; Roony, B.; Mandeville, T., 2003: "Phenomenological Turbulence in Innovation and Knowledge Systems", in: *Prometheus*, 21,2: 231–244.
Hedgecoe, A.; Martin, P., 2003: "The Drugs Don't Work: Expectations and the Shaping of Pharmacogenetics", in: *Social Studies of Science*, 33,3: 327–364.
Hinnells, M., 1993: "Environmental Factors in Products: How to Gather the Evidence", in: *Design Studies*, 14(4): 457–475.
Hirsch, P.M.; Gillespie, J., 2001: "Unpacking Path Dependence: Differential Valuations Accorded to History Across Disciplines," in: Garud, R.; Karnøe, P. (Eds.): *Path Dependency and Creation* (Mahwah, New Jersey: Lawrence Erlbaum).
Hobday, M., 1998: "Product Complexity, Innovation and Industrial Organization", in: *Research Policy*, 26: 698–710.
Hughes, T., 1983: *Networks of Power: Electrification in Western Society, 1880–1930* (Baltimore, MD: Johns Hopkins University Press).
Hoffman, P., 2001: *Tomorrow's Energy* (Cambridge, MA: MIT Press).
Jamison, A., 1998: "The Shaping of the Global Agenda: The Role of Non-governmental Organisations", in: Lash, S.; Szerszynski, B.; Wynne, B. (Eds.): *Risk, Environment and Modernity* (London: Sage).
Jamison, A., 2001a: "Science, Technology and the Quest for Sustainable Development", in: *Technology Analysis and Strategic Management*, 13,1: 9–22.
Jamison, A., 2001b: *The Making of Green Knowledge* (Cambridge: Cambridge University Press).
Kemp, R., 1994: "Technology and the Transition to Environmental Sustainability: The Problem of Technological Regime Shifts", in: *Futures*, 26,10: 1023–1046.

Kemp, R.; Rip, A.; Schot, J., 2001: "Constructing Transition Paths Through the Management of Niches", in: Garud, R.; Karnøe, P. (Eds.): *Path Dependency and Creation* (Mahwah, New Jersey: Lawrence Erlbaum): 269–299.

Kemp, R.; Schot, J.; Hoogma, R., 1998: "Regime Shifts to Sustainability through Processes of Niche Formation: The Approach of Strategic Niche Management", in: *Technology Analysis and Strategic Management*, 10: 175–196.

Kline, S.J., 1985: "What is Technology?", in: *Bulletin of Science and Technology*, 1: 215–218.

Koch, C., 2000: "The Ventriloquist's Dummy? The Role of Technology in Political Processes", in: *Technology Analysis and Strategic Management*, 12(1): 199–238.

Koch, C., 2001: "Enterprise Resource Planning: Information Technology as a Steamroller for Management Politics?", in: *Journal of Organizational Change Management*, 14: 64–78.

Kovalsky, N.; Haluza-DeLay, R., 2011: Homo-Energeticus: An Ellulian Analysis of the Alberta Tar Sands; at: http://www.academia.edu/1216875/Homo_energeticus_Jacques_Ellul_on_the_Alberta_Oilsands (7 May 2013).

Kozinets, R.V., 2008: "Technology/Ideology: How Ideological Fields Influence Consumers' Technology Narratives", in: *Journal of Consumer Research*, 34(6): 865–881.

Kroes, P., 2001: "Technical Functions as Dispositions: A Critical Assessment", Techne, 5,1: 1–16.

Lampel, J., 2001: "Show and Tell: Product Demonstrations and Path Creation of Technical Change", in: Garud, R.; Karnøe, P. (Eds.): *Path Dependency and Creation* (Mahwah, New Jersey: Lawrence Erlbaum): 303–328.

Latour, B., 2000: "When Things Strike Back: A Possible Contribution of Science Studies", in: *British Journal of Sociology*, 51,1: 105–123.

Levidow, L., 2001: "Precautionary Uncertainty: Regulating GM Crops in Europe", in: *Social Studies of Science,* 31,6: 845–78.

Low, P.; Ward, S. (Eds.) 1998: *British Environmental Policy in Europe* (London: Routledge).

McCormick, J., 2001: *Environmental Policy in the European Union* (Basingstoke: Palgrave).

Maley, T., 2004: "Max Weber and the Iron Cage of Technology", in: *Bulletin of Science Technology and Society*, 24: 69–85.

Milanese, B.; Buhrs, T., 2007: "Marrying Strands of Ecological Modernisation: A Proposed Framework", in: *Environmental Politics*, 16,4: 565–583.

Milne, R., 2012: "Pharmaceutical Prospects: Bio-pharming and the Geography of Technological Expectations", in: *Social Studies of Science*, 42: 290–306.

Mitcham, C., 1994: *Thinking Through Technology: The Path Between Engineering and Philosophy* (Chicago, IL: University of Chicago Press).

Moore, R.C., 1998: "Hegemony, Agency, and Dialectical Tension in Ellul's Technological Society", in: *Journal of Communication*, Summer: 129–144.

Moore, R.C., 2001: "Environmental Issues and the Watchdog Role of the Media: How Ellul's Theory Complicates Liberal Democracy", in: *Bulletin of Science Technology and Society*, 32 (6): 325–333.

Narayanan, V.K., 2001: *Managing Technology and Innovation for Competitive Advantage* (Upper Saddle River, NJ: Prentice Hall).

Nicholls, A.; Opal, C., 2005: *Fair Trade: Market Driven Ethical Consumption* (London: Sage Publications).

Nowotny, H., 2005: "The Increase of Complexity and its Reduction", in: *Theory Culture and Society*, 22: 15–31.

Peters, S.R., Coles, A.-M., 2006: "Strategic Innovation in Sustainable Technology: The Case of Fuel Cells for Vehicles", in: *International Journal for the Environment and Sustainable Development*, 5,4: 338–354.

Prabhaker, P., 2000: "Who Owns the Online Consumer?", in: *Journal of Consumer Marketing*, 17,2: 158–171.

Roden, D., 2011: In and Out of Control: Self-augmenting and Autonomous Technique; at: http://www.academia.edu/296976/In_and_Out_of_Control_Self-Augmenting_and_Autonomous_Technique (7 May 2013).

Rose, E., 2003: "The Errors of Thamus: An Analysis of Technology Critique," in: *Bulletin of Science Technology and Society*, 23: 147–156.
Rycroft, R., 2002: *Technology-Based Globalization Indicators: The Centrality of Innovation Network Data*. George Washington University Occasional Paper Series, 7 October.
Rydin, Y., 2010: "Planning and the Technological Society: Discussing the London Plan", in: *International Journal of Urban and Regional Research*, 34,2: 243–259.
Rosenberg, N., 1983: *Inside the Black Box: Technology and Economics* (Cambridge: Cambridge University Press).
Scott-Ruse, M., 2005: "Technology and the Evolution of the Human: from Bergson to the Philosophy of Technology", in: *Essays in Philosophy, A Biannual Journal*, 6,1; at: http://commons.pacificu.edu/eip/vol6/iss1/27 (7 May 2013).
Schot, J., 1992: "The Policy Relevance of the Quasi-Evolutionary Model: The Case of Stimulating Clean Technologies," in: Coombs, R.; Saviotti, P.; Walsh, V. (Eds.): *Technological Change and Company Strategies* (London: Academic Press).
Shapere, D., 1998: Building on What we have Learned: the Relations Between Science and Technology", in: *Techne*, 4,2: 105–120.
Skea, J., 1994: "Environmental Issues and Innovation," in: Dodgson, M.; Rothwell, R. (Eds.): *The Handbook of Industrial Innovation* (Aldershot: Edward Elgar).
Smith, A., 2003: "Transforming Technological Regimes for Sustainable Development: A Role for Alternative Technology Niches?", in: *Science and Public Policy*, 30,2: 127–135.
Smith, A., 2006: "Green Niches in Sustainable Development: The Case of Organic Food", in: *Environment and Planning C: Government and Policy,* 24: 439–458.
Smith, A.; Kern, F., 2007: *The Transitions Discourse in the Ecological Modernisation of the Netherlands*. SPRU Electronic Working Paper Series 160, University of Sussex.
Son, W.C., 2004: "Reading Jacques Ellul's 'The Technological Bluff' in Context", in: *Bulletin of Science Technology and Society*, 24: 518–533.
Summerton, J., 1999: "Power Plays: The Politics of Interlinking Systems", in: Coutard, O. (Ed.): *The Governance of Large Technical Systems* (London: Routledge): 93–113.
Thomson, I., 2000: "From the Question Concerning Technology to the Quest for a Democratic Technology: Heidegger, Marcuse, Feenberg", in: *Inquiry*, 43: 203–216.
Torgerson, D., 2000: "Farewell to the Green Movement? Political Action and the Green Public Sphere", in: *Environmental Politics*, 11,1: 133–145.
Tsoi, J.; Steward, F.; Coles, A-M., 2008: "Nanoparticle Innovation and Paper Fibre Recyclability —Mapping Niches as Emergent Socio-technical Networks", in: *Journal of Cleaner Production*, 16,8/9: 957–966.
Urry, J., 2005: "The Complexities of the Global", in: *Theory Culture and Society*, 22: 235–254.
Vanderburg, W.H., 2004: "The Autonomy of Technique Revisited", in: *Bulletin of Science Technology and Society*, 24: 515–517.
Van der Sluijs, J.; Eijndhoven, J.; Shackley, S.; Wynne, B., 1998: "Anchoring Devices in Science for Policy: The Case of Consensus Around Climate Change", in: *Social Studies of Science*, 28,2: 291–323.
Van Lente, H., 2000: "Forceful Futures: From Promise to Requirement", in: Brown, N.; Rappert, B.; Webster, A. (Eds.): *Contested Futures: A Sociology of Prospective Techno-science* (Aldershot: Ashgate): 43–64.
Wallace, D., 1995: *Environmental Policy and Industrial Innovation Strategies in Europe, USA and Japan* (London: Earthscan).
Winner, L., 1978: *Autonomous Technology: Technics Out-Of-Control as a Theme in Political Thought* (Cambridge, MA: MIT Press).
Winston, B., 1998: *Media, Technology and Society: a History from the Telegraph to the Internet* (London: Routledge).

Chapter 9
Promoting Sustainable Consumption—a View from the Ground

Mandy Meikle

Abstract The chapter is based on a talk given at the SCORAI workshop in London entitled "What to do if your community is not ready for Transition". It considers the issues that need to be confronted by activists seeking to promote sustainable consumption and production in local communities, focusing on a case in which I have been closely involved, in rural Scotland. The chapter identifies actions taken and skills and resources required to enable these to be implemented. However it also outlines why initiatives fail and some ideas for increasing the chances of success.

Keywords Charitable organizations · Community activism · Community projects · Environmental activism · Scotland · Transition towns · Wind farms

9.1 Introduction

"There is no possibility of all people on earth ever rising to rich world per capita levels of consumption of energy, minerals, timber, water, food…", said Ted Trainer, writing for FEASTA (2011), a Dublin-based sustainability think-tank. "Most people have no idea of the magnitude of the overshoot, of how far we are beyond sustainable levels of resource use and environmental impact", Trainer continues. I agree with Trainer's unpalatable analysis, which sets the context for my personal transition from environmental activism into community activism.

In their 2013 briefing, the *Institute for Public Policy Research* (IPPR 2013) considers best practice for achieving sustainable consumption in the UK. One of the 12 case studies is the Transition Network, an entirely voluntary-sector scheme coordinating multiple, 'bottom up' local campaigns to promote sustainable consumption. Transition Initiatives (or Transition Towns, as they are sometimes called) are local and community-based but require a 'special interest' for people to become involved. Many fledgling Transition groups begin with a screening of a film which

Mandy Meikle, Ph.D., independent researcher and activist, South Lanarkshire, Scotland, UK; e-mail: m.meikle@reforestingscotland.org.uk.

A. Genus (ed.), *Sustainable Consumption*, The Anthropocene: Politik—Economics—Society—Science 3, DOI 10.1007/978-3-319-29665-4_9

explains the inherent unsustainability of modern, industrial capitalism, followed by a debate about what could be done locally to reduce energy demand and consumption. This in itself is a limiting process, excluding anyone who has never considered the future through such a negative lens or who does not believe that anything they do will make a difference.

While involved at the fringes and supportive of the Transition movement from its outset, trying the Transition model in my own community never progressed beyond 'mulling', the term used for groups and individuals who are interested but never actually become a Transition initiative. In the small, rural community in which I live, where there is neither public transport nor mains gas, it is unlikely that a call to reduce consumption would create much interest. So the question remains of how communities can become more resilient to an uncertain, resource-constrained future if people don't want to engage in such issues? The answer lies in focusing on what a community is ready to engage in.

As the welfare state contracts and local authority services decline, communities will increasingly have to 'fend for themselves' (*The Independent* 11 May 2015). So important will this be, that many more individuals must become actively involved in their communities now to avoid the 'burn-out' of key players in the future. Fortunately, in post-referendum Scotland, this is happening with many more people now being politically active and awake to the idea of grassroots change—a trend which has continued such that Scotland now has 56 SNP MPs out of a possible 59 Scottish seats in the UK Parliament. But do we all want the same thing? And how often is that 'wish' for sustainable consumption? What makes some people choose to reduce their consumption of goods they want *and* can afford to buy?

The three questions addressed in the presentation were:

1. What actions are being taken by activists, which may reduce consumption or at least make it more sustainable?
2. What kinds of resources/skills/support do practitioners need to make projects happen and durable?
3. What makes initiatives fail?

9.2 What Actions Are Being Taken on the Ground?

Woolfords, Auchengray and Tarbrax are small settlements located in a rural area in north-east Clydesdale, in South Lanarkshire, Scotland. The area lies at almost 1,000 ft above sea level on the edge of the Pentland Hills, and consists of farmland, open moorland and some commercial forestry. The area is rich in wildlife and local history. In the past, this area had a thriving local economy based around the coal, lime and shale mines of Cobbinshaw, Tarbrax and nearby Baads Mill. There were train stations at Cobbinshaw, Tarbrax and Auchengray. Auchengray was the last of these to close, in 1966, and was one of the stops for the Caledonian Railway on its route between Carlisle and Edinburgh (the West Coast Main Line).

Being rural yet also close to sizable centres of population in the central belt of Scotland, this area has been subjected to a large number of wind farm proposals in recent years. Not all have been approved, but the cumulative impact is becoming significant. In August 2011, a public meeting was held to discuss local wind farms but there was no consensus over what to do and more than a little hostility. One development, the six-turbine Muirhall wind farm, had been built by local company Muirhall Energy Ltd. People understood that 'community benefit' had to be released by developers to those living with this 'industrialization of the countryside'. While Muirhall wind farm was at the application stage, the community was encouraged by the developer to form a community trust. This attempt failed, for reasons beyond my knowledge. This failure had fuelled much of the hostility as Muirhall wind farm was approved and built yet no money could come *directly* to the community, as had been promised. 'Promised', that is, *if* a local trust had been established—which it wasn't. Without such a body, community benefit could only go to the local authority and people found access prohibited by form-filling and bureaucracy.

Muirhall Energy Ltd. later applied for a 2-turbine extension and after another, more convivial, public meeting in September 2011, I and a few other local residents began work to set up a community trust, initially as a project of an existing local group without charitable status, but with a bank account. This community trust would have charitable status and be able to access community benefit from the Muirhall extension, if approved, and from any other local developments—whether wind farm, opencast coal mining or landfill (we have them all!).

Woolfords, Auchengray and Tarbrax Improvement Foundation (WAT IF?) received charitable status in November 2012 and is a *Scottish Charitable Incorporated Organization* (SCIO). A SCIO is a legal form unique to Scotland, which was introduced on 1 April 2011 and allows Scottish charities to incorporate without becoming companies. A SCIO is able to enter into contracts, employ staff, incur debts, own property, sue and be sued. There is little underlying law, as would be the case with a company, and the SCIO sources nearly all of its powers and rules from its own constitution, making that document of critical importance. There are important differences between a SCIO and other charity types in Scotland, for example the Land Reform Act 2003 excludes the use of a SCIO as a legal vehicle for Scottish community right-to-buy. While most of the Trust's area of influence is within the local authority area of South Lanarkshire, a small proportion is within neighbouring West Lothian. Between October 2011 and March 2013, regular public meetings were held and articles printed in the local community newsletter. Funds were raised from South Lanarkshire's Leader Programme and South Lanarkshire Rural Communities Trust to carry out an independent community consultation in January 2013, from which a *Community Action Plan* (CAP) was produced to guide the Trust's activities over the next five years.

Approval was granted to Muirhall extension and an agreement reached that the Trust would receive £50,000 per year in community benefit, in addition to a one-off payment of £18,647 when construction began. The one-off payment was received in September 2013 and quarterly instalments of £12,807 began in September 2014. The two turbines were, at the time of construction, the largest onshore wind turbines in the UK (Muirhall Energy 2015), so it seems 'fair' that we also have one of the most generous benefit rates from wind at £8,088.25 per MW per annum. The developer, who lives locally, was keen that the community got as much from these two new turbines as they would have if a trust had been formed when the original six-turbine development was built.

The response rate to the community consultation was almost 30 %, with a total of 205 individuals, eight farms and nine representatives of community groups returning completed questionnaires. While the majority (71.3 %) of questionnaires returned came from the villages of Woolfords, Auchengray and Tarbrax, almost one third came from other, smaller settlements and farms in the area. The results provided a representative sample of views from the population and different interest groups in the area, and an evidence base and mandate to the Trust for future work in the area.

According to the Scottish Index of Multiple Deprivation (The Scottish Government 2012), this area is amongst the 5 % most access-deprived areas of Scotland, and transport and access to services came out highly in the community consultation. There is no scheduled bus service (although there is a dial-a-bus service for all ages but the service is not always available) and the vast majority of residents own a car. However, having a positive influence on public infrastructure is a long-term aim. Specific concerns include getting to doctor's appointments 8 miles away and getting to the shops (the nearest being 4 miles away). If the Trust could run a community minibus or provide a local 'shop', this may reduce individual car use or increase local produce consumption. Depending on how projects develop, some may encourage a reduction in consumption but it is not the basis of the Trust.

People need to see things change but the changes need to be sustainable. Our projects need to be visible and the first has been to refurbish the disused village hall in Woolfords; Auchengray and Tarbrax both have functioning village halls. The majority of the funding for this project came from a local landfill trust, who paid the contractor directly, with match funding coming from our regular donations from the Muirhall extension, the two-turbine extension which led to the formation of the Trust.

9.3 Practitioners' Needs

Communities vary. Our community is rural, scattered and disadvantaged in terms of infrastructure, having neither mains gas nor public transport. Depending on one's world-view, some might see this as an advantage—you do not miss what you have never had. But most see this as something to be rectified. Activists vary too—and by 'activist', I mean someone who works, usually unpaid, for a cause they believe in. WAT IF? does not organize protests at the local town hall, but it does engage with local authorities and councillors.

As indicated above, I do not believe that society will *choose* to consume less. *The changes we need to make will be imposed by nature—we will use less when there is less to use.* This realization, that the simplification of our complex way of life is unlikely to be orchestrated or proactively planned, moved me away from environmental activism and towards community activism; the most important thing anyone can do is to try to build resilience into their community in whatever way best suits the local context (i.e. the community and its activists). Others will lead the way for different reasons. The IPPR briefing notes that the success of a Transition initiative "is largely dependent upon those involved".

A key skill is communication. Not just with the wider world, but within the community and within the group of active members. There are a number of small groups in the area, as well as people who have planted flowers and shrubs at their own expense. A resident from Tarbrax, who had seen recent improvements in Woolfords, wondered why Tarbrax had not had similar from the Council and seemed amazed when told that the improvements had been carried out and paid for by a few individuals.

One reason why our efforts have been successful so far is that we have people with the confidence to communicate with developers in a friendly but professional manner. The Trust has stated its neutrality with respect to wind farm proposals from the start and we avoid 'deals' struck to improve the chances of a planning application being approved. A new, 22-turbine wind farm was granted planning permission in summer 2014 and we are now working out community benefit payments with the developer. Dealing with two developers who genuinely seem to want community benefit to benefit communities, rather than merely tick the right boxes, is a vital stroke of luck that not every community will have.

The basic resources and skills required by any community group are similar whether you are campaigning at a global, national or local level. The core group behind the Trust have, between them, years of experience in business, the voluntary sector, environmental campaigning, working with offenders, landscape gardening, research, writing, parenting, employing others, being self-employed—*transferable skills*. Knowing who to approach is also important, as is trust. During the early days of forming WAT IF?, I was supported by a neighbour's father, a retired civil servant who knew the basics of writing a constitution and went on to become a co-opted Trustee. However, we decided to become a SCIO which, as a relatively new entity, not many people knew about. Through voluntary sector experience, we knew to contact the *Development Trusts Association Scotland* (DTAS) and the Scottish Council for Voluntary Organizations (SCVO) for help with writing our constitution. DTAS were exceptional in the free help they provided us with, especially as we are not a Development Trust *per se* (a key aim of which is to generate income through enterprise and the ownership of assets; WAT IF? does not have a trading arm, yet).

Having a friend who worked in the renewable energy industry helped with learning about agreements, such as a Memorandum of Understanding. And having a core member who also runs her own local business gave us access to other local professionals, such as builders, architects, lawyers and accountants. General discussions with other organizations can lead to new ways of operating. The idea to have our development officer, who was contracted in October 2014, working from the newly-opened Woolfords Hall came from a much earlier meeting with

Fauldhouse Community Development Trust (FCDT), who were doing similar things but in a more urban environment. FCDT had rented office space from the Council and were offered the chance to buy part of the building, giving them a base in which to hold events and a 'drop-in' facility, making the project more accessible.

So what could academics provide to help community activists? Case studies and examples would be of use. A resource base, such as an online repository (or wiki) of case studies and/or an FAQ page would allow access to other local community initiatives. A simple form could be drawn up, the completion of which by various community groups would allow a database of case studies to develop. Perhaps one question could determine whether a group was a Transition Initiative or not, to gauge which types of community groups are succeeding in reducing consumption. Information to help activists access reliable information (e.g. to back up a funding application) and which highlights ways over the common hurdles faced would also be beneficial, as would training in how best to work with communities, with people in general, not just on 'sustainable consumption' itself. What does lead to a change in behaviour?

9.4 What Makes Initiatives Fail?

WAT IF? has achieved a lot in less than four years and has, thankfully, avoided any one of its key activists from 'burning out'. If someone has to take time out, so be it—fewer tasks will be completed in any given time but the group will remain functional. Communication is important here too.

It might be interesting to consider how many people have both the academic skills to study global issues, such as climate change and resource depletion, and the social skills to work in their community to increase cooperation and thus resilience, to communicate the need to consume differently, if not less. Which is more important in achieving change on the ground? How many promising initiatives have failed due to the inability of a lead person to delegate, compromise and/or work within a group? What has helped a failing group to survive and thrive? Fortunately, the core group of WAT IF? activists consists of a very good mix with respect to skills and experience—and outlook. We certainly keep each other going.

The loss of a key person is certainly a common reason for an initiative to fail but as more people from the community become involved, this should relieve the pressure on the main activists. The lessons learned may seem obvious but they are key for *durability*:

1. *The actions of any community group must be relevant to the community*
   Saying 'reduce consumption' does not resonate with many. People tend to care more about 'saving money' or 'getting fit' so consider how projects might save money, or improve health (a future project will be a heritage trail). All the potential projects in our action plan came from the community. It is for the Trust

to interpret, prioritize and raise funds for these, but we can emphasize certain aspects. The heritage trail would restore a right of way between two villages. People are interested in local industrial and natural heritage and enabling people to walk the moors and learn what is there, might build attachment to this place. For example, we have two SSSIs, including Cobbinshaw Moss (494 ha), which is the largest area of intermediate bog (i.e. sharing features of both raised and blanket bog) left in Britain and is the largest of a string of bogs along the south-western edge of the Pentlands' watershed. Another project is to create a community garden and allotments in association with the local primary school, which is currently being rebuilt, and the Council.

2. *Never assume that others know what you are doing or why*
   Even if you feel that you have said it repeatedly. People may attend public meetings but they will all remember different aspects of what has been said. The Trust's development officer has been able to focus on communication, using a logo based on our CAP on all materials, from banners to emails, producing a newsletter to inform people of what has been achieved and future priorities, and liaising with other local groups and decision-makers.
   It is worth pointing out that without the 'unrestricted' funding from Muirhall, it would have been much more difficult for the Trust to take on a development officer. It is not easy to fund raise to employ someone—even a project officer attached to a specific project is not considered suitable by many funders. Our development officer is young and full of energy, qualified in rural development and has exceeded our expectations. But she has to earn a living and could not have taken the Trust forward as a volunteer.
3. *Never assume that others see the world in the same way as you do ...*
   This applies to those in the wider community as well as to other activists and is all the more important to bear in mind when not part of a 'special-interest' group. An example might be when negotiating with a developer over the timing of community benefit payments. Is it better to have a larger sum up front and less per MW over the lifetime of the wind farm or less up front and a larger per MW contribution? The answer would depend on whether one believed that the value of money would be higher or lower in the future.
   ... but never forget that people can and do change if they see a reason to.
   If our community can cooperate and become more cohesive over a range of community projects, it will be better prepared to fend for itself as local authority funding dries up. Some people simply do not have the time to commit to community activism but a lack of confidence, in either their own abilities or the project itself, often lies at the route of inaction. If people are inspired they will reprioritize their time so that they can get involved, using their skills where they see fit, and the more people are involved, the less likely an initiative is to fail. It might change over time but it will continue with its work and adapt to whatever the future holds.

9.5 The Future…

WAT IF? has made potential wind farm developers aware of its presence, meeting with them and explaining its ambitions. However, if the Trust did access a 6-figure sum, would it make or break us? Or is access to community benefit going to be what makes or breaks a community as local authority budgets are cut further? Only time will tell and it will tell of diversity, of similar projects having different outcomes depending on what a place has to offer and what its needs are. Examples of communities fighting for their rights are inspiring (see: Riddoch 2013; Young and Young 2012) but I know of no repository for such. While the Transition movement has certainly informed and guided me, the message of reducing consumption has been put aside until such times as it becomes relevant to this community.

References

FEASTA (The Foundation for the Economics of Sustainability), 2011: The Transition Towns movement: Its Huge Significance and a Friendly Criticism; at: http://www.feasta.org/2011/04/06/the-transition-towns-movement-its-huge-significance-and-a-friendly-criticism/ (11 May 2015).

IPPR (The Institute for Public Policy Research), 2013: Sustainable Consumption in the UK: A Selection of Case Studies; at: http://www.ippr.org/assets/media/images/media/files/publication/2013/02/sustainable-consumption-UK_Feb2013_10302.pdf (11 May 2015).

Muirhall Energy, 2015: Muirhall Windfarm Extension; at: http://www.muirhallenergy.co.uk/muirhallwindfarmext.html (11 May 2015).

Riddoch, L., 2013: *Blossom: What Scotland Needs to Flourish* (Edinburgh: Luath Press).

The Independent, 2015: Councils Rely on Local Street Champions to Pick Up Litter Prune Hedges and Grit Minor Roads as Funds Run Out; at: http://www.independent.co.uk/news/uk/politics/councils-rely-on-local-street-champions-to-pick-up-litter-prune-hedges-and-grit-minor-roads-as-funds-run-out-9985738.html.

The Scottish Government, 2012: Scottish Index of Multiple Deprivation, 2012: at: http://simd.scotland.gov.uk/publication-2012/ (11 May 2015).

Young, A.; Young, E., (2012): *The New Road: Charting Scotland's Inspiration Communities* (Glendaruel: Argyll Publishing).

Chapter 10
Conclusion

Audley Genus

Abstract This concluding chapter summarizes the work of book and indicates future avenues for research on sustainable consumption. The chapter reconsiders what has been learned from the foregoing chapters and the workshop in which research reported therein was previously presented. It does so while reflecting upon previous literature in diverse fields, discussing how this connects with the themes addressed in the book. Some implications for policy are highlighted.

Keywords DIY design · Environmental policy-making · Grassroots activism · Institutional change · Sharing economy · Social practices

10.1 Introduction

The book was conceived as a report and reflection on a workshop organized by the European affiliate of the Sustainable Consumption Research and Action Initiative to identify developments in thinking and practice which have the potential to reduce unsustainable consumption. Unsustainable consumption is a critical element of the global greenhouse gas emissions which have been increasing over a number of decades, contributing to harmful climate change. Our understanding of unsustainable consumption remains in need of development, as does appreciation of the remedial or transformative actions that are or might be taken. In relation to this the book has identified: types of initiatives (the 'what' of transformation); categories and roles of actors involved or not involved in such actions (the 'who'); and processes by which actions are accomplished (the 'how' of consumption-related social change). Specifically the book brought together contributions having a focus on one or more of: (a) design; (b) innovation, and relations among science, technology and society; and (c) practices of consumption. Some of the recurring issues

---

Audley Genus, Ph.D., YTL Professor of Innovation and Technology Management, Small Business Research Centre, Kingston Business School, London, UK; Email: a.genus@kingston.ac.uk.

A. Genus (ed.), *Sustainable Consumption*, The Anthropocene: Politik—Economics—Society—Science 3, DOI 10.1007/978-3-319-29665-4_10

covered included the extent to which the phenomena under scrutiny are capable of realising a fundamental change in patterns of consumption and production. They invite questions about approaches which have been argued to engender well-being or economic development less reliant on the exploitation of material resources, such as the sharing of services, DIY production or active design. For example, are recent developments early manifestations of deep-seated social transformation or more in the way of surface level change, which actually serves to reinforce the status quo? Is there an over-reliance on the actions of iconoclastic entrepreneurs and social innovators? Are culture and/or social practice underplayed and what is their significance to policy-making? The merits of cross-disciplinary approaches and their capacity to address or to generate the relevant research questions and problems represents another important element of the discussion, one which requires further elaboration in this conclusion.

The chapters above represent much of the content of the workshop on which this book is based. They have been concerned with design activism and the work of practitioners 'on the ground', and how professional designers and researchers might be facilitative of this (Chap. 1, by Genus and Thorpe; Chap. 2, by Salvia and Cooper; and Chap. 9 by Meikle). They have also been concerned with issues such as the relation between national culture, interpersonal trust and social practice and its relevance to (un)sustainable consumption (Chap. 7, by McGreevy and Akitsu). Chapters have connected technology development, innovation and social structures and the implications of 'technological society' for sustainable consumption (Chap. 8, by Coles). Several chapters remarked on the phenomena of rebound and Diderot effects, for example in relation to the spread of DIY design or repair (Chap. 2), sharing (e.g. in relation to accommodation, Chap. 5, by Netter) and explicable with reference to the uncertain nature of innovation (Chap. 8). Shifting and competing discourses, moreover, constitute technology development, the promises and expectations of innovation, and the uses and disappointments of innovations (Chap. 8). Further, the chapters have addressed the communication of ideas about sustainable consumption through narratives, for example in terms of the availability cascade approach taken to analyse the 'hype' of the sharing economy (Chap. 5) but also in relation to the sharing of skills for DIY design and repairing goods, and how micro-organizations communicate sustainability with consumers of 'slow-fashion' (Chap. 6 by Henninger et al.). A concern with design and consumption practices permeated the book. At the same time, as has been recognized recently elsewhere (e.g. Cohen et al. 2013), the book has demonstrated that claims for emerging movements and phenomena, again linked to the sharing economy, are exaggerated. However, in no way can a volume as brief as this hope to capture the full range and depth of discussions which took place over two days of a workshop and subsequently over several months (including at other SCORAI workshops). Mindful of this the concluding chapter reflects on what may be learned from the book and the workshop taken together, placing their contribution in the context of the wider research literature on the new economics, socio-technical transitions and social practices (c.f. Cohen et al. 2013), and policy and initiatives 'on the ground'. It also suggests future agenda for research on diverse themes and in relation to the work and interaction of various protagonists whose activities bear on practices, policies and innovation related to sustainable or reduced consumption. The discussion in the following section is organized according to the broad themes covered by contributions to the book and the workshop.

10.2 Revisiting the Themes of the Book

As originally conceived the workshop themes were listed in the call for papers as follows:

1. Actions for developing and diffusing sustainable consumption practice;
2. Relations among and roles for researchers and practitioners in enabling sustainable consumption;
3. New perspectives and research methods, mindful of the increasing calls for inter- or multi-disciplinary research to tackle societal 'grand challenges', and the potential and limitations associated with working across academic disciplines; and
4. Integrating sustainable consumption and production.

These themes evolved so that ultimately the workshop papers and discussions and chapters of the book addressed the following:

1. DIY design
2. The sharing (or 'solidaristic') economy
3. Grassroots activism
4. Interactions between consumption and production; and
5. Social practices

10.2.1 DIY Design

In relation to the first of these themes contributors argued that design practices have the potential to make the resource implications of modern consumerism visible (c.f. Thorpe 2012). Furthermore sustainability-orientated design may highlight connections between consumption and long term, rather than ephemeral, well-being. This approach to design can transform the nature of consumption by demonstrating that a slower pace of stimulation can engender consumer satisfaction. At the same time it was argued that a pronounced cultural shift will be implicated in social relations which place greater value on collective rather than individual actions and behaviour, with profound consequences for the processes by which our identities develop and our social positions are understood. Indeed the book identified ways in which design practices might contribute to sustainable collective DIY design (Chap. 2), and offered a tool for the design of innovative products based on the analysis of user practices (Chap. 3 by Piscicelli et al.). Beyond those mentioned in the book, contributions to the workshop referred to numerous other examples, such as the expandable urban mobility jacket which provides a built-in alternative to plastic carrier bags or the notion of design with intent. With respect to the latter there was frequent reference at the workshop to 'pattern languages' and techniques employed by designers to guide what people what and how people consume, such as the Design with Intent toolkit by Dan Lockton.[1] In creating new infrastructures for commitment, design projects often tackle physical limitations to activities that improve social and environmental values. Between them the book and the workshop discussed examples of infrastructural design which have the potential to reduce the demand for energy. Specific instances include green roofs and rooftop gardens, the 'Re-done Bike' concept and lunar resonant street lights.

There are a number of interventions and approaches which could elicit the aforementioned changes, some of which are already in evidence, as observed by contributors to the workshop and in previous other work. They include the formulation and implementation of labelling and rating systems, which may render hidden values 'visible', and 'slow design' (Thorpe 2012). A number of examples of slow design were given by workshop contributors and include flock knitwear of which fibres might be traced back to specific animals, or on which clothing tags provide information about the animal and its location and breeding. Taking things further the point was made, repeatedly, that developments in the direction of "collaborative consumption" constitute and convey a narrative about making, ownership and use in society, an alternative storyline that induces people to rethink the nature of short-term and long-term satisfaction and well-being.

One of the essential tasks considered necessary by chapter authors and other workshop delegates is the delineation of the factors which promote and diffuse DIY design. In addition it is necessary to understand the nature of and the potential contribution of 'design activism' to the reduction of unsustainable consumption. This takes in questions surrounding the prevalence of 'DIY urbanism', the scope and role of design/designers and their relationship to other spheres such as research and politics. A key question that was raised at the workshop concerned what all this design activism is for, and this issue was taken up again in the chapters above. For example, the chapter by Henninger et al. begs the question of whether slow fashion as practised by some micro-organizations is merely another way of more efficiently producing more, though high quality, goods with reduced inputs. The question needs to be asked whether any more fundamental transformation of consumption/production relations and models attends such a development, particularly when the focus of analysis is on communication from seller to buyer rather than the mutuality of interactions between the two. Already mentioned above in

[1]The toolkit may be downloaded from the websites: http://www.danlockton.com/dwi/Download_the_cards; http://architectures.danlockton.co.uk/dan-lockton/ and also via a link to the work of Christopher Alexander and colleagues on pattern languages at: http://www.jacana.org.uk/pattern/P14.htm.

connection with design intent, 'pattern languages' was a suggested design principle for (re) creating—in potentially democratic and transdisciplinary ways—how and where we live and work. In such a process the implicit values underpinning sustainable design are made explicit in the grammar of language.

10.2.2 Sharing and the Solidarity Economy

The emerging literature on the new economy, sharing and self-provisioning is as yet inconclusive. Commentators such as Juliet Schor, for example, assert the role of consumer-citizens as sustainability entrepreneurs operating locally in collectives which transcend reliance on individual or household action (Schor 2010, 2014; Schor/Thompson 2014). The book and the workshop provided many examples of initiatives which are illustrative of the sharing economy. These included examples of re-used clothing, shared accommodation and the service in which cars are publicly shared for the final stage of local trips, the remainder of a journey having been undertaken by mass transit. However others (Offer 2006; Thorpe 2012) have commented on the difficulties of cultivating such 'strategies for commitment' to longer term well-being and sustainability, whether this has its origins in community- or personally-based activities. SCORAI London workshop delegates sought to probe critically the reality and myth of the sharing or solidaristic economy (e.g. Cohen 2014; Goodman 2014), as well as the importance of values and trust therein. Delegates considered the capacity for international capital to undermine or co-opt citizen action and modes of provisioning based on social solidarity. More broadly, the need for a culturally sensitive perspective of sustainable consumption was highlighted, as was the argument that some apparently innovative practices masked what should more insightfully be viewed as contributory to the building or reinforcement of a more resilient yet unsustainable capitalism. The workshop contributions explored the phenomenon and challenges associated with the recreation of the 'commons' and, relatedly, the key issue of 'upscaling', or the more widespread diffusion of currently marginal (possibly) sustainable practices. Again, emphasis was placed on the need for context sensitivity in our work and for debate between policy-makers and other actors regarding emerging trends and the implications for sustainable consumption. Rather, more potentially effective interventions were seen as being based on promoting multiplication of initiatives sensitive to local cultural, economic and historical circumstances. The developing agenda, it is suggested (e.g. by Røpke 2013; Netter, this volume; see also a recent issue of the *Journal of Peer Production* 2014) needs however to address the limitations of the various sharing economy archetypes as well as their possible contribution to the transformation of prevailing systems of production and consumption. This applies to peer-to-peer, not-for-profit forms emphasized in this book but also to other variations on 'sharing' e.g. based on business-to-peer relations and a for-profit orientation.

10.2.3 Grassroots Activism

Chapter 9, by Mandy Meikle, and workshop presentations and discussions embraced a range of issues connected with the role and work of environmental and community activists (e.g. in Transition Town groups), including the implications of such activities for local sustainability initiatives. There was a concern that local environmental campaigning about sustainable consumption was falling on deaf ears and that merely repeating such messages might not mean much to many people, who thus might not feel that they 'own' initiatives. Meikle identified key factors in the failure of such initiatives and of the roles that university researchers can play to help communities 'see' how things can change for the better, both for the benefit of the community as well as in terms of realising more sustainable living. Whilst these observations stem from anecdotal evidence from her own experience which are not presented as scientifically valid, they do tally with the findings from recent researches on the topic (Middlemiss/Parrish 2010; Seyfang/Smith 2007; Young/Middlemiss 2012). Aspects of Meikle's chapter are redolent of Berkhout's (2006) comments regarding visions of future society representing 'bids' made by activists in attempting (but partially) failing to persuade local citizens to enrol voluntarily to collective visions, in this case connected with environmental campaigning. The WAT-IF case is a kind of grassroots initiative exemplifying relatively newly established networks involving various citizens and organizations and (the promise of) renewable—and also non-renewable—energy technologies and energy demand reduction. As previous research on socio-technical transitions has suggested, a variety of visions and expectations co-exist among the local population, some of which have already 'failed' to be realized (so far!) (Geels/Smit 2000). Otherwise the diffusion of a sustainable energy or consumption storyline has given way to a community activism narrative that appears to play rather better with a large number of local residents in some countries (Berkhout 2006) opposed to 'industrialized' wind energy generation technology. Thus in relation to innovation of sustainable energy technologies, in the UK for example, environmental campaigners represent actors more certain and confident of the future benefits of preferred renewable energy technologies, whereas a large number of other groups and citizens prefer 'alternative' (but not wind power) generation technologies and see themselves as marginalized from the networks promoting the adoption of renewables (Brown/Michael 2003).

One way of understanding the social change required is, as suggested by delegate and activist Tom Henfrey of the Schumacher Institute, to conceive of sustainable consumption as a cultural project, in which culture could be understood as shared beliefs about the world, the structure of relationships with the world, and a set of ideas about the world and institutions associated with them. Thought of in this way the pervasive culture of unsustainable consumption is in need of fundamental transformation relating to the notion (presented above in Chap. 1) that in market economies people are 'born to buy' (Schor 2004); the way research is designed and conducted; the boundary between activism and research; and the way we produce and consume food, *inter alia*. Chapters above and workshop papers and discussions examined the emergence of ‘grassroots prototypes’ such as fablabs, hackerspaces and makerspaces, into which anyone can enter if they wish to learn about making or repairing all kinds of products (Smith 2014a; Salvia and Cooper, this volume). At the workshop Adrian Smith, of the Science Policy Research Unit at University of Sussex, remarked on the commitment to openness and collaboration in such spaces, including collaboration among unlikely partners, and explored the implications of such phenomena in terms of the emergence of new meanings of production and consumption. He was though wary of ‘excited claims’ that such developments amounted to, for example, a third industrial revolution, while remaining hopeful about the prospects for socially useful production and human-centred design. Like other chapter authors and workshop delegates Smith took an historical perspective, his arguments informed by accounts of previous experiments and technology networks such as the Lucas Plan in the 1970s and at the Greater London Council in the 1980s. Then and now it is not clear whether the object of such ventures was or is to promote the design of accessible technology prototypes, or something more wholeheartedly political and ideological such the democratization of technology development (Smith 2014b).

10.2.4 Interactions Between Consumption and Production

Both book chapters and workshop contributions addressed interactions between consumption and production, and included work on new sites and entrepreneurs connected with potentially sustainable consumption/production, such as urban farm-(er)s and designers and wearers of slow fashion, and the multiple social practices which need to be understood in order to enable the diffusion of energy-efficient lighting, for example. A core element of the discussion concerns the role of innovation in sustainable consumption (and in reducing consumption per se). There are two aspects of this which have featured in the chapters of the book. One aspect involves what researchers refer to as the expectations (Berkhout 2006; Borup et al. 2006; Brown/Michael 2003) and imaginaries (Jasanoff/Sang-Hyun 2009, 2013) associated with innovations and the extent to which we should expect innovation (whether in products, processes, practices or social organization) to deliver sustainable or reduced consumption. It is a common observation that innovation can engender process efficiencies and product development which merely result in ‘rebound’ effects in which resource use is exacerbated. Perhaps it is time to probe more deeply into this phenomenon in the relation to the workings and limits of the ‘technological society’ (Coles, this volume; Ellul 1964), including the arguably ‘inevitable’ separation of production from consumption and the prevailing dominant discourse which make technological systems appear to us as natural and unquestionable (Ellul 1980). Another aspect involves the diffusion of innovation and practice. Here the book has provided accounts of emerging practices and business models. It is recognized that typically such forms of potentially more sustainable consumption may not have diffused widely and that the reasons for this limited institutionalization have much to do with connections among prevailing patterns and practices of consumption, relations among producers and consumers, and what consumption means to citizen-consumers in acquisitive market-orientated societies. Attention is drawn to a complex of factors, involving the function and use of technologies as well as their design and production, the societal function of technology and the cultural values and discourses implicated with related visions and practices (Geels 2002, 2004; Piterou and Steward in this volume; Rip and Kemp 1998; Shove 2003).

10.2.5 Social Practice

The matters of concern to this book are manifold, being implicated with innovative business models, user and design practices and a variety of governance and cultural phenomena implicated in diverse empirical settings. Previous work had focussed on the policy and practical interventions required to elicit behavioural change or to reorient attitudes of consumers (DECC 2009; DEFRA 2008; IPCC 2014; Stern 2007), often employing mono-disciplinary approaches, notably rooted in behavioural economics. The book and workshop contributions have added to the growing volume of work critical of models emphasising the rational choices and behaviour of individual consumers, instead bringing to the fore collective practices and values and their (un)sustainability (Shove 2003; Shove et al. 2012). Contributions have recognized the centrality of both national culture to practice (Chap. 7 by McGreevy and Akitsu) and of everyday practices (Chap. 3 by Piscicelli et al., and Chap. 4 by Piterou and Steward) to unsustainable of consumption.

The chapters and workshop papers have tended to be informed by diverse sources, favouring cross-disciplinary approaches to analysing practice. One example of this includes the employment of different notions of practice and contributions from social psychology and social practice theory to analyse the relevance of various elements of practice to individual consumption (Piscicelli et al. in this volume). Another is Charlotte Jensen's paper for the London workshop, on lighting practices which moves the focus away from energy efficient lights. Instead Jensen employs a combination of social practice theory, institutional theory and the sociology of translation to analyse what people do with lighting, why and how, as well as to diagnose the persistence of such practices and sources of change, which entail social and technical transformation. Further, Karin Dobernig's workshop paper analyses the phenomenon of urban farming through two lens: as social practice, and in relation to emerging alternative food networks which include activist urban farmers but also local authorities and others who make rooftop space available to be farmed, for example. Other contributions, for example those by Piterou and Steward (in this volume) on book production and the practice of reading, and Greene et al. (2014) on the measurement of mobility practices over the life course, offer a blend of historical perspective with socio-technical analysis and/or social practice theory (c.f. Schatzki et al. 2001; Shove/Walker 2014). Such perspectives are necessary to gain a proper understanding of the context, process and performance of sustainability-related innovations, the ‘life course’ of consumers’ user practices e.g. in relation to transportation or using energy in the home, and of past exemplars such as the socially useful production movement of the 1970s. In contrast to some earlier work empirical analysis of practice in a range of domains both inside and outside of the home allows for more extensive and deeper insights into the nature and origins of sustainability-related practices. Between them the book and the workshop papers examined practices related, for example, to food consumption, book reading, transport, domestic lighting, urban farming, and DIY design, production and repair related to furniture, industrial machines, urban spaces, and re-use of scrap materials. Contributions underscored the significance of combinations of social practices, institutional rules, entrepreneurial design activists (e.g. urban farmers), and supportive policy and social structures and material infrastructure to making ‘real’ transformations which have the potential to endure.

10.2.6 Looking Back and Looking Ahead

Reflecting on the above a number of points may be made by way of summarising findings and indicating possible avenues for future inquiry and action in practice. These are discussed in the following sub-sections.

10.2.7 DIY Design and Grassroots Activism

Caution needs to be exercised regarding the matter of what realistically may be achieved by the agency of activists and others. Chap. 9, by Mandy Meikle, drew attention to the work of academic researchers and how this could inform grassroots initiatives. She argued that academic research had a role to play in generating and sharing case studies of local environmental or related community schemes, from which activists and other practitioners could learn and draw inspiration. The open space sessions of the workshop discussed the possible contribution of ‘pracademics’; language use by academic researchers which excludes others; the role of laypeople in drafting calls for research funding and applications for funding, possibly as ‘acaditioners’, a term invoked by a lay delegate to the workshop. Roles that university researchers can or should play in effecting such transformation include collaborating with practitioners to share the findings of research, case studies and so on but, moreover, possibly to identify new research problems with non-professional researcher partners. Suggested questions that need to be addressed in future research include: what is the motivation underlying DIY design and innovation? What does it achieve in relation to reducing (unsustainable) consumption? Who is left out of such design processes? How are such processes to be funded anyway?

10.2.8 *The Sharing Economy*

Fundamental social and technical change in the direction of more sustainable living need to be seen in the light of social structures inherent in contemporary capitalism. Some of the contributors here have argued that the reproduction of (national) culture and international structural features of society attenuate possible shifts (for example in the consumption of food and relations between farmers and consumers) and the framing of what is required (e.g. in relation to the problems and solutions generated in the process of innovation and technology development). A central task is for future research to assess the prevalence and significance of different types of initiative associated with the 'new', sharing, or solidarity economy. This includes examination of the availability of (high-tech) resources required to enable fab-labs, for example, to operate, as well as of the claim that such initiatives are more environmentally sustainable than mainstream practices.

Communication represents another theme requiring further scrutiny. Chapters of the book have explored the use of online media to promote sustainable consumption as well as to share skills in co-design. However it has also demonstrated how the detrimental impact of availability cascades via which novel ideas and initiatives diffuse can mean that sustainability consumption becomes merely the latest 'fix', which ultimately is set to disappoint. Moreover the degree to which online communication between firms and potential customers is uni-directional (i.e. from firm to customer) rather than mutual is likely to feed the view that such developments are tantamount to 'window dressing', thus only serving to reinforce existing patterns of consumption and social relations rather than to transform society.

10.2.9 *Practice Theory*

There is a need for further reflection and research on social practices and practice theory. Within the SCORAI network there is some concern that the insights obtained from research founded on social practice perspectives may be gained at the cost of over-emphasising individual- or household-level practices, and underplay more general social and political phenomena implicated in consumption. Relatedly, as indicated above there is a requirement for more work on implications of national cultural differences for the generation and (non-)transmission of more sustainable consumption practices across national borders, distinct from a concern to probe the propensity of global consumer culture to diffuse unsustainable consumption practices.

It may be argued that an emphasis on people as carriers of practices (a) reduces the extent to which they are active agents in reproducing, not reproducing and creating practices; and (b) ignores or downplays the role of other carriers of practices. It is interesting that proponents of practice theory refer to the 'reproduction of institutions' and 'institutional projects' but typically do not draw explicitly on research informed by institutional theory or on the nature of 'discourse institutions' in environmental policy-making (Hajer/Versteeg 2005; Schmidt 2008). This may be due to the association of institutional approaches with the carrying of institutions by passive adherents to institutional rules, whereas contemporary thinking focuses on the dynamics of institutional change and the 'paradox of agency' (Greenwood/Suddaby 2006; Sine/David 2003). Questions to be posed now concern but are not limited to how people create and establish new ways of thinking about and practising (e.g. sustainable consumption) while at the same time being embedded in institutionalized fields of rules of thought, language and action. From an academic point of view this is all the more interesting given the following. First, consider Giddens' (1984) remark that of the greatest significance for our understanding of social life are rules and resources that are 'locked into in the reproduction of institutionalized practices …' (Giddens 1984: 22). Such rules may be manifest in language, formally codified or informal, or subject to strong or weak sanctions if not followed. Second, consider Bourdieu's observations of the fundamental role that types of capital and language play in defining the (economic and environmental) 'fields' and in establishing the rules which 'define the ordinary functioning of the field[s]', and in and between which there is contestation (Wacquant 1989: 39–40).

An examination of institutional rules informed by insights from institutional theory, as well as key contributions such as the above, provides a potentially complementary approach to the analysis of entities of social practice (driving, food shopping etc.) and recurrent performances. Allied to discourse analysis such an approach would address the role in changing patterns of consumption of formal and informal regulative, normative and cultural rules, symbols/language, artefacts, and relational networks in institutionalized (and institutionalizing) social action in economic and environmental domains (Scott 2008; Fairclough 2001; c.f. Genus 2014a, in press; Genus/Theobald in press). It could add to developing understanding of the bases of compliance or divergence with existing social conventions (c.f. Spurling et al. 2013), including the social sanctions that may be applied to ensure adherence. The approach also highlight connections between changing regulative (e.g. governmental) rules and practices. It would do so recognising that formally constituted laws and regulations do not mandate (sustainable) practice but if accepted as legitimate may be of significance to the disruption of prevailing practices and the establishing and embedding of new ones.

If applied, a discourse institutional approach could, arguably, generate insights related to the observation that practice is about what is said (or read), by whom, how and where in conjunction with what is done and the meanings, competences and things that have been recognized as elements of practice. Such a viewpoint would examine the nature and 'career' of practices of the everyday kind to constitute routinized actions taken by 'bundles' of individuals, things, knowledge, and language. It would analyse the discourses operating more generally that govern the availability of things and knowledge and the legitimacy of what it is that is practised, which is necessary for (continued) institutionalization. Approaches informed by an understanding of discourses and institutions have the potential to provide a bridge between practices (and nests of linked practices) and wider social institutions and structures of which they are part. It is argued that the policy relevance of practice theory is to emphasize and inform interventions which can help build networks that have the potential to make more sustainable practice possible and contribute to the undoing of unsustainable ones (Shove et al. 2012). Here, chapter and other workshop contributors have drawn attention to cultural, discursive and socio-economic, normative and regulatory institutions which provide the resources and historical legacies that inhabit our understanding of what and how we consume.

10.2.10 Research and Engagement Agenda

In a number of instances the SCORAI London contributions call for the replication of the research presented to other sites or for the inclusion of other or more actors. For example, Chap. 6 (by Henninger et al.) suggests that the views of customers be incorporated into research on the communication strategies of micro-organizations in the slow fashion sectors, whilst the 'TRACES' approach they investigate is examined in other industries. The potential and limits of cross-disciplinarity is an area of concern, however. It is apparent that variations of practice theory-related research exist and that researchers are attempting to generate novel questions and insights either by combining practice theory with other approaches (e.g. social psychology), or are applying it in parallel to other approaches (such as institutional theory or network analysis). The wide range of work on this encompasses that which emphasizes the relationship between individual consumption and elements of practice and how this relates to behaviour and design, research on the cultural shaping of practice and that which explicitly focuses on user(s) practices.

It is apparent from our discussions that SCORAI contributors are aware of the need to debate the underpinning assumptions, merits, limits and implications of behaviour change, practice-theoretic and hybrid approaches. However it is clear that for SCORAI and other researchers alike, there is still much to be done to articulate the differences and tensions regarding underlying assumptions about knowledge, nature and research conduct, which could debilitate our efforts but yet provide a platform on which to build appreciative investigations. At the same time the question remains concerning whether and how researchers should seek to combine different perspectives/knowledge, and how this might be done effectively in ways which do not do a disservice to previously unfamiliar fields, or risk the employment of incompatible or incommensurate work. Further, there is a debate which has begun but will need to be taken further regarding the academic and policy significance and desirability of *trans-* or *post-*disciplinarity (Rau/Fahy 2013). Reflecting on the contributions to this edited volume, there is an orientation towards 'weak' forms of multi- and inter-disciplinarity in which the foundations and conduct of the research could be more explicitly articulated in relation to the different academic disciplines invoked. Generally, the contributions do seek to engage with ideas in cognate rather than distant fields of research. Similarly, engagement with non-researchers appears to take a 'weak' rather than a 'strong' form of co-inquiry and in certain cases collaboration with research subjects is not very evident (Genus 2014b). (The civil society engagement which features in SCORAI Europe research activities, often involves practitioners and activists who are employed or funded by research organizations at least part of the time and facilitation processes more friendly to academics than others, albeit that it is characterized by some rather longstanding collaborations with certain organizations such as the Green Dependent Institute and WAT-IF). Consider this alongside: (a) the argument that the 'silo' quality of academic discipline-driven research is counter-productive to the progress of social science and the need to tackle grand challenges connected with environmental sustainability and climate change (Sayer, in Rau/Fahy 2013); and (b) the view that new—not necessarily discipline-based—research agenda and questions are generated from collaborative engagement between researchers and non-researchers (Shove 2010). On the first argument it is apparent that both discipline-based and cross-disciplinary contributions may be insightful and add to understanding of policy and practice. The pertinent issue concerns the quality, currency and originality of the work conducted, whatever the disciplinary base(s). On the second argument, for SCORAI and doubtless other researchers it is clear that more needs to be done to advance inclusivity beyond the 'usual suspects' and to develop more fully engaging processes (e.g. in other spaces than researcher-oriented events and venues c.f. Chilvers 2008 on the tyranny of participation). This will require reflection on the part of researchers and non-researchers about the questions which need to addressed, and the benefits and effective realization of such engagement and cross-disciplinarity, including on the part of funders and users of engaged research. This in turn requires a sustained dialogue about what engagement and cross-, trans- or post-disciplinarity could be, over and above stale considerations of the 'impact' of research, culture change in universities and familiar, dominant behaviour-change models of sustainable consumption.

10.2.11 Policy and Governance

In relation to policy, and more generally the governance of sustainable consumption, the implication of the book is that interventions are needed which act on the institutionalized cultures and practices which reproduce unsustainability and catalyse those which have the potential to realise transformation to more sustainable ways of life. This will require those formally responsible for making policy to be persuaded of the need to move away from individual behaviour-focused interventions where this prevails (Shove et al. 2012). At this juncture it is worth noting a point discussed at the London workshop. This centred on the view that practice theory may not constitute social *science* in the sense that scientific theories enable predictions to be made but rather a perspective of social action and transformation. There are implications of this observation connected with the credibility of research(ers) attempting to engage with policy-makers who may be predisposed towards accepting quantitative evidence as sound(er) science and wary of findings based on qualitative research designs, as is much of the work reported in this book. Fundamentally this may be a matter of extending the practice of working with policy (and other) actors as research projects are designed and executed, to enhance their understanding of, or to debate, the merits of particular methodologies to be employed. It may also require researchers to develop methods for better appreciating and learning from disparate studies of phenomena occurring across different geographical and temporal locations, without glossing local but important peculiarities.

As emphasized in a wealth of research on systems innovation and transition management other actors are variously involved in the governance of innovation (e.g. Geels 2002, 2004; Rip/Kemp 1998; Rotmans et al. 2001). To some extent this has been recognized by policy-makers, too. In the UK, for example, governments have observed that climate change is not likely to be tackled successfully without the actions of communities, firms and other actors in society (DECC 2009). The governance process is known to be fragmented and uncertain, in different countries one in which the responsibilities of different actors and their influence over decision-making varies over time and geographically. Taking for example the promotion of DIY design and RE-DIY policy-makers could (continue to) provide support for local demonstration or self-help workshops, or funding for collaborative networks between entrepreneurs, universities and grassroots or local initiatives.

The question arises as to what will allow new or different perspectives of sustainability to gain salience and, in relation to 'degrowth' or the 'new economy' in what form, both in terms of concept and in terms of specific commitments that might be made. One aspect of an answer to this query involves better understanding of how protagonists negotiate the paradox of agency, which in turn requires further attention to how institutionalized practices persist yet may be undone and supplanted, or recognized as starting points, the building blocks on which durable changes must be founded (c.f. Spurling et al. 2013). This is in part likely to be a matter of understanding how new (or prevailing) practices, whether related to DIY design (or not sharing the use of a car), are rendered as legitimate to others and embedded (or dislodged or reconfigured) as rules to be followed, as well as their physical, material and knowledge content. An incremental approach, working with the here and now of unsustainable practices and cultures of consumption and involving multiple actors, rather than an 'overthrow' approach to behaviour change, may not fit the urgency of the challenges faced nor carry any guarantees of success. It, however, does have the advantage of concurring with what has been learned from over several decades of research in policy analysis, technology policy and innovation studies (Collingridge 1992; Lindblom 1990; Smith/Kern 2009). Overall, an updated version of this demands attention to the ways in which institutionalized language and other rules and practice in micro-worlds create and recreate macro-worlds, which in liberal democratic societies tend to privilege individual choice and short-termist market solutions over collective approaches to sustaining our world. Further it calls into question the conditions which make reflexivity possible about the ways in which we live and whether and how this needs to change, and ultimately the nature and extent of the academic, public and policy roles researchers may play as they interact with others (Burawoy et al. 2004).

References

Berkhout, F., 2006: "Normative Expectations in Systems Innovation", in: *Technology Analysis and Strategic Management*, 18,3–4: 299–311.

Borup, M.; Brown, N.; Konrad, K., 2006: in: *Technology Analysis and Strategic Management*, 18,3–4: 285–298.

Brown, N.; Michael, M., 2003: "A Sociology of Expectations: Retrospecting Prospects and Prospecting Retrospects", in: *Technology Analysis and Strategic Management*, 15,1: 3–18.

Burawoy, M.; Gamson, W.; Ryan, C.; Pfohl, S.; Vaughan, D.; Derber, C.; Schor, J., 2004: "Public Sociologies: a Symposium from Boston College", in: *Social Problems*, 51,1: 103–130.

Chilvers, J., 2008: "Delivering Competence: Theoretical and Practitioner Perspectives and Effective Participatory Practice", in: *Science, Technology and Human Values*, 33: 155–185.

Cohen, M.J., 2014: *The Illusory Promises of the Sharing Economy* (SCORAI Europe Workshop: London): September 30–October 1.

Cohen, M.J.; Szejnwald Brown, H.; Vergragt, P., 2013: *Innovations in Sustainable Consumption: New Economics, Socio-technical Transitions and Social Practices* (Cheltenham: Edward Elgar).

Collingridge, D., 1992: *The Management of Scale* (London: Routledge).

DECC (Department of Energy and Climate Change), 2009: *UK Low Carbon Transition Plan, 2009: National Strategy for Climate and Energy* (Norwich: The Stationery Office).

DEFRA (Department of Environment Food and Rural Affairs), 2008: *A Framework for Pro-Environmental Behaviours* (London: DEFRA).

Ellul, J., 1964: *The Technological Society* (New York: Vintage Books).

Ellul, J., 1980: *The Technological System* (New York: Continuum).

Fairclough, N., 2001: *Language and Power* (London: Longman).

Geels, F.W., 2002: "Technological Transitions as Evolutionary Reconfiguration Processes: A Multi-level Perspective and a Case-Study", in: *Research Policy*, 31: 1257–1274.

Geels, F.W., 2004: "From Sectoral Systems of Innovation to Socio-technical Systems: Insights about Dynamics and Change from Sociology and Institutional Theory", in: *Research Policy*, 33: 897–920.

Geels, F.W.; Smit, W., 2000: "Failed Technology Futures: Pitfalls and Lessons from a Historical Survey", in: *Futures*, 32: 867–885.

Genus, A., in press: "Sustainability Transitions: A Discourse-Institutional Perspective", in: Brauch, H.G., et al. (Ed.): *Handbook on Sustainability Transition and Sustainable Peace* (Cham: Springer).

Genus, A., 2014a: "Governing Sustainability: A Discourse-Institutional Approach", in: *Sustainability*, 6,1: 283–305.

Genus, A., 2014b: "'Co-inquiry' for Environmental Sustainability: A Review of the UK Beacons for Public Engagement", in: *Environment and Planning C: Government and Policy*, 32,3: 491–508.

Genus, A.; Theobald, K., in press: "Creating Low Carbon Neighbourhoods: A Critical Discourse Analysis", in: *European Urban and Regional Studies*.

Giddens, A., 1984: *The Constitution of Society: Outline of the Theory of Structuration* (Cambridge: Polity).

Goodman, M., 2014: "The Fair Trade Consumer-Citizen is Dead! Long Live the Fair Trade Corporate-Citizen!", SCORAI Europe workshop, London, 30 September–1 October.

Greene, M.; Rau, H.; Fahy, F., 2014: "Mobilising Memories: Measuring Mobility Practices Across the Life Course", SCORAI Europe workshop, London, 30 September–1 October.

Greenwood, R.; Suddaby, R., 2006: "Institutional Entrepreneurship in Mature Fields: The Big Five Accounting Firms", in: *Academy of Management Journal*, 49: 27–48.

Hajer, M.; Versteeg, W., 2005: A Decade of Discourse Analysis of Environmental Politics: Achievements, Challenges, Perspectives", in: *Journal of Environmental Policy and Planning*, 7,3: 175–84.

IPCC [Blanco, G.; Gerlagh, R.; Suh, S.; Barrett, J.; de Coninck, H.C.; Diaz Morejon, C.F.; Mathur, R.; Nakicenovic, N.; Ofosu Ahenkora, A.; Pan, J.; Pathak, H.; Rice, J.; Richels, R.; Smith, S.J.; Stern, D.I.; Toth, F.L.; Zhou, P.], 2014: "Drivers, Trends and Mitigation", in: Edenhofer, O.; Pichs-Madruga, R.; Sokona, Y.; Farahani, E.; Kadner, S.; Seyboth, K.; Adler, A.; Baum, I.; Brunner, S.; Eickemeier, P.; Kriemann, B.; Savolainen, J.; Schlömer, S.; von Stechow, C.; Zwickel, T.; Minx, J.C., (Eds.): *Climate Change 2014: Mitigation of Climate Change. Contribution of Working Group III to the Fifth Assessment Report of the Intergovernmental Panel on Climate Change* (Cambridge, UK and New York, NY, USA: Cambridge University Press).

Jasanoff, S.; Sang-Hyun, K., 2009: "Containing the Atom: Sociotechnical Imaginaries and Nuclear Power in the United States and South Korea", in: *Minerva*, 47: 119–146.

Jasanoff, S.; Sang-Hyun, K., 2013: "Sociotechnical Imaginaries and National Energy Policies", in: *Science as Culture*, 22,2: 189–196.

Journal of Peer Production (2014): Shared Machine Shops. Issue 5, October; at: http://peerproduction.net/issues/issue-5-shared-machine-shops (5 May 2015).

Lindblom, C.E., 1990: *Inquiry and Change: The Troubled Attempt to Understand and Shape Society* (New Haven: Yale University Press).

Middlemiss, L.; Parrish, B.D., 2010: "Building Capacity for Low-Carbon Communities: The Role of Grassroots Initiatives", in: *Energy Policy*, 38: 7559–7566.

Offer, A., 2006: *The Challenge of Affluence: Self-control and Well-being in the US and Britain since 1950* (Oxford: Oxford University Press).

Rau, H.; Fahy, F., 2013: "Sustainability Research in the Social Sciences—Concepts, Methodologies and the Challenge of Interdisciplinarity", in: Fahy, F.; Rau, H., (Eds.): *Methods of Sustainability Research in the Social Sciences* (London: Sage): 3–24.

Rip, A.; Kemp, R., 1998: "Technological Change", in: Rayner, S.; Malone, E.J., (Eds.): *Human Choice and Climate Change,* vol. 2. *Resources and Technology* (Columbus, Ohio: Battelle Press): 327–399.

Røpke, I., 2013: "Ecological Macroeconomics: Implications for the Roles of Consumer Citizens", in: Cohen, M.; Brown, H.; Vergragt, P., (Eds.): *Innovations in Sustainable Consumption: New Economics, Socio-technical Transitions and Social Practices* (Cheltenham: Edward Elgar): 48–64.

Rotmans, J.; Kemp, R.; Van Asselt, M., 2001: "More Evolution than Revolution: Transition Management in Public Policy", in: *Foresight—the Journal of Future Studies, Strategic Thinking and Policy,* 3: 15–31.

Schatzki, T.R.; Knorr-Cetina, K.; Savigny, E., (Eds.), 2001: *The Practice Turn in Contemporary Theory* (London: Routledge).

Schmidt, V., 2008: "Discursive Institutionalism: The Explanatory Power of Ideas and Discourse", in: *Annual Review of Political Science*, 11: 303–326.

Schor J., 2004: *Born to Buy: The Commercialized Child and the New Consumer Culture* (New York: Simon and Schuster).

Schor J., 2010: *Plenitude: The New Economics of True Wealth* (New York: Penguin Press).

Schor, J., 2014: Debating the Sharing Economy. Great Transition Initiative (October); at: http://greattransition.org/publication/debating-the-sharing-economy (5 May 2015).

Schor, J.; Thompson, C.J., (Eds.), 2014: *Sustainable Lifestyles and the Quest for Plenitude: Case Studies of the New Economy* (New Haven: Yale University Press).

Scott, W.R., 2008: *Institutions and Organizations: Ideas and Interests* (3rd ed.) (Thousand Oaks, CA: Sage).

Seyfang, G.; Smith, A., 2007: "Grassroots Innovations for Sustainable Development: Towards a New Research and Policy Agenda", in: *Environmental Politics*, 16,4: 584–603.

Shove, E., 2003: *Comfort, Cleanliness and Convenience: The Social Organization of Normality* (Oxford: Berg).

Shove, E., 2010: "Social Theory and Climate Change Questions Often, Sometimes and Not Yet Asked", in: *Theory, Culture and Society*, 27,2–3: 277–288.

Shove, E.; Pantzar, M.; Watson, M., 2012: *The Dynamics of Social Practice: Everyday Life and How it Changes* (London: Sage).

Shove, E.; Walker, G., 2014: "What is Energy for? Social Practice and Energy Demand", in: *Theory, Culture and Society*, 31,5: 41–58.

Sine,W.D.; David, R.J., 2003: "Environmental Jolts, Institutional Change, and the Creation of Entrepreneurial Opportunity in the US Electric Power Industry", in: *Research Policy*, 32: 185–207.

Smith, A., 2014a: "Grassroots Prototyping Past and Present", SCORAI Europe workshop, London, 30 September–1 October.

Smith, A., 2014b: Technology Networks for Socially Useful PRODUCTION. Journal of Peer Production, 5; at: http://peerproduction.net/issues/issue-5-shared-machine-shops (2 June 2015).

Smith, A.; Kern, F., 2009: "The Transitions Storyline in Dutch Environmental Policy", in: *Environmental Policy*, 18: 78–98.

Spurling, N.; McMeekin, A.; Shove, E.; Southerton, D.; Welch, D., 2013: *Interventions in Practice: Re-framing Policy Approaches to Consumer Behaviour*. Sustainable Practices Research Group Report, September 2013; at: http://www.sprg.ac.uk/uploads/sprg-report-sept-2013.pdf (4 June 2015).

Stern, N., 2007: *The Economics of Climate Change—The Stern Review* (Cambridge: Cambridge University Press).

Thorpe, A., 2012: *Architecture and Design versus Consumerism: How Design Activism Confronts Growth* (Abingdon: Earthscan/Taylor and Francis).

Wacquant, L.J.D., 1989: "Towards a Reflexive Sociology: A Workshop with Pierre Bourdieu", in: *Sociological Theory*, 7,1: 26–63.

Young, W.; Middlemiss, L., 2012: "A Rethink of How Policy and Social Science Approach Changing Individuals' Actions on Greenhouse Gas Emissions", in: *Energy Policy*, 41: 742–747.

Kingston University

Kingston University is the largest higher education provider in South West London, with nearly 21,000 students enrolled on full and part-time courses. Its four campuses are located within a 4-mile radius of the Kingston upon Thames town centre, which is 25 min from central London.

Kingston University consistently ranks among the top institutions for student applications, is a growing force in research and a pioneer in entrepreneurship and e-learning.

Offering a comprehensive range of undergraduate and postgraduate study programmes, Kingston University provides students with a choice of subjects reflecting their interests and the needs of industry. It is committed to opening up higher education to the whole community and encouraging students from under-represented and disadvantaged backgrounds to further their studies. One in 10 Kingston University students comes from a family with no previous involvement in university study.

Research plays a central role in the University's activities. Through a variety of individual cutting-edge projects and the development of multi-disciplinary centres of research excellence, the University has made significant strides in creating a broad range of high impact research. Kingston University received a huge boost to its research as a result of the Government's latest research evaluation exercise—the Research Excellence Framework 2014—with 60 % of its research being rated as world-leading and internationally excellent.

Kingston University plays an active role in nurturing innovation and enterprise. By producing applied research, developing technology transfer and sharing knowledge it has become a driving force in forging strong links between education and the business community.

The Higher Education Business and Community Interaction Survey 2013–14 reported that, for the 6th year running, Kingston was one of the top universities in the country for the number of graduates starting up their own companies. The University also has impressive graduate start-up turnover, with firms launched by former students notching up a combined total of nearly £30 million in 2013–14.

A. Genus (ed.), *Sustainable Consumption*, The Anthropocene:
Politik—Economics—Society—Science 3, DOI 29, DOI 10.1007/978-3-319-29665-4

Developments in teaching, learning, research and facilities have all contributed to positioning Kingston University at the heart of education and economic development in the region.

As at January 2015, the estimated annual expenditure stimulated by Kingston University in the regional economy was £481 million.

For more information
Telephone: 020 8417 9000; Website: http://www.kingston.ac.uk

About the Contributors

Motoki Akitsu (Japan), Kyoto University, Japan is Professor of Philosophy of Agricultural Science in the Graduate School of Agriculture at Kyoto University and working as a council member on several domestic and international academic associations. He has been studying cultural construction and social problems in rural societies not only in Japan, but also in Asian, African, and European countries. He has recently begun research projects on the promotion of ethical food consumption in Japan and Asian countries to support the creation of sustainable agrifood systems. The projects employ action and participatory research methods to expand upon practice theory and the ethical and pedagogical needs to promote sustainable food consumption.

Address: Graduate School of Agriculture, Kyoto University, Kyoto, Japan
Email: akitsu@kais.kyoto-u.ac.jp
Website: http://kyouindb.iimc.kyoto-u.ac.jp/e/tP0kM.

Panayiota J. Alevizou (UK), University of Sheffield, UK, is a Lecturer in Marketing at the University of Sheffield Management School, where she teaches contemporary marketing management and retail & services marketing. Her research focuses on sustainability labeling, eco-labeling, and ethical marketing in the context of fast-moving consumer goods and apparel. Panayiota joined the School as a lecturer after several years of working as a marketing consultant. She has presented her work in various national and international conferences and has published in journals such as Journal of Marketing Management, Journal of Marketing Communications, and the International Journal of Consumer Studies.

Address: Department of Marketing, University of Sheffield Management School, University of Sheffield, Sheffield, UK
Email: p.j.alevizou@sheffield.ac.uk
Website: http://www.sheffield.ac.uk/management/staff/alevizou/index.

Ranis Cheng (UK), University of Sheffield, UK, is a Lecturer in Marketing at the Management School, University of Sheffield. She obtained her Ph.D. from Manchester Metropolitan University. Her doctoral thesis explored the desired and perceived corporate identity within the UK fast fashion retail sector. Her research interests are corporate identity and corporate brand management. She is a member

A. Genus (ed.), *Sustainable Consumption*, The Anthropocene: Politik—Economics—Society—Science 3, DOI 29, DOI 10.1007/978-3-319-29665-4

of Chartered Institute of Marketing. She has published in the European Journal of Marketing and Journal of Product and Brand Management.

Address: Department of Marketing, University of Sheffield Management School, University of Sheffield, Sheffield, UK
Email: r.cheng@sheffield.ac.uk.

Anne-Marie Coles (UK), University of Greenwich, UK, is Senior Lecturer in Strategic Management in the Faculty of Business, Greenwich University and currently leader of the Sustainability, Technology and Innovation Research (STIR) group. Her research is concerned with elucidation of the complex, dynamic factors that affect development of new artefacts, their subsequent diffusion and use. Anne-Marie's analytical approach is to examine the social embedding of technologies through reconfiguration of heterogeneous socio-technical networks. Specific themes are: non-linear socio-technical path creation; development and adoption of sustainable technologies; and knowledge-based small firms.

Address: Business School, University of Greenwich, London, UK
Email: a.coles@gre.ac.uk
Website: http://www2.gre.ac.uk/about/faculty/business/study/sms/staff/anne-marie-coles.

Tim Cooper (UK), Nottingham Trent University, UK, is Professor of Sustainable Design and Consumption at Nottingham Trent University and Co-Director of the £6.2m Centre for Industrial Energy, Materials and Products. Tim was a construction industry economist prior to posts at the New Economics Foundation and Sheffield Hallam University. A specialist in product lifetimes, his research interests are multidisciplinary, embracing sustainable design, consumer behaviour, public policy and environmental values. His work has been funded by the European Commission, EPSRC, Defra and WRAP and has included collaborative projects with industry in the clothing and electronic goods sectors. He is Contributing Editor of *Longer Lasting Products* (Gower 2010).

Address: UK INDEMAND Research Centre, Nottingham Trent University, Nottingham, UK
Email: t.h.cooper@ntu.ac.uk
Website: http://www.ntu.ac.uk/apps/staff_profiles/staff_directory/124788-0/26/Tim_Cooper.aspx.

Tom Fisher (UK), Nottingham Trent University, UK, is Professor of Art and Design at Nottingham Trent University UK. A graduate in Fine Art he has worked as a designer and maker of furniture, and wrote his Ph.D. in the Sociology department at the University of York that concentrated on everyday experiences of plastic materials. His current research focuses on the materiality of human/object relationships and their implications for sustainability. In this he draws on his background as a maker and on perspectives from the sociology of consumption.

Address: School of Art and Design, Nottingham Trent University, Nottingham, UK
Email: tom.fisher@ntu.ac.uk
Website: http://www.ntu.ac.uk/apps/staff_profiles/staff_directory/124149-0/26/Tom_Fissher.aspx.

Claudia Henninger (UK), University of Sheffield, UK, is an early career researcher at the University of Sheffield, where she teaches aspects of branding. Her research focuses on sustainability in the fashion industry, corporate identity, micro-organisations, and value co-creation. Claudia has been involved in a variety of projects in the area of sustainability marketing and the creative and cultural industries. Her work has been presented at both national and international conferences and she has published in the area of marketing and management.

Address: Department of Marketing, University of Sheffield Management School, University of Sheffield, Sheffield, UK
Email: c.e.henninger@sheffield.ac.uk
Website: http://www.sheffield.ac.uk/management/staff/chenninger/index.

Steven R. McGreevy (Japan), Research Institute for Humanity and Nature, Kyoto, Japan is an Assistant Professor at the Research Institute for Humanity and Nature (RIHN) and has a background in agriculture and rural sustainable development from Kyoto University (Ph.D., 2012). His research focuses on novel approaches to rural revitalization utilizing local natural resources and the relinking of patterns of food consumption and production at local communities in Japan. He leads a RIHN Feasibility Study entitled "Lifeworlds of Sustainable Food Consumption and Production: Agrifood Systems in Transition" exploring the transformation of social practices related to food and agriculture at various sites in Asia.

Address: Research Institute for Humanity and Nature, Center for Research Development
Email: srmcgreevy@chikyu.ac.jp
Website: http://archives.chikyu.ac.jp/archives/AnnualReport/Viewer.do?prkbn=R&jekbn=E&id=501.

Mandy Meikle (UK), Woolfords, Auchengray and Tarbrax Improvement Foundation (WATIF), South Lanarkshire, Scotland, UK, has been speaking on peak oil issues since 2004. She is an environmental and community activist working with the WATIF community trust in South Lanarkshire in Scotland. Mandy also edits the Reforesting Scotland Journal and undertakes both independent and contract research on climate justice.

Address: South Lanarkshire, Scotland, UK
Email: m.meikle@reforestingscotland.org.uk
Website: http://www.watif.scot/.

Mariale Moreno (UK), Cranfield University, UK, is a Research Fellow at the RECODE Network at Cranfield University. She has collaborated at the Centre for Industrial Energy, Material and Products; an EUED inter-university research project between industry and academic partners looking at reducing materials and energy demand. Her work focuses on user-centred design, consumer behaviour, sustainable production and consumption, and business opportunities towards achieving a Circular Economy. She completed her Ph.D. at Loughborough University on user-centred design and sustainable consumption. She has also collaborated with the Royal Society of Arts and the Helen Hamlyn Centre for Design on topics around behavioural change and sustainability.

Address: Cranfield University, UK
Email: m.moreno@cranfield.ac.uk
Website: http://www.cranfield.ac.uk.

Sarah Netter (Denmark), Copenhagen Business School, Denmark, is a Ph.D. Fellow at the Centre for Corporate Social Responsibility in the Copenhagen Business School and is also affiliated with the MISTRA Future Fashion Program. She is researching the diffusion of sustainable innovations and the adoption of sustainable fashion consumption practices. Sarah's work examines young consumers' acceptance of innovative forms of sustainable fashion consumption by investigating cases of in-store recycling systems and collaborative fashion consumption. The aim is to identify drivers and barriers of these practices and ultimately to provide grounds for investigating how these practices influence consumers' behaviour in all phases of their fashion consumption.

Address: Department of Intercultural Communication and Management, Copenhagen Business School, Frederiksberg, Denmark
Email: sn.ikl@cbs.dk
Website: http://www.cbs.dk/en/research/departments-and-centres/department-of-intercultural-communication-and-management/staff/snikl#profile.

Caroline J. Oates (UK), University of Sheffield, UK, is a Senior Lecturer in Marketing at the University of Sheffield Management School, where she teaches marketing communications and directs the Postgraduate Research Programme. Her research focuses on ethical issues and challenges in marketing, particularly sustainability and marketing to children. She has published widely in both these fields, in journals such as Psychology & Marketing, Sociology, Journal of Marketing Management, Social Business, and Young Consumers. She is the co-author/co-editor of two books on advertising to children.

Address: Department of Marketing, University of Sheffield Management School, University of Sheffield, Sheffield, UK
Email: c.j.oates@sheffield.ac.uk
Website: https://www.sheffield.ac.uk/management/staff/oates.

Laura Piscicelli (UK), Nottingham Trent University, UK is a Ph.D. candidate in Sustainable Consumption at Nottingham Trent University. She holds an M.Sc. in Product-Service System Design and a B.Sc. in Industrial Design from Politecnico di Milano. Her current research combines insights from social psychology and social practice theory to understand the role of values in the acceptance, adoption and diffusion of collaborative consumption. Laura's research interests are in the areas of design and sustainability, including consumer behaviour, design for behaviour change, product-service systems, user-centred design and the collaborative economy.

Address: School of Architecture Design and the Built Environment, Nottingham Trent University, Nottingham, UK
Email: laura.piscicelli@ntu.ac.uk
Website: http://www.ntu.ac.uk/apps/staff_profiles/staff_directory/4d209b6d-d9f8-4acb-9ace-b7ef29d3bd80-0/26/profile.aspx?text=Laura%20Piscicelli.

Athena Piterou (UK), University of Greenwich, UK, is Lecturer in Sustainability at the University of Greenwich. She completed her Ph.D. at Brunel University. The thesis examined the development of electronic books as a disruptive innovation and implications for print-on-paper sustainability. She is a Visiting Fellow at the Policy Studies Institute, University of Westminster where she produced a network analysis of the events organised by the Sustainable Development Research Network. Her research follows a relational approach to innovation and applies social network analysis methods to the examination of hybrid networks. This method was developed to map sustainable energy technologies in London.

Address: Business School, University of Greenwich, London, UK
Email: a.piterou@gre.ac.uk
Website: http://www2.gre.ac.uk/about/faculty/business/study/sms/staff/athina-piterou.

Giuseppe Salvia (Italy), Politecnico di Milano (Italy) is a Research Fellow at Politecnico di Milano (Italy) where he investigates the current self-producing and making trend (i.e. DIY) with a focus on grassroot innovations and development of skills. Giuseppe is interested in the design role in a society where "everyone designs" in order to foster sustainable consumption and production. His Ph.D. research investigated the satisfactory component of potentially sustainable practices, as individual and collaborative making and transforming. He has also collaborated in research projects on product longevity, design strategies for sustainable consumption, industrial ecology and life cycle assessment, bio-inspired design approaches, materials innovation, and expressive-sensorial dimensions of materials.

Address: School of Design, Politecnico di Milano, Milano, Italy
Email: Giuseppe.Salvia@polimi.it
Website: polimi.academia.edu/GiuseppeSalvia.

Fred Steward (UK), Policy Studies Institute, UK is Professor of Innovation and Sustainability at the Policy Studies Institute in the UK. His primary research interest is in 'transformative innovation'—pervasive, radical, system-wide social and technological change. His approach to this is a synthesis between innovation network concepts and sociotechnical transition theory. The focus of his research is the role of innovation in addressing the global challenge of climate change and environmental sustainability, and the implications of this for policy. Fred is a member of several international committees: the Dutch Knowledge & System Innovation programme, the Sustainable Consumption Research network and the IHDP Industrial Transformation programme. He is a member of the Royal Society committee on Global Environmental Change.

Address: Policy Studies Institute, University of Westminster, London, UK
Email: f.steward@psi.org.uk
Website: http://www.psi.org.uk/site/people_detail/professor_fred_steward.

Ann Thorpe (UK), University College London/activist, UK, is in sustainable design and the spatial and material politics that surround it. Ann has published a number of papers and two books, The Designers Atlas of Sustainability and Architecture and also Design versus Consumerism. Her work examines design's role in sustainable consumption, activism, and innovation, particularly moving from reformist to transformative policies. Ann has lectured internationally on these topics and audiences describe her accessible and generously illustrated talks as "brain-opening," "intriguing and insightful," and full of "unusual angles."

Address: Department of Science, Technology, Engineering and Public Policy, University College London, London, UK
Email: ann@designers-atlas.net
Website: https://www.ucl.ac.uk/steapp/people/thorpe.

About the Editor

Audley Genus (UK), YTL Professor of Innovation and Technology Management at the Small Business Research Centre, Kingston University, Kingston upon Thames, has research interests in the areas of innovation and entrepreneurship, technology policy and sustainable consumption and production. He publishes regularly in high impact journals such as *Research Policy*, *Applied Energy* and *Environment and Planning* and has published three single-authored books. He is a member of the editorial board of *Technology Analysis and Strategic Management* and the steering committee of the *Sustainable Consumption Research and Action Initiative* (SCORAI) Europe. Audley is a member of the *European Association for the Study of Science and Technology* (EASST), the *British Academy of Management*, the *Sustainable Development Research Network* and the *Sustainability Transitions Research Network*.

Selected publications: Coles, A-M., Piterou, A., and Genus, A. (in press). Sustainable energy projects and the community: mapping single building use of microgeneration technologies in London, *Urban Studies*; Genus, A., and Theobald, K. (in press). Roles for University Researchers in Urban Sustainability Initiatives: the UK Newcastle Low Carbon Neighbourhoods project, *Journal of Cleaner Production*; Genus, A., and Theobald, K. (in press). *Creating Low Carbon Neighbourhoods: a Critical Discourse Analysis, European Urban and Regional Studies*; Attar, A., and Genus, A. (2014) Framing Public Engagement: a Critical Discourse Analysis of GM Nation? *Technological Forecasting and Social Change* 88: 241–250; Genus, A. (2014) 'Co-inquiry' for Environmental Sustainability: a Review of the UK Beacons for Public Engagement, *Environment and Planning C: Government and Policy* 32(3): 491–508; Genus, A., and Mafakheri, F. (2014). A Neo-institutional Perspective of Supply Chains and Energy Security: the Case of Bioenergy, *Applied Energy* 123: 307–315; Genus, A. (2014). Governing Sustainability: A Discourse-Institutional Approach, *Sustainability* 6(1): 283–305;

A. Genus (ed.), *Sustainable Consumption*, The Anthropocene: Politik—Economics—Society—Science 3, DOI 29, DOI 10.1007/978-3-319-29665-4

Genus, A. (2012). Changing the Rules? Institutional Innovation and the Diffusion of Microgeneration, *Technology Analysis and Strategic Management*, 24(7): 711–727; Genus, A., and Coles, A.-M. (2008). Rethinking the Multi-level Perspective of Technological Transitions, *Research Policy* 37(9): 1436–1445.

Address: Prof. Audley Genus, YTL Professor of Innovation and Technology Management, Small Business Research Centre, Kingston Business School, Kingston University, Kingston Hill, Kingston upon Thames, Surrey, KT2 7LB, UK
Email: a.genus@kingston.ac.uk
Website: http://business.kingston.ac.uk/staff/professor-audley-genus and http://www.afes-press-books.de/html/APESS_03.htm.

About this Book

The book originates from the work of contributors to initiatives and global networks promoting and pursuing lines of enquiry that recognise and probe relationships among sustainable consumption, design and production, and the implications of these for new economic activity and the way we live and govern ourselves. The book features contributions from social scientists (e.g. from innovation studies, marketing, social psychology, sustainable design, and sociology) and practitioners to generate a short-list of research perspectives and topics around which future research and actions in practice should be orientated. There are eight contributory chapters plus an Introduction and Conclusion (on policy, research and practical implications). Chapters cover: perspectives/methodological insights; empirical work integrating consumption and production; site-specific case studies; and reflections on initiatives in practice.

This book offers a:

1. holistic treatment of sustainable consumption and production (and thus leads to better appreciation of the range of issues to be confronted in properly understanding and achieving sustainable economies and societies);
2. presents new perspectives on the issues (helps readers to think about sustainable consumption/production and innovation in novel ways); and
3. unusually spans theory, empirical research, action initiatives and policy implications

Contents

A. Genus (ed.), *Sustainable Consumption*, The Anthropocene:
Politik—Economics—Society—Science 3, DOI 29, DOI 10.1007/978-3-319-29665-4

6. Claudia E. Henninger, Panayiota J. Alevizou, Caroline J. Oates and Ranis Cheng: Communicating Sustainability: The Case of Slow-Fashion Micro-organisations
7. Steven R. McGreevy and Motoki Akitsu: Steering Sustainable Food Consumption in Japan: Trust, Relationships, and the Ties that Bind
8. Anne-Marie Coles: The Potential for Sustainable Production and Consumption in a Technological Society
9. Mandy Meikle: Promoting Sustainable Consumption—A View from the Ground
10. Audley Genus: Conclusion

More on this book is at: http://www.afes-press-books.de/html/APESS_03.htm.

Index

A. Genus (ed.), *Sustainable Consumption*, The Anthropocene: Politik—Economics—Society—Science 3, DOI 29, DOI 10.1007/978-3-319-29665-4

MIX
Papier aus verantwortungsvollen Quellen
Paper from responsible sources
FSC® C105338

If you have any concerns about our products,
you can contact us on
ProductSafety@springernature.com

In case Publisher is established outside the EU,
the EU authorized representative is:
Springer Nature Customer Service Center GmbH
Europaplatz 3, 69115 Heidelberg, Germany

Printed by Libri Plureos GmbH
in Hamburg, Germany